"Finally! A to-do manual on how best to *keep* the money our investments *make!* Most investors—and most investment managers—invest as though taxes can't be managed (or worse, don't exist). **Doug Rogers has studied these issues as much as almost anyone in the finance world and has assembled a commonsense guide to help navigate our investment choices with an eye on the tax man's take.**"

> ROBERT D. ARNOTT
> Chairman, Research Affiliates, LLC
> Editor, *Financial Analysts Journal*

"This is the definitive work on this complex and rapidly evolving subject. Doug Rogers covers an array of topics—including security analysis, portfolio construction methodologies, the manager search process, asset allocation, and technology developments—in a way that everyone can immediately apply to more effectively manage wealth from an after-tax perspective. **Whether you are an investor, portfolio manager, investment consultant, private banker, financial adviser, accountant, or estate attorney, *Tax-Aware Investment Management* will give you the knowledge to allow you to differentiate yourself in today's competitive environment.**"

> THOMAS J. BOCZAR, CFA, ESQ.
> Chairman, Private Wealth Management Committee,
> New York Society of Security Analysts (NYSSA)

"Doug Rogers combines his many years of experience with a high degree of technical knowledge to create an innovative guide with a fresh perspective on tax-aware strategies. In my opinion it is an **essential tool for private investors and wealth management professionals to manage portfolios holistically and effectively.**"

> RALPH C. RITTENOUR JR.
> Chairman and CEO, CTC Consulting, Inc.

Tax-Aware
Investment Management

Also available from Bloomberg Press

The Investment Think Tank:
Theory, Strategy, and Practice for Advisers
edited by Harold Evensky and Deena B. Katz

Retirement Income Redesigned:
Master Plans for Distribution
edited by Harold Evensky and Deena B. Katz
(Available April 2006)

Family Wealth—Keeping It in the Family:
How Family Members and Their Advisers Preserve Human,
Intellectual, and Financial Assets for Generations
by James E. Hughes Jr.

Managing Concentrated Stock Wealth:
An Adviser's Guide to Building Customized Solutions
by Tim Kochis

The PPLI Solution: Delivering Wealth Accumulation,
Tax Efficiency, and Asset Protection Through
Private-Placement Life Insurance
edited by Kirk Loury

Wall Street Secrets for Tax-Efficient Investing:
From Tax Pain to Investment Gain
by Robert N. Gordon with Jan M. Rosen

———————————

A complete list of our titles is available at
www.bloomberg.com/books

Tax-Aware
Investment Management

THE ESSENTIAL GUIDE

Douglas S. Rogers

BLOOMBERG PRESS

NEW YORK

First edition published 2006
1 3 5 7 9 10 8 6 4 2

Library of Congress Cataloging-in-Publication Data

Rogers, Douglas S.
    Tax-aware investment management : the essential guide / Douglas S. Rogers.
       p. cm.
    Summary: "Illustrates how investment strategies for tax-exempt accounts don't work for individuals subject to taxes. Offers techniques for comparing tax-efficiency of mutual funds, hedge funds, and investment managers, and presents more-sophisticated strategies for offsetting gains against losses in wealth planning, portfolio management, and estate planning. Includes results of historical research, 100 tables and charts"--Provided by publisher.
    Includes bibliographical references and index.
    ISBN 1-57660-180-3 (alk paper)
    1. Investments--Taxation--United States--Handbooks, manuals, etc. 2. Portfolio management--Handbooks, manuals, etc. I. Title.

HG4910.R655 2006
332.6--dc22   2005030613

CONTENTS

ACKNOWLEDGMENTS

Tax-Aware Investment Management: The Essential Guide embodies the collective wisdom of many people with whom I have been fortunate enough to interact during my investment career. I want to acknowledge those who have supported my efforts and provided me many of the insights necessary to complete this work. I apologize to anyone I may have inadvertently missed in my attempt to give credit where it is due.

I extend my gratitude to Ralph Rittenour Jr., to Jeffrey Grubb, and to my other associates at CTC Consulting for their backing of this project. I am especially mindful of the support of Don Lindow and Chris Arvani who recognized early on in my career my desire to take on new and exciting research pertaining to the nuclear decommissioning trust (NDT) industry. My participation at NDT conferences and my interaction with Arland Brusven, David Krause, James Meehan, Joanne Howard, Mary Jo Dempsey, Thomas Tuschen, Eric Knause, Mary Miller, and others only heightened my enthusiasm. Michael Brilley and Gene Sit encouraged me to submit my first article for publication on tax-aware investment management, which set the stage for other projects to follow. Similar appreciation is extended to Louise Wasso-Jonikas and Michael Radford for encouraging my involvement in CFA Institute (formerly AIMR) activities and public speaking.

Lee Price has always been a respected mentor, and to serve with him on both AIMR Subcommittees on After-Tax Reporting has been an honor and privilege. I will always be indebted to the members of the Subcommittee. Their response to the SEC proposal for after-tax returns on mutual funds and recommended revisions to the existing standards would not have been possible without the assistance of Pauline Pilate and Alecia Licata. Stanley Lee and Liz Miller of the New York Society of Security Analysts have been consistent supporters of this topic and related issues.

I am truly thankful for the willingness of Tad Jeffrey, James Garland, Robert Arnott, Joel Dickson, Jack Bogle, Peter Bernstein, Marc Moulton, Brian Langstraat, David Stein, and Bob Breshock to share their experiences on critical research and product development. Jay Whipple III, Ron Surz, James Hollis, and Matt Schott have played critical roles in furthering my understanding of systems technology. Robert Gordon and

Thomas Boczar played a similar role with tax issues as they relate to hedge fund investing. Leslie Giardani and her research offered valuable insight into the future direction of the insurance industry. Tony Rochte and his associates at Barclays shared their knowledge of exchange-traded funds, as did Gary Gastineau. William Reichenstein, William Jennings, and James Poterba were thoughtful enough to introduce me to the leading contributors from academia. Don Phillips was gracious enough to allow the use of after-tax return data from Morningstar Principia. While stock pickers always seem to take center stage over those whose special expertise is in fixed income, it has been a joy to share ideas with passionate bond portfolio managers like Guy Davidson, Christine Todd, and Paul Jungquist.

Harold Evensky was instrumental in introducing me to Jared Kieling, who has supported the project with sage editorial advice. Jeffery Yablon was kind enough to share his quotes from *Tax Notes* that appear as epigraphs throughout the book.[1] Encouragement from Nancy Jacob, Jean Brunel, and Dave Spaulding to continue to publish has been a driving force that has culminated in this effort.

This book could not have completed without the continued encouragement of close friends and relatives. Last, and most important, I thank my children and my wife, Soon Hee, for their unwavering support and sacrifices made during the many evenings and weekends that were needed to complete this text.

Chapter Notes

1. The tax-related quotations that open each part and chapter were compiled and arranged by Jeffery L. Yablon, "As Certain as Death: Quotations About Taxes (2004 Edition)," *Tax Notes* vol. 102, no. 1 (January 5, 2004): 99-116.

The Importance of Tax-Aware Investment Management

Our Constitution is in actual operation; everything appears to promise that it will last; but nothing in this world is certain but death and taxes.

—BENJAMIN FRANKLIN
FOUNDING FATHER

Taxes have been a permanent part of the social-political landscape in the United States since the Sixteenth Amendment to the Constitution was ratified in 1913. Soon thereafter, President Woodrow Wilson approved the form of federal income taxation that we know today. Initially affecting only the wealthy, it was not until after World War II that the federal income tax began to have a significant impact on the economic well-being of the average citizen.[1]

Although no one enjoys paying them, taxes serve an important purpose. Taxes are the source of revenue that enables the government to build the infrastructure necessary to maintain and enhance our quality of life and to provide for the common defense. And like the prices of securities, taxes will change! The prices of securities fluctuate daily as market participants assess the importance of the various forces affecting the economy, whereas tax rates change more slowly, reflecting government policies and spending. Since the adoption of the federal income tax, tax policy has become an increasingly important stimulus tool with each successive administration. Therefore, major change in the tax code is expected to be the norm rather than the exception. For this reason, tax-aware investment practices are essential to maximizing wealth.

Tax-aware investment management refers to the application of sound judgment that results in optimal results after all taxes and fees have been paid. It is *not* about avoiding the payment of taxes through questionable accounting or estate planning or simply attempting to pay no tax. Rather, it is about maximizing what is left after taxes have been paid. For example, if an investor has the choice between two securities with similar features, it is foolish to avoid purchasing the one that will require a tax payment if it offers a superior net overall result. If the investor receives a higher after-tax return through effective tax-aware investment management, the money manager makes a reasonable profit, the government collects its revenue, and we have achieved the best of all worlds—everyone involved in the process has gained something of value.

In the more than ninety years that the federal income tax has been with us, you would think that academic institutions and professional certification programs would have paid sufficient attention to tax-aware investment management to train people and develop products to serve the needs of the taxable investor. Unfortunately, this is not the case. A shortage of educators and trained professionals in tax-aware investing persists because of an earlier emphasis on retirement plans and charitable organizations, which are exempt from the payment of taxes.[2] All too often, modern portfolio theory concepts that have emerged from the tax-exempt account arena as gospel are naively applied to taxable accounts by well-intentioned individuals, resulting in less-than-optimal, costly solutions. The lack of attention to taxes in the investment process is so severe that most professionals in the investment management industry are unaware that about half of the trillions of dollars of liquid assets in the United States are subject to taxation.

Fortunately, it is not all gloom and doom for individual taxpayers, trusts, and corporations with significant taxable assets. There are several bright spots. First, over the past decade, a group of dedicated practitioners has emerged to make significant contributions to the body of knowledge needed to serve taxable accounts. Second, uniform standards for reporting returns on an after-tax basis are now in place for most mutual funds, and a growing number of separate account managers[3] are adopting them for their clients and for the purpose of constructing composite results for marketing purposes. Third, some managers are modifying buy-and-sell decisions to incorporate the impact of taxes, and innovative tax-efficient products, such as exchange-traded funds, are rapidly gaining recognition and acceptance. Fourth, traditional methods are being analyzed in order to better position assets in both taxable and tax-exempt accounts for ultimate wealth creation. Furthermore, advancements in systems technology are currently improving the capability and scale of these processes.

Tax-aware investment management involves four critical elements:

1 Utilizing after-tax assumptions in the asset allocation process
2 Allocating asset classes and managers/funds according to the characteristics of each investment entity

3 Tax-aware equity manager positioning
4 Identifying tax-aware managers/funds

Implementing these steps has the potential to add from 0.5 to 2.5 percent annually to bottom-line performance or wealth creation. The exact amount of value added can vary significantly between taxable account relationships for each element, ranging from 0 to 1.5 percent or more depending on the complexity of the investment opportunity. The four elements interact and complement one another. For example, you may allocate a tax-inefficient manager to a tax-exempt account where lack of attention to tax management is not an issue or replace the manager with another strategy that may create tax benefits that can be used beyond the replacement manager. This process lends itself to creativity and innovative solutions all within a simple understanding of the tax code. A tax-aware solution will take into account the investment time horizon, tax characteristics of the investment entities involved (e.g., personal taxable account assets, 401(k) retirement plans, and individual retirement accounts), the client's tax profile, projected returns, permissible asset classes, and structure (e.g., funds vs. separate accounts vs. limited partnerships) of the investment portfolios. Most important, it takes a knowledgeable and experienced professional to implement and orchestrate a tax-aware investment management process. It is not unrealistic for a high-net-worth family to gain approximately 0.5 percent from using after-tax assumptions for asset allocation, 1.0 percent from locating managers/funds according to the characteristics of each investment entity, 0.4 percent from optimally combining equity managers in a manner quite different than the pension-consulting approach, and 0.6 percent from using tax-aware managers for the taxable accounts. All four of the elements are important and ignoring one or more leads to a less than optimal solution.

Tax-aware investing is equally important to investors regardless of the magnitude of wealth. If an ultra-affluent family with $100 million in liquid assets does not take advantage of the benefits of tax-aware investing, it is unlikely to change their lifestyle. However, it will certainly impact the wealth of future generations and, if not employed, lessen the chances of achieving and perpetuating a family dynasty. For a twenty-five-year-old investor, a 1 percent advantage on a $10,000 portfolio will mean having an additional $4,889 for retirement some four years later. With a 2 percent enhancement the initial investment doubles in slightly more than thirty-five years, and the individual will have $12,080 extra at retirement. Thus, for the average investor, properly employing the critical elements of tax-aware investing can mean the difference between enjoying retirement according to plan or perhaps having to continue to work well beyond age sixty-five. Whether you are an investor, a portfolio manager, or a financial adviser for taxable clients, employing the elements of tax-aware investment management will allow you to significantly improve net after-tax results to the benefit of wealth creation and maintenance. This is the distinguishing value proposition between the management of traditional tax-exempt accounts and the evolving body of knowledge pertinent to achieving optimal results with taxable accounts.

With interest rates bottoming in 2003, and the Federal Reserve continuing to increase the funds rate, the fixed income markets are unlikely to achieve compelling returns anytime soon. Although the equity markets experienced a favorable rebound in 2003 and 2004, and corporate earnings improved measurably, valuations are still at high levels when compared with historical norms. Thus, the consensus of strategists at the beginning of 2005 is that the markets are unlikely to deliver their previous averages of 11 percent for stocks and 6 percent for government bonds over the next ten years. Furthermore, no strategists are predicting a repeat of the spectacular results achieved during the 1980s and 1990s. In this type of market environment, the impact of taxes accounts for a greater percentage of the total return.

The taxpayer in the United States has experienced three years of favorable tax legislation (from 2001 through 2003) and the second Bush administration has already expressed the goal of simplifying the tax code. Moreover, the president hopes to make permanent the tax code changes implemented during his first term and potentially to eliminate the estate tax altogether. The annual government budget deficit is looming at $400 billion, however, and the financial soundness of the Social Security system remains a concern. For these reasons, many are questioning Congress's ability to maintain the favorable maximum federal tax rate of 15 percent on qualified dividends and long-term capital gains. These and other tax issues will be hotly debated in the years ahead because no one seems satisfied with the status quo. For both the taxable investor and the adviser serving taxable accounts, personal beliefs regarding the tax code are not important. What does matter is how maximum value can be extracted from the available opportunities. This is especially true today because we are in a low-return environment, and the gap between applying a tax-aware solution or not can result in an annual difference of 2 percent or more. A working knowledge of the evolution of the tax codes, reporting standards, portfolio construction, and allocation of assets in a tax-aware manner is as valuable today, if not more so, as it was when the federal income tax was established.

Chapter Notes

1. Touis Allen Talley, "CRS Report on History of Federal Taxes," *CRS Report for Congress,* January 19, 2001, 1–8, http://www.taxhistory.org/thp/readings.nsf (accessed July 7, 2004).

2. Under Section 4940 of the Internal Revenue Code, charitable organizations may be subject to a tax of 2 percent on net investment income.

3. Throughout this book the term *separate account* is used in its traditional meaning, i.e., an established account with a money manager, rather than the retail-oriented wrap account industry where a bundle of investments and services is provided for a single fee.

PART ONE

EVOLUTION OF KNOWLEDGE PERTAINING TO TAX-AWARE INVESTMENT MANAGEMENT

A person doesn't know how much he has to be thankful for until he has to pay taxes on it.

—ANN LANDERS
(QUOTING AN ANONYMOUS SOURCE)

CHAPTER 1

The Evolution of Tax-Aware Investment Management

Only God knows where we got our tax system.

—SAM GIBBONS
MEMBER OF CONGRESS

The current body of knowledge pertaining to tax-aware investment management emerged in the early 1990s. With the passage of the Employee Retirement Income Security Act of 1974 (ERISA), investment firms and academic institutions allocated their resources with an eye toward issues in the expanding and highly profitable tax-exempt account area.[1] As a result, during the 1970s and 1980s, most firms assigned their best and brightest managers to manage portfolios and serve clients for whom taxes simply were not a factor.

While plenty of assets were being managed by the trust departments of banks, and by a select group of managers that focused on the needs of property and casualty insurance companies, very little was published on how to manage assets effectively when taxes were a factor. In addition, the mutual fund industry was growing rapidly, but most firms viewed their mutual fund offerings as an opportunity to enhance revenue by reaching investors who could not qualify for their separate account minimums, utilizing the same process for their tax-exempt accounts. The taxable assets were there, but the investment management industry needed a catalyst.

Decommissioning Nuclear Power Plants

The initial call to action for the investment management industry came, oddly enough, from a market niche that most people are unaware of. In 1984, Title 26, Section 468A of the Internal Revenue Code was amended to allow electric utilities to claim a deduction for costs related to decommissioning the nation's 103 nuclear-powered generating plants.[2] With the average estimated cost of decommissioning exceeding $200 million, a small group of investment managers saw a major market opportunity. They began to analyze the impact of taxes and to modify their portfolio strategies to distinguish themselves from the competition. Electric utilities first turned to their pension managers for advice, but they knew that more had to be done. The Utility Pension Fund Study Group, founded in 1969, began a series of annual conferences to discuss topics related to the efficient management of retirement assets.[3]

In 1989, Arland D. Brusven, treasurer of Northern States Power Company, added a half-day to the agenda in order to include issues pertaining to nuclear decommissioning trusts.[4] The response was overwhelming. More attendees sat through the sessions on nuclear decommissioning than in the sessions devoted to pension management.[5] The first Nuclear Decommissioning Trusts (NDT) Fund Study Group Conference to address the interests of electric utilities and money managers was held in Wrightsville Beach, North Carolina, in 1990. In recent years, the event has attracted more than 150 attendees, and at least that many are expected in 2006.

The presentations by investment managers initially analyzed the impact of taxes on the NDT funding process and might be considered primitive by today's standards, but they were a step in the right direction. After only a few years, the level of sophistication of the presentations improved dramatically. Perhaps the most important result of the nuclear decommissioning experience is that the investment management industry could no longer operate in a vacuum and continue to disregard the impact of taxes on investment returns. Furthermore, the managers who achieved meaningful market share in this niche were those who effectively communicated all relevant factors that affect the day-to-day portfolio construction and management process to the parties involved.

For the NDT industry, the basic relevant factors include cost estimates; the estimated remaining life of the reactor; an understanding of the applicable federal, state, and local tax codes; allocation of assets among trusts subject to different tax rates; and the evolution of regulatory matters. Unlike taxable corporate assets, nuclear reactors have an estimated life of approximately forty years. The future liability or decommissioning is funded through two trusts. The electric utilities first funded a "qualified trust" using an annual amount agreed upon by regulators that could be deducted for tax purposes. However, the amount permitted to fund the qualified trust typically fell short of the total estimate to complete the decommissioning of the reactor. As a result, the utilities have been allowed to fund the shortfall in a "nonqualified trust." Although nonqualified trusts do not receive the initial favorable tax treatment of qualified trusts, there have been periods where they were given great latitude with permissible asset classes, and the tax rates on taxable income and realized gains have been advantageous. The types of asset classes and the tax profiles of the two different types of trusts have been quite different and have evolved over the years. Therefore, all involved in the process have been confronted with an extremely complex form of asset/liability management. Not only were managers challenged to provide more tax-efficient portfolio strategies, but consultants had to adjust their tax-exempt account procedures to include taxes in asset class assumptions and conduct the overall optimization on an after-tax basis. Additionally, they had to address the optimal positioning of asset classes between the qualified and nonqualified trusts, taking into account various regulatory restrictions and evolving tax treatment. While the parameters of nuclear decommissioning trusts differ from those of other types of taxable accounts, it became clear that investment professionals need to be cognizant of all relevant factors in order to achieve optimum after-tax returns. The importance of the annual decommissioning conferences cannot be understated—this forum proved to be and continues to be the leading think tank from which many of the tax-aware investing ideas and concepts evolved that have become second nature in tax-aware investing today.

High-Net-Worth Investors

Bank trust departments had been serving the needs of taxable investors for decades, but without a high level of sophistication. Recognizing a market for consulting services tailored to high-net-worth families, Ralph C. Rittenour Jr. founded Capital Trust Co. in Portland, Oregon, in 1981, which eventually became CTC Consulting. Nancy L. Jacob, the former dean of the University of Washington Business School, joined Rittenour later. While the partnership would not last, and Jacob would eventually establish her own firm, what emerged during their professional relationship had a profound effect on the industry.

For years, investment professionals and consultants attempted to adjust returns of assets for the so-called tax haircut, or impact on investment returns, and to position them in a way that improved or optimized overall results. For a relationship with one vehicle or entity, such as a pension plan, 401(k) plan, or trust, a spreadsheet solution was satisfactory. But when multiple vehicles or entities entered the picture, the solution was often less than desirable in at least one aspect. With funding from CTC, Jacob teamed with Marc Moulton to develop the first commercially available software program that truly accounted for the impact of taxes—PORTAX. Other consulting firms, investment management firms, and banks were developing similar products for use with their internal clients, but none of these could be purchased for independent use.

Although it is a complex tool to learn and master, the beauty of PORTAX is that it enables the investor to incorporate the impact of the tax implications of various entities, cash flows, and time in the optimization process. It also allows the user to quantify the impact of tax-efficient asset location, a topic that Jacob, Jean L. P. Brunel of Brunel Associates, and Gregory Friedman of Greycourt & Co. had addressed in previous collaborations for articles and public presentations. PORTAX, available from Windermere Investment Associates, is still considered to be the system of choice by managers working with sophisticated clients and complex taxable situations.

Publicizing the Need

The adage about the squeaky wheel getting the grease certainly applies to the investment community's reaction to the article "Is Your Alpha Big Enough to Cover Its Taxes?" by R. H. ("Tad") Jeffrey and Robert Arnott, which appeared in the *Journal of Portfolio Management* in the spring of 1993.[6] The article highlights how less than 20 percent of the mutual funds the authors analyzed outperformed the Vanguard 500 Index Fund on an after-tax basis. At the same time that Jeffrey and Arnott were working on their article, Stanford professor John B. Shoven and graduate student Joel M. Dickson initiated a working paper titled "Ranking Mutual Funds on an After-Tax Basis." Although there had been no collaboration between the two parties, both studies pointed to the fact that managers were ignoring the impact of taxes. The results of the studies, covered in greater detail in chapter 3, provided the evidence that was needed to shock fund managers into paying attention to tax issues. Managers were on notice that their failure to address taxes in the portfolio management process was apparent and that the investing public would begin to hold them to a higher standard of accountability.

Jeffrey and Arnott, along with Shoven and Dickson, brought the neglect of managers to center stage, but a standard method of measuring results on an after-tax basis was needed. In response to requests from clients, Lee N. Price, of Rosenberg Capital Management, approached the Association for Investment Management and Research (AIMR) with the idea of developing standards for reporting after-tax returns, similar to what was in place for before-tax returns.[7] At the 1993 NDT Fund Conference, Price announced his vision and the AIMR Subcommittee for After-Tax Reporting was formed. The Subcommittee, co-chaired by Price and Robert E. Pruyne, consisted of working professionals who had extensive experience with taxable accounts. The standards were adopted by AIMR in 1994, but only a few firms, primarily those with nuclear decommissioning accounts, implemented them.

SEC Issues a Proposal

The importance of this initial work, spearheaded by Price, cannot be underestimated since it addressed many of the key concepts and laid the foundation for future initiatives. Once again, however, a major catalyst was needed to achieve a lasting result, and that catalyst proved to be the escalation of private wealth in the late 1990s. With the favorable returns of the equity markets during this period, an increasing number of investors were becoming concerned, if not downright upset, about the capital gains distributions from their mutual funds. The Securities and Exchange Commission (SEC) began to research after-tax reporting and issued a proposal for public comment in March of 2000. The U.S. House of Representatives underscored the importance of the subject by passing the Mutual Fund Tax Awareness Act of 2000 in April, introduced by Congressman Paul Gilmour and adopted by a vote of 385–2.[8] The AIMR subcommittee was reconstituted, with the author, Douglas S. Rogers, as chairman. A dozen uniquely qualified and dedicated Subcommittee members worked selflessly over a three-year period first to respond to the SEC's initiative and later to make recommendations to the AIMR board and the Investment Performance Council (IPC). Most mutual funds are now required to provide after-tax returns in the prospectus. Revisions to the separate account standards for those firms with the desire to adopt them went into effect in January 2005.

Conferences to Share Information

Another key development in the evolution of tax-aware investment management has been in education, or the dissemination of information. Initiatives by the Family Office Exchange (FOX) and the Institute for Private Investors (IPI), under founders Sara Hamilton and Charlotte B. Beyer, respectively, addressed the needs of the influential buyer in the marketplace—the high-net-worth family. Both FOX and IPI managed to bring together buyers and providers in a manner that facilitated an open exchange of information, forcing all parties to seek a higher level of knowledge and sophistication. The effort reinforced the lessons learned through the nuclear decommissioning experience. Since high-profile families and individual investors are easier to identify with than nuclear reactors and have influence with other buyers in the marketplace, these and similar education efforts by other organizations and universities are what finally brought home to the profession the importance of tax-aware investing.

Perhaps the most important conferences on the topic of tax-aware investing have been those held by AIMR. The Investment Counseling for Taxable Investors Conference held in November 1998 was the first of these annual events that attracted speakers with expertise in various taxable-account-related fields.[9] These meetings captured an enormous amount of intellectual thought of the day, and the published AIMR Conference Proceedings can be ordered from the organization. For anyone serving high-net-worth individuals and families, these publications are considered an essential element of the manager's professional library. Although some of the articles focus on the needs of the ultra-affluent, the concepts presented can be applied to almost all taxable-account opportunities.

Baby Boomers Cause a Shift

With more than fifteen years of progress in the theoretical approach to tax-aware investment management, and with after-tax reporting standards now in place, the emphasis is shifting toward implementing strategies through scalable software solutions that take into account the unique characteristics of each client relationship. Surprising to many is the current emphasis on allocating research-and-development dollars to developing systems for smaller accounts and the retail segment of the investment business. Thus, rather than software development trickling down from the more sophisticated portion of the market, it is now building momentum from demand that was created following the SEC's mandate that mutual funds provide after-tax return information. Many believe this is occurring because as the wealth of the baby boomers increases, these investors are shifting their assets from mutual funds to wrap accounts. They naturally ask the question, "If your firm can provide after-tax returns on your mutual funds, why can't you do it here when the fees are higher?" Which portion of the market gets there first is really not important. What is significant is that the state of tax-aware investment management has never been better: progress is being made and the future is promising.

Chapter Notes

1. U.S. Department of Labor, Employee Benefits Security Administration, http://www.dol.gov (accessed July 27, 2004).

2. Title 26 of the Internal Revenue Code, http://frwebgate.access.gpo.gov (accessed July 27, 2004).

3. Utility Pension Fund Study Group, http://www.upfsg.com, (accessed July 27, 2004).

4. Nuclear Decommissioning Trust Fund Conference, http://www.ndtconference.com (accessed July 27, 2004).

5. Arland Brusven, in discussion with the author, July 17, 2004.

6. Robert H. Jeffrey and Robert D. Arnott, "Is Your Alpha Big Enough to Cover Its Taxes? The Active Management Dichotomy," *Journal of Portfolio Management* (Spring 1993): 15–25.

7. The Association for Investment Management and Research changed its name to the Chartered Financial Analysts Institute (CFAI) in 2004.

8. Securities and Exchange Commission, "SEC Requires Disclosure of Mutual Fund After-Tax Returns," news release, January 22, 2001.

9. Association for Investment Management and Research, *AIMR Conference Proceedings: Investment Counseling for Private Clients* no. 2 (1999).

CHAPTER 2

The Sources and Impact of Taxes on Investment Returns

Taxation, in reality, is life. If you know the position a person takes on taxes, you can tell their whole philosophy. The tax code, once you get to know it, embodies all the essence of life: greed, politics, power, goodness, charity.

—SHELDON S. COHEN
FORMER INTERNAL REVENUE SERVICE COMMISSIONER

An understanding of how taxes affect investment returns is essential to a portfolio manager's ability to add value net of fees and taxes. When the knowledge is combined with skill, managers can evolve from reacting to tax consequences to developing proactive procedures to benefit from them. The impact of taxes on investment returns can be broken down into the following areas:

❏ Components of total return and the level of taxation imposed on each
❏ Holding period of the investment
❏ Tax consequences of selling and buying securities
❏ Fees

Using this model, the individual who is new to tax-aware investment management should be able to determine, with the assistance of the two methodologies most commonly used to measure after-tax returns, which types of securities and investment styles are best suited for taxable accounts.

Income Component of Investment Return

Investment returns consist of three components: income, appreciation, and the reinvestment of income. The third component—reinvestment of income—is not a significant factor for short periods of analysis but has a meaningful impact for longer periods. Not all income is treated equally. For example, the United States and Italy are the only two countries in the world to offer tax-exempt bonds. To cite another example, a significant provision of the Jobs and Growth Tax Relief Reconciliation Act of 2003 is the lowering of the tax rate on "qualified" dividends from the ordinary income rate to the more favorable rate for long-term capital gains. Yet although most dividends qualify for the lower rate, taxed at a maximum rate of 15 percent, the majority of income distributed from real estate investment trusts (REITs) does not. As of December 31, 2004, common stocks in the United States provided a dividend yield of 1.6 percent, whereas REITs were offering a yield of approximately 4.6 percent. Let's assume an investor anticipates a 10 percent total return on stocks and REITs over the next year, and that he can go into the market and purchase a unit of each for $100. If the investor does not hold the units in a tax-deferred account and is subject to the highest federal tax rate, then the common stock investment will generate $1.60 in dividends, causing a tax of $0.24 ($1.60 dividend taxed at 15 percent). The REIT investment, however, will generate $4.60 in nonqualifying dividends taxed at the maximum rate on ordinary income, resulting in a tax of $1.61 ($4.60 dividend taxed at 35 percent). Several sources report that up to 25 percent of REITs generate qualified dividends, but the general consensus of portfolio managers serving this niche suggests that qualified dividends from REITs are quite rare.

The key common to these examples is that the nature of the income matters. If you have the opportunity, place investments that generate a high level of taxable income—in the preceding example, REITs—in tax-deferred accounts!

Pre-Liquidation and Post-Liquidation Return

Prior to 2003, stock dividends in the United States were taxed at the ordinary income rate. This created a disparity in the potential after-tax returns between two stocks offering similar overall results when there was a meaningful difference in their dividend yields. In the last twenty-five years or so, the maximum rate on ordinary income has fallen from 50 percent to 35 percent, and the rate on long-term capital gains from 39.9 percent to 15 percent. In addition, common stock dividend yields have fallen from 5 percent to approximately 1.6 percent. A few select years were analyzed

Source: Douglas S. Rogers

FIGURE **2.1** *Projected After-Tax Returns on a 10 Percent Total Return in Common Stocks*

YEAR	AVERAGE STOCK YIELD	TAX ON DIVIDENDS	TAX ON LT GAINS	ONE YEAR		FIVE YEARS	
				PRE-LIQ.	POST-LIQ.	PRE-LIQ.	POST-LIQ.
1978	5.0%	50.0%	39.0%	7.25%	5.00%	6.97%	5.50%
1994	3.0%	39.6%	28.0%	8.53%	6.04%	8.26%	6.81%
2000	1.2%	39.6%	20.0%	9.18%	6.04%	8.93%	7.46%
2005	1.6%	15.0%	15.0%	9.47%	6.82%	9.29%	8.17%

to create projected after-tax returns in **FIGURE 2.1** using a before-tax total rate of return of 10 percent in common stocks and applying the average dividend yields of the time.[1]

In the calculations we assume a 10 percent annual realization of available capital gains and show returns over one-year and five-year periods for both pre- and post-liquidation returns. Pre-liquidation returns assume that only the dividend payments and gains realized are taxed, whereas post-liquidation returns incorporate the tax impact of pre-liquidation returns and also take into account the complete liquidation of all outstanding capital gains and losses. While actual before-tax returns proved to be quite different from the assumed 10 percent, this process enables us to see how the yield characteristics of the market and the tax code create different circumstances for the taxable investor attempting to formulate strategy. In this case, having knowledge of the past may prove beneficial if history repeats itself and tax rates begin to rise during the next decade.

How we calculate after-tax returns can influence our decisions. Therefore, we disclose after-tax returns on both a pre- and post-liquidation basis. Fans of pre-liquidation returns believe these are most appropriate when analyzing returns of individuals, since the tax code allows for a step-up in the cost basis of securities at death. Supporters of the post-liquidation methodology point to the fact that most portfolios or securities are liquidated or sold many times and that you need to emphasize the cost of making these moves to get the investor's attention. Because there are valid reasons for both, they will be shown whenever possible throughout the text. A 10 percent before-tax total return, 10 percent annual capital gains generation, market dividend yield of 1.6 percent, and

FIGURE **2.2** *Trends in Pre- and Post-Liquidation After-Tax Returns*

YEARS	PRE-LIQUIDATION	POST-LIQUIDATION
1	9.47%	6.82%
10	9.16%	8.44%
20	9.04%	8.63%
30	8.98%	8.70%
40	8.95%	8.74%
50	8.94%	8.77%

Source: Douglas S. Rogers

current provisions of the tax code were applied to achieve the after-tax returns shown in **FIGURE 2.2**. When there is a positive unrealized capital gains position, pre-liquidation after-tax returns will be greater than the post-liquidation after-tax returns. As the figure shows, there is one peculiarity of pre- and post-liquidations returns: one series has the tendency to decrease over time while the other increases.

As Figure 2.2 shows, pre-liquidation after-tax returns tend to have a slight downward trend, whereas post-liquidation returns increase and are applied when investment managers wish to highlight the beauty of compounding tax-free over extended periods of time. The buy-and-hold investor takes full advantage of this concept, as he understands that his best tax break may be not to sell and thus avoid realizing capital gains. This makes sense as long as the value of the security is not falling and the general trend for taxes is decreasing or stable.

Holding Period of an Investment

If we go back just a few years to the time when dividends were taxed as ordinary income at 39.6 percent and long-term capital gains at 20 percent, we can analyze how the level of taxable income can have a significant impact on potential after-tax returns.

The rate of taxation on dividends and short-term capital gains is the same, so naturally all one-year returns, regardless of the dividend yield, show a reduction of 3.96 percent, in **FIGURE 2.3**, from the before-tax total rate of return of 10 percent. Note the meaningful differences, especially

FIGURE **2.3** *Impact of Taxable Income on After-Tax Returns When the Tax on Dividends Is Greater Than the Long-Term Capital Gains Rate*

DIVIDEND YIELD	ONE YEAR		FIVE YEARS	
	PRE-LIQ.	POST-LIQ.	PRE-LIQ.	POST-LIQ.
1%	9.25%	6.04%	9.00%	7.49%
3%	8.48%	6.04%	8.34%	7.16%
5%	7.82%	6.04%	7.68%	6.84%

Source: Douglas S. Rogers

of the pre-liquidation after-tax returns, when comparing the results of the 1 percent and 5 percent dividend yield portfolios. The gap narrows with the five-year post-liquidation after-tax returns of the 1 percent and 5 percent portfolios, but the difference is still significant. Higher portfolio yield is typically associated with value-oriented stock selection.[2] Although it is not the purpose of this text to debate whether value outperforms growth on a persistent basis, all things being equal, lower-yielding buy-and-hold portfolios offer the potential for higher after-tax returns when the tax on dividends is greater than the tax on long-term capital gains.

Trading activity that results in the realization of positive capital gains is costly to after-tax returns. However, it must be understood that low turnover is not necessarily a guarantee of a high level of tax efficiency and when relied on can lead to erroneous conclusions. The Dodge & Cox Stock Fund is known to have an enviable record of long-term performance, typically ranking in the top 10 percent of all similarly managed funds. Although it has a portfolio turnover rate that averages 20 percent or less in most years, it still loses about 1.75 percent annually to the payment of taxes from dividend and capital gains distributions.[3]

Perhaps the best way to understand the dilemma faced by the taxable investors in the Dodge & Cox Stock Fund is through the "pipe analogy" developed by Glyn A. Holton.[4] Holton likens building an unrealized capital gains position to water entering a pipe. Water continues to fill the pipe and eventually what goes in must come out the other end as taxable or realized gains. Holton equates the length of the pipe to the level of trading activity. The length or capacity of the pipe dictates how much time passes before the pipe is filled, the amount of water held, and the average amount of time it takes for water to fill the pipe. Lower trading activity

FIGURE **2.4** *The Impact of Capital Gains Realization on After-Tax Returns*

RATE	ONE YEAR		TWENTY YEARS	
	PRE-LIQ.	POST-LIQ.	PRE-LIQ.	POST-LIQ.
0%	6.82%	6.82%	9.76%	9.03%
5%	6.82%	6.82%	9.35%	8.81%
10%	6.82%	6.82%	9.04%	8.63%
25%	6.82%	6.82%	8.43%	8.21%
50%	6.82%	6.82%	7.80%	7.69%
100%	6.82%	6.82%	6.82%	6.82%

Source: Douglas S. Rogers

is equivalent to a longer pipe, which needs more time and water to fill it. The Dodge & Cox Stock Fund is a seasoned product and the capacity of its "pipe" has grown with ever-increasing assets. However, water needs to figuratively trickle from its pipe, or the turnover must fall well below the historical 20 percent level, if the fund wants to lower the tax bite. This is because it takes extremely low levels of capital gains realization to truly be tax-efficient, as the pre- and post-liquidation returns for the twenty years shown in **FIGURE 2.4** highlight.

It may be unrealistic to think that a product can be managed to generate 0 percent capital gains, but it is being done—and with great success, as we will see in later chapters. For this exercise, the capital gains realization rate is the percentage of capital gains realized when compared with the amount of appreciation during the past year, plus the amount of the previous unrealized capital gains outstanding in the portfolio at the beginning of the period.

Tax Consequences of Selling and Buying Securities

A common phrase—"the good, the bad, and the ugly"—has been used to describe trading activity. Discussing these in reverse order, "ugly" trading activity leads to capital gains taxed at the highest level of taxation, which is currently 35 percent for individuals when securities are held for a period of one year or less. The only reason Figure 2.4 does not show a 6.5 percent return in both the pre- and post-liquidation columns for the one-year time period is that qualified dividend income is currently taxed at the more favorable long-term capital gains rate of 15 percent. The key here is that if you hold the security for one day more than a year, you can save 20 percent on the realized portion of the capital gain position! If you trade in the short term, and generate gains, you have to outperform the typical manager through stock selection by 2.5 percent a year—a daunting task in more efficient areas of the market—just to keep up with the average manager, and this does not take into account the cost of commissions, the bid/ask spread between security prices, or settlement costs.

"Bad" trading activity results in the realization of capital gains that are subject to the rate of tax on long-term capital gains. While this rate has been lowered from 20 percent to 15 percent beginning in 2003, it is still costly and should still be avoided, if possible. Most actively managed stock portfolios still have their fill of "bad" trading activity, as the vast majority of them are managed by individuals who fail to account for the impact of taxes prior to selling a security with embedded gains and reinvesting the proceeds in another security. This is evident in the average annual turnover rate for equity mutual funds, which has ranged from a low of 55 percent in 2003 to a high of 81 percent in 1987.[5] The more favorable rate in 2003 is most likely due to the greater flows to passive funds rather than to a change in trading habits of portfolio managers. As the last column of Figure 2.4 shows, it takes levels of capital gains realization of less than 5 percent annually to stay competitive on an after-tax basis. This may sound difficult, but it is possible to realize low levels of capital gains, which leads us to the final type of trading activity.

It is not a sin to take gains. The objective for taxable-account managers is to achieve the highest after-tax return possible, rather than paying no taxes. Therefore, if a portfolio has achieved a substantial profit in a particular stock, and there are clear signs that the fundamentals of the company are deteriorating, sell the position in the most efficient manner possible. This is not the time to become a "tax hero," as we learned all too well with technology issues after the spring of 2000. Taking gains when the outlook is for rapidly falling prices is certainly good trading activity. Another type of "good" trading activity that may be less obvious involves analyzing the sale and purchase of two securities on an after-tax basis. If a purchase candidate offers superior return potential when the tax payment on that security is incorporated in the analysis, then the trade makes sense.

The best-known "good" turnover in tax-aware investment management circles is the potential for realizing losses when they are available in taxable account portfolios. This can be a difficult concept for even the most seasoned investors to grasp. It may appear at first that a manager is purposely losing money for the client. We don't want to get carried away like Michael Douglas's character in the movie *Wall Street* who says "greed is good," but unlike in the tax-exempt account arena, losses can have genuine economic value for taxable accounts when properly managed. If there is a nice feature within our tax code, it is that losses can be used to offset realized gains. If they cannot be applied initially, they may be "saved" for the future, and in some cases indefinitely. You may also hear, "Trading or turnover for taxable accounts is like cholesterol, in that our doctors inform us there are both good and bad forms of cholesterol." If cholesterol is a permanent part of our daily existence, then why not focus on taking advantage of the good cholesterol and reduce the negative impact of the bad form of cholesterol as much as possible? The same thought should be applied to trading activity and the realization of capital gains. No portfolio manager wants to purposely lose money, but the market does not go up everyday. So take advantage of the naturally occurring volatility of security prices and "harvest" losses when it makes economic sense to do. Besides, "tax-loss harvesting" reduces the cost of the other two forms of "good" trading activity when gains have to be realized.

We've often heard that there is no such thing as a free lunch. Tax-loss harvesting may not be a free lunch—there are trading costs associated with the process—but it may be the closest thing to a free lunch in the investment management industry, and avoiding it may ultimately represent a missed opportunity with true economic value. As my father once said, "It may not be the best thing going, but it sure beats what is in second place!" In the past decade, great strides have been made in the understanding and execution of the tax-loss harvesting trade. There is simply no longer a valid excuse for the failure of managers serving taxable accounts to understand the strengths and weaknesses of tax-loss harvesting and to know when and how it should be applied.

Impact of Fees

Fees are the last factor that affects after-tax returns. Because fees take away from net wealth creation, tax-aware investors consider fees a form of taxation. Fees come in many forms, all of which are worthy of scrutiny. For the purpose of this discussion, however, we will focus on all-encompassing annual portfolio or fund management fees along with any sales load. Studying the impact of fees can be an extremely worthwhile exercise because many fees are not readily apparent to the investor.

Like taxes, fees serve a purpose. There is nothing wrong with charging a reasonable fee for a value-added product or service. No one is in the investment management business to work for free. The question the

FIGURE **2.5** *The Impact of Fees on After-Tax Returns*

FRONT LOAD	FEE RATE	ONE YEAR		TWENTY YEARS	
		PRE-LIQ.	POST-LIQ.	PRE-LIQ.	POST-LIQ.
None	0.0%	9.47%	6.82%	9.04%	8.63%
None	0.2%	9.26%	6.61%	8.82%	8.41%
None	0.5%	8.94%	6.30%	8.50%	8.09%
None	1.0%	8.42%	5.77%	7.97%	7.54%
None	1.5%	7.89%	5.25%	7.43%	7.00%
4.5%	1.0%	3.54%	1.01%	7.72%	7.30%

tax-aware manager or investor must ask is whether the fees are reasonable for the value that a particular product or service contributes to wealth creation. The sad fact is that in many cases the answer is no, and we owe it to ourselves and to clients to determine what makes the most economic sense. With the average fees for common stock mutual funds at 1.5 percent per year and index funds at or below 0.2 percent, **FIGURE 2.5** suggests that fees are a form of taxation and that they really do matter.

The first row of information in the figure suggests a 0 percent fee scenario, and you might think the manager is working for free. The fact is that large index portfolios often put their securities out for lending to broker-dealers, which may generate sufficient revenue to create, in essence, close to a free or zero-cost proposition. Fees make it extremely difficult for the product-based adviser dealing with a limited number of offerings to compete in the tax-aware arena today. When you look at the last row in Figure 2.5, it becomes clear that even with a mild front-end load, it takes many years before this type of product can catch up with its no-load counterparts, unless the fund is generating extremely strong positive results through superior security selection that is likely to generate a high level of capital gains. This is especially true for military personnel, who are often approached by advisers extolling the merits of using front-end-loaded funds and dollar-cost averaging into the market over an extended period of time. The underlying logic of these systematic savings plans is sound, since overseas deployments make it particularly challenging for military personnel to manage their financial affairs. However, when the product is not tax-efficient, the military investor with limited upside earnings potential can find himself, ten or so years down the road, barely able to afford to pay the tax on the fund's capital gain distribution without liquidating shares. If the manager has the potential to produce a superior return, he should be compensated with an appropriate fee. However, when taxes are accounted for, it comes as no surprise that many managers are falling short of a reasonable after-tax return objective.

In summary, when tax-aware practitioners or investors are cognizant of the causes and ultimate impact that taxes have on investment returns, they can better manage the process to maximize future results. This means identifying products that are advantageous for taxable accounts while positioning others in tax-exempt accounts where they will be least detrimental to wealth creation. To assist in the process, managers should take into account the following principles:

❏ When the tax rate is higher on taxable income than on long-term capital gains, all else being equal, lower-yielding portfolios have an advantage.

❏ Extending the holding period, especially beyond one year, enhances after-tax returns.

❏ Trading activity can significantly influence after-tax returns.

❏ It takes extremely low levels of capital gains realization to be tax-efficient.

❏ Fees are a form of taxation, and they do matter.

With an understanding and an appreciation of these principles, you are in a position to fully comprehend how seminal research and the processes and products that subsequently developed have benefited the taxable investor.

Chapter Notes

1. Ibbotson 2003 Yearbook, *Stocks, Bonds, Bills and Inflation* (Chicago: Ibbotson Associates, 2003).

2. Douglas S. Rogers, "After-Tax Equity Returns for Non-Qualified Nuclear Decommissioning Trusts," *Financial Analysts Journal* (July-August 1992): 70–73.

3. Morningstar Principia (June 30, 2004).

4. Glyn A. Holton, "Transient Effects in Taxable Equity Investment," *Financial Analysts Journal* (May–June 1994).

5. *Mutual Fund Fact Book 2004* (Washington, D.C.: Investment Company Institute, 2004), 65.

CHAPTER 3

Seminal Research

And it came to pass in those days, that there went out a decree from Caesar Augustus that all the world should be taxed.

—NEW TESTAMENT

Experienced advisers often wonder why it took until the 1990s before tax-aware investment management began to gain traction. One of the many reasons for this was the lack of research available to the investment community and investors. To conduct any type of analysis takes two main ingredients: knowledgeable individuals to conduct the exercise and a means to measure results on the subject they wish to investigate. The first research ingredient was present in academics, such as George M. Constantinides, a noted professor at the University of Chicago, who wrote several outstanding articles in the early 1980s.[1] His work addresses optimal trading of both stocks and bonds, and he coauthored an article with Myron S. Scholes on asset pricing that takes into account the impact of personal taxes. Furthermore, a review of his references quickly reveals there had been a great deal of work taking taxes into account by noted individuals in the 1970s. However, the more-sophisticated research of the time emphasized how taxes influenced the pricing of securities, rather than whether or not analysts and portfolio managers took them into consideration. The other essential ingredient is having a way to measure results. Unfortunately, we still do not have databases or methods to accurately measure after-tax results of separate account managers in any meaningful way. To do this we must still rely on information from mutual funds, which is historically still a relatively young industry. Whereas the first fund was launched in Boston in 1924, the real structure and regulatory framework for the industry was not put into place until 1940, and the number of funds did not surpass 500 until 1978.[2]

"Is Your Alpha Big Enough to Cover Its Taxes?" published in the *Journal of Portfolio Management* in the spring of 1993, was the first article to use mutual fund tax-related information to truly capture the impact on investment returns.[3] The story behind this article is worth sharing, as it offers several valuable lessons.[4] The article was coauthored by Robert D. Arnott and Robert H. Jeffrey. At the time the article was prepared, Arnott was the president of First Quadrant, a firm recognized for quantitative investing and insightful research. Most recently, he founded his own firm, Research Affiliates, and is the portfolio manager of the highly successful PIMCO All Asset Fund. Known as a prolific author and coauthor of numerous articles on an array of investment-related subjects, Arnott also serves as editor of the *Financial Analysts Journal*, the research journal of the CFA Institute. Robert "Tad" Jeffrey is a hands-on practitioner and has published several noteworthy articles, as well.

In 1974, Jeffrey's family's company sold a manufacturing subsidiary for cash. Therefore, the family had to make a major adjustment from managing operating companies to overseeing a taxable portfolio. Having been a history major, Jeffrey had to learn quickly. It was probably a blessing in disguise that he did not have a formal investment education, as his thinking was not inhibited by traditional portfolio management practices.

Jeffrey made a very wise move by asking none other than Peter L. Bernstein to assist as a consultant to the company. Bernstein had been a teacher at Williams College. Shortly after his departure, Jeffrey enrolled there as a student. They met later and developed a warm friendship over the years, and Jeffrey affectionately refers to Bernstein as his professor.

Bernstein introduced Jeffrey to some of the most noted personalities in academia, investment management, and pension consulting. Throughout the 1980s Jeffrey sent letters to these individuals, such as the late Peter O. Dietz of Frank Russell Co., seeking more efficient ways to manage taxable assets.[5] Meanwhile, Jeffrey continued to hear of firms that could possibly address his special need but that they had all the business they could handle from the mainstream and would find it uneconomical to divert their resources. Jeffrey even sent Jack Bogle of Vanguard a letter suggesting launching a product similar to the Windsor Fund that would explicitly take the impact of taxes into consideration, but Vanguard would not directly address the need until some nine years later when it launched the "Tax-Managed" series of funds in 1994.[6]

Like Tad Jeffrey, Rob Arnott was concerned about the impact of taxes on his own portfolio. Knowing that both individuals had a passionate interest in the subject, Bernstein introduced them after one of Arnott's articles on taxable account investing had been rejected by *Financial Analysts Journal*. As Arnott tells the story, he had written an internal piece on how trading affects after-tax results and shared it with Jeffrey. After reading the article, Jeffrey remarked, "This is great, but we need to put something in English so the average individual can understand it!" To address Jeffrey's concern about simplicity, they decided on a more real-world versus theoretical approach. They compared the after-tax performance of all funds classified by Morningstar as "growth" and "growth and income" that had at least $100 million in assets throughout the period of 1982 to 1991. Obviously, there is survivor bias in the study, as many lesser-performing funds that could not attract and maintain the $100 million threshold were eliminated. Rather than apply the maximum federal tax rates for individuals, they applied a 35 percent rate so that the results would apply to the various types of taxable accounts. The results from seventy-one funds studied were compared with the Vanguard 500 Index Fund, and also with a fictional "Closed-End Index 500" as a better benchmark, since mutual funds are subject to tax implications from shareholder redemption activity. The latter is a valid comparison because, as Jack Bogle has stated, close scrutiny on redemption activity did not begin until sometime later, and the after-tax results of the Vanguard 500 Index Fund would have been higher if current controls had been in place.[7] **FIGURE 3.1** gives the key results of their study.

Source: Robert H. Jeffrey and Robert D. Arnott, "Is Your Alpha Big Enough to Cover Its Taxes?" *Journal of Portfolio Management* (Spring 1993)

FIGURE 3.1 *Number of Large Actively Managed Mutual Funds of Seventy-One That Outperformed the Respective Index Fund (1982–1991)*

TOTAL RETURN	"CLOSED-END INDEX 500"	VANGUARD 500 INDEX
Pretax	15	15
After Capital Gains Taxes	5	10
After Capital Gains and Dividend Taxes	6	9
After All Taxes Including Deferred	10	13

Readers, especially those in the investment management community, were shocked to discover not that only 21 percent (15 out of 71) funds beat the Vanguard 500 Index Fund on a pretax basis but that only 13 percent (9 out of 71) outperformed on an after-tax basis, once taxes on capital gains and dividend distributions were accounted for. This method of calculation is now known as the "pre-liquidation methodology," as the tax on the unrealized capital gain or loss position is not taken into account. Since large-capitalization stock index funds have very little turnover in their holdings, capital gains distributions are primarily attributable to shareholder activity or mergers and acquisitions that are consummated as a taxable cash transaction rather than as a tax-free exchange of shares. Therefore, all else being equal, index funds are likely to have greater embedded unrealized capital gains positions than actively managed funds that are consistently generating capital gains through the sale and purchase of individual securities. Even with the most conservative post-liquidation calculation only 17 percent (13 out 71) of the funds outperformed the Vanguard 500 Index Fund on an after-tax basis.

Of the thirteen mutual funds that outperformed the Vanguard 500 Index Fund on an after-tax basis, only two did so by a meaningful margin (see **FIGURE 3.2**). These were the CGM Capital and Fidelity Magellan funds managed by legendary managers Ken Heebner and Peter Lynch, respectively. The helm of Fidelity Magellan has changed hands several times since Peter Lynch managed the fund, but neither fund has repeated

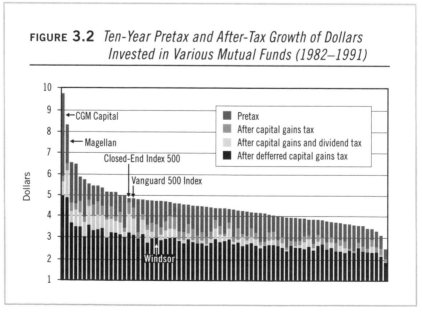

FIGURE **3.2** *Ten-Year Pretax and After-Tax Growth of Dollars Invested in Various Mutual Funds (1982–1991)*

Source: Robert H. Jeffrey and Robert D. Arnott, "Is Your Alpha Big Enough to Cover Its Taxes?" *Journal of Portfolio Management* (Spring 1993)

Source: Morningstar Principia (January 2005)

FIGURE **3.3** *Ten-Year After-Tax Performance (for the Ten Years Ending 12-31-2004)*

MUTUAL FUND	RETURN AFTER TAXES ON DISTRIBUTION	RETURN AFTER TAXES ON DISTRIBUTION & SALE
CGM Capital Development	8.60%	8.31%
Fidelity Magellan	8.54%	8.11%
Vanguard 500 Index	11.32%	10.34%

over the past ten years, as **FIGURE 3.3** shows.[8] Part of the two funds' inability to outperform an index fund can be explained by their growth style of investing being out of favor for the past five years. However, the point of this example is to highlight how difficult it is to outperform the index on after-tax basis over a long period of time and then to repeat the feat in the future.

Even after more than a decade, "Is Your Alpha Big Enough To Cover Its Taxes?" is still considered the seminal article in tax-aware investing, as it clearly demonstrated the difficulty in attempting to outperform a low-fee, large-capitalization index fund on after-tax basis when relying on traditional portfolio management practices. The study also highlighted how tax consequences are more a factor of the holding period and their impact diminishes as turnover increases. Its impact on the industry has been profound, as it underscored the amount of research that needed to be done into taxable-account investing.

Over the years, financial services entrepreneur Charles Schwab developed a supportive relationship with Stanford University. He funded the Charles R. Schwab Professor of Economics position, which was filled by professor John B. Shoven.[9] After launching the Schwab 1000 Index Fund with the thought of offering a product with a favorable tax orientation, Charles Schwab approached Shoven to conduct two studies. The first study was to illustrate the impact taxes have on mutual fund returns. Schwab was hoping the conclusions of the study would support his vision of a need for a tax-aware fund, and the market would therefore embrace his firm's new product.

To satisfy Schwab's request, Shoven enlisted Joel M. Dickson, a graduate student who had a special interest in mutual funds, to cowrite the working paper, titled "Ranking Mutual Funds on an After-Tax Basis." [10]

The project kept the coauthors busy, as they soon found out that the data they obtained from the Investment Company Institute (ICI) required a lot of scrubbing before they could draw meaningful conclusions with any degree of confidence. They analyzed returns going back ten, twenty, and thirty years and applied tax rates applicable to low-, middle-, and high-tax-bracket families. Dickson and Shoven noticed the Vanguard 500 Index Fund improved in relative performance, moving from 78.9 on a before-tax basis to the 85.0 on after-tax basis. They also calculated that if the small amount of capital gains distributed had been zero, then the performance would have ended up at the 91.8 percentile. These results were consistent with findings of Arnott and Jeffrey and supported the conclusion that mutual fund managers were paying little attention to the impact of taxes.

Dickson and Shoven analyzed 147 of the largest growth and growth and income mutual funds from 1983 to 1992 using ICI data. Since the first index mutual fund did not come about until 1976, they focused their attention on how managers changed in relative ranking between before- and after-tax performance in relation to their turnover rates. When they looked at the performance of individual funds, they found some interesting surprises. As might be expected the fund with the lowest turnover, Franklin Growth (only 3.2 percent annually), jumped 33.8 percentiles in ranking, but the fund with the highest turnover, Fidelity Value (296 percent), improved more than any other fund with a jump of 35.4 percentiles. The Dickson and Shoven study shows only a small negative correlation between turnover and the pre- to post-tax performance ratios. Moreover, the coauthors believed the results were not statistically significant. In essence, what their study proved is that you simply could not make broad sweeping statements about portfolio turnover and the impact on after-tax performance. At the time they probably did not envision how sage the comment "We feel that managing a fund so as to defer all capital gains realizations is feasible" would prove to be some ten years later, as the Schwab 1000 Index Fund has not made a capital gain distribution since its inception in 1991. Actually, this statement was really a prelude of more things to come, as Charles Schwab's second request was for Shoven to address methods that could be used to operate a mutual fund without generating capital gains. Just a year after publishing the first paper, they would coauthor "A Stock Index Mutual Fund Without Net Capital Gains Realizations."[11] The importance of this work will be covered in greater detail in chapter 9, which addresses methods used to outperform index funds on an after-tax basis in detail.

In 2000, Rob Arnott revisited the subject he had addressed seven years earlier with the follow-up paper "How Well Have Taxable Investors

Source: Robert H. Jeffrey and Robert D. Arnott, "'Is Your Alpha Big Enough To Cover Its Taxes? The Active Management Dichotomy," *Journal of Portfolio Management* (Spring 1993): 15–25

FIGURE **3.4** *Margin of Gain and Shortfall vs. Vanguard Index 500*

TOTAL RETURN	WON	AVG. MARGIN OF GAIN	LOST	AVG. MARGIN OF SHORTFALL
Pretax Returns	15	1.8%	56	−1.9%
After Capital Gains	5	1.0%	66	−3.5%
After Capital Gains and Dividend Taxes	6	0.9%	65	−3.1%
After All Taxes Including Deferred	10	1.1%	61	−2.4%

Been Served in the 1980's and 1990's?"[12] With his associates Andrew L. Berkin and Jia Ye, he went back to the original study and came up with an interesting observation that, upon further analysis, the magnitude of the average margin of shortfall by the large number of funds underperforming was much greater than the average margin of gain on the funds that outperformed the Vanguard 500 Index Fund on an after-tax basis (see **FIGURE 3.4**).

With the growth in the mutual fund industry there were now many more funds to analyze. Therefore, the longer time horizon and the greater number of observations could reinforce the validity of or possibly refute their earlier findings. They studied three time horizons: ten years (1989–1998), fifteen years (1984–1988), and twenty years (1979–1988). Depending on the period and type of calculation method, only 4 percent to 16 percent of the mutual funds consistently having more than $100 million in assets outperformed the Vanguard 500 Index Fund on after-tax basis. Therefore, this study produced results similar to those of the original study and validated the claims made years earlier.

In this study, the coauthors also subtracted the before-tax return differential from the after-tax results between the funds and the Vanguard 500 Index Fund to achieve a "pure tax effect." There are several interesting observations (see **FIGURE 3.5**). First, since the Vanguard 500 Index Fund has outperformed most funds on a before-tax basis, the differential is not as dramatic as previously shown. Second, the total column is always negative, which shows that the average fund pays more taxes than the index fund. Lastly, note how the percentages improve in each case

FIGURE **3.5** *Mutual Fund Pure Tax Effect vs. Vanguard 500 Index Fund*

	AHEAD OF VANGUARD 500 INDEX	
	NUMBER OF FUNDS	MARGIN ABOVE VANGUARD 500
10-Year Results (1989–1998)		
After Capital Gains Taxes	6 2%	0.21%
After Capital Gains and Dividend Taxes	31 31%	0.39%
After Liquidation	125 35%	0.50%
15-Year Results (1984–1998)		
After Capital Gains Taxes	7 3%	0.26%
After Capital Gains and Dividend Taxes	17 8%	0.60%
After Liquidation	53 26%	0.60%
20-Year Results (1979–1998)		
After Capital Gains Taxes	5 3%	0.37%
After Capital Gains and Dividend Taxes	16 10%	0.75%
After Liquidation	44 27%	0.56%

when you go from the row marked "After Capital Gains" to the row marked "After Capital Gains and Dividend Taxes." Common stock mutual funds can apply the income from dividends to offset fund expenses, which lowers the tax burden to the shareholder. Since fees of actively managed funds are much higher than the 20 basis points or less for the Vanguard 500 Index Fund this tax saving is meaningful.

This also addressed the issue of survivor bias, which was not addressed earlier. As expected, when this factor was taken into account the results favored the Vanguard 500 Index Fund even more. As with the previous study, information provided by Morningstar made this study possible.

| BEHIND VANGUARD 500 INDEX | | | |
NUMBER OF FUNDS		MARGIN ABOVE VANGUARD 500	TOTAL
349	98%	−1.68%	−1.65%
324	91%	−1.27%	−1.12%
230	65%	−0.47%	−0.13%
196	97%	−1.63%	−1.56%
186	92%	−1.20%	−1.05%
150	74%	−0.53%	−0.23%
157	97%	−1.49%	−1.43%
146	90%	−1.00%	−0.83%
118	73%	−0.56%	−0.25%

Source: Robert D. Arnott, Andrew L. Berkin, and Jia Ye, "How Well Have Taxable Investors Been Served in the 1980's and 1990's?" *Journal of Portfolio Management* vol. 26, no. 4 (Summer 2000): 84–94.

After-tax investing is a noble objective, but is there evidence to suggest that investors have taken notice? In their paper, "Do After-Tax Returns Affect Mutual Fund Inflows?" authors Daniel Bergstresser and James Poterba of the MIT Department of Economics offered evidence to suggest that high tax burdens are associated with lower gross inflows, and mutual funds that offer higher after-tax returns attract greater inflows.[13] They studied a large sample of equity mutual funds from 1993 to 1999. It is encouraging that Bergstresser and Poterba discovered that investors took noticeable steps to protect themselves, as it was not until the end of this period that the financial press began to address in a meaningful way the adverse financial consequences from potential large capital gains distributions.

Review of the key articles on tax-aware investing highlights four important factors. First, change in the financial management industry requires a vision. Both Tad Jeffrey and Charles Schwab addressed an issue that others ignored. Through two decades of persistence and interaction with countless professionals Jeffrey should be designated as the "father of tax-aware investing," and due to his financial support Charles Schwab be known as "the godfather of tax-aware investing." The second point is it often takes gifted individuals to communicate the dreams of others. Therefore, we need to be thankful that Rob Arnott, John Shoven, and Joel Dickson recognized the issue and were able to communicate their conclusions in a manner that allowed practitioners and investors to take action. Third, the content of materials available to the investor will continue to improve as needs are addressed by service providers and regulators. To demonstrate how the industry has progressed, refinements in the Morningstar Principia database now allow individual investors to conduct their own after-tax mutual fund analysis—which would rival the pioneering work done by researchers with advanced degrees only a decade ago—on almost any asset class in a matter of minutes! Fourth and lastly, while most stock funds have underperformed the Vanguard 500 Index Fund on an after-tax basis, it does not mean all funds should or will underperform in the future. Since we now understand what causes lackluster after-tax performance, enlightened practitioners are now offering and creating distinctive services and products. However, compelling results cannot be achieved unless investors or their trusted advisers are able to identify the growing number of uniquely qualified tax-aware professionals in the marketplace today.

Chapter Notes

1. George M. Constantinides and Myron S. Scholes, "Optimal Liquidation of Assets in the Presence of Personal Tax," *Journal of Finance* vol. 35, no. 2(1980): 439–449; George M. Constantinides, "Capital Market Equilibrium With Personal Tax," *Econometrica* 51 (1983): 611–636; George M. Constantinides, "Optimal Stock Trading With Personal Taxes: Implications for Prices and the Abnormal January Returns," *Journal of Financial Economics,* 13 (1984): 65–89; George M. Constantinides, "Optimal Bond Trading With Personal Taxes," *Journal of Financial Economics,* 13 (1984): 299–335.

2. Investment Company Institute, *Mutual Fund Fact Book* 2004 (Washington, D.C.: Investment Company Institute, 2004), 105.

3. Robert H. Jeffrey and Robert D. Arnott, "Is Your Alpha Big Enough To Cover Its Taxes? The Active Management Dichotomy," *Journal of Portfolio Management* (Spring 1993): 15–25.

4. Robert D. Arnott, Peter L. Bernstein, John C. Bogle, and James P. Garland and Robert H. Jeffrey, in discussion with the author, August 30, September 1, September 2, and August 4, 2004, respectively.

5. Robert H. Jeffrey to Peter O. Dietz, April 26, 1983.

6. Robert H. Jeffrey to John C. Bogle, May 29, 1985.

7. John C. Bogle, in discussion with the author, September 2, 2004.

8. Morningstar Principia, June 30, 2004.

9. Joel M. Dickson, in discussion with the author, September 21, 2004.

10. Joel M. Dickson and John B. Shoven, "Ranking Mutual Funds on an After-Tax Basis," NBER Working Paper no. 4393, National Bureau of Economic Research, July 1993.

11. Joel M. Dickson and John B. Shoven, "A Stock Index Mutual Fund Without Net Capital Gains Realizations," NBER Working Paper no. 4717, National Bureau of Economic Research, April 1994.

12. Robert D. Arnott, Andrew L. Berkin, and Jia Ye, "How Well Have Taxable Investors Been Served in the 1980's and 1990's?" *Journal of Portfolio Management* vol. 26, no. 4 (Summer 2000): 84–94.

13. Daniel Bergstresser and James Poterba, "Do After-Tax Returns Affect Mutual Fund Inflows?" *Journal of Economics* vol. 63, no. 3 (2002): 381–414.

CHAPTER 4

The Tax-Aware Practitioner

What is one really trying to do in the investment world? Not pay the least taxes, although that may be a factor to be considered in achieving the end. Means and end should not be confused, however, and the end is to come away with the largest after-tax rate of compound.

—WARREN BUFFETT

When individuals hear their first presentation or read their first article on tax-aware investing, they often ask, "How do you identify or become a tax-aware practitioner?" This is an excellent question, since there is no direct route available to acquire the body of knowledge required to effectively serve taxable accounts. Although it is difficult to pinpoint a specific qualification as the telltale sign of excellence, there are four traits shared by all elite tax-aware practitioners:

❑ Knowledgeability
❑ Inquisitiveness
❑ Patience
❑ Passion

This chapter is devoted to individuals who appreciate the value of tax-aware investment management and desire to sharpen their skills for the benefit of their clients. These traits and their development are especially important, not only for people just entering the industry but also for investors who are evaluating their providers' potential to serve them properly in the future.

Knowledgeability

The process of acquiring knowledge begins with education. Many academic institutions offer outstanding programs that build a base of knowledge in finance, accounting, and personal financial or estate planning. The area that today is perhaps most aligned with incorporating taxes in making investment decisions is personal financial planning. To screen for a potential fit, the college-bound student should start with one of the dozen or so college guides available in bookstores or on the Internet. Another excellent source is the Certified Financial Planner Board of Standards website (www.cfp.net), which lists more than eighty schools that offer undergraduate and graduate programs.

Most practitioners begin their careers by first obtaining degrees in accounting, finance, or law. Although these academic majors consider taxes in one form or another, none of them adequately address the impact of taxes on security buy and sell decisions, portfolio construction, policy development, or asset allocation and location. To illustrate how little information is available to students: the leading college textbook *Investments,* Fifth Edition, by Bodie, Kane, and Marcus, is approximately a thousand pages, and devotes only three pages to the impact taxes have on investment considerations and asset allocation.[1] The author could mention instances where noted titles actually misstate the impact of taxes on investment returns, but the objective of this text is to enlighten readers about the benefits of tax-aware investing rather than to criticize the sins and neglect of the past.

To add compelling value with taxable accounts, practitioners need to have at least a basic working knowledge of the taxes their clients are subject to. It is unrealistic to expect one individual to know everything there is about investing, the tax code, or estate planning, but when in doubt, tax-aware practitioners need to know where to locate—or whom to contact to obtain—accurate information. Additionally, they must be aware of how the payment of taxes affects the returns of permissible securities identified by the client. Moreover, they must be able to see the benefit of the optimal allocation of various categories of assets and investment styles between taxable and tax-deferred accounts to achieve the highest after-tax returns possible. Lastly, they must understand how to measure success and realize that tax-aware investing and reporting are evolving art forms, as opposed to sciences.

Upon entering the private sector, sincere practitioners will generally obtain one of the following professional designations, depending on their employment specialty:

❑ Chartered Financial Analyst (CFA), a globally recognized standard for measuring the competency and integrity of analysts—The CFA program's self-study curriculum allows even the busiest investment professional to participate. The curriculum develops and reinforces a fundamental knowledge of investment principles. The three levels of examination verify a candidate's ability to apply these principles across all areas of the investment decision-making process. And the program's professional-conduct requirements demand that both CFA candidates and charter holders adhere to the highest standards of ethical responsibility.[2]

❏ Certified Financial Planner (CFP), a certification that consumers recognize, respect and demand—Before applying for the CFP certification examination, candidates need to complete the education requirements set by the CFP Board. There are more than 285 academic programs at colleges and universities from which to choose, plus certain degrees and professional credentials fulfill the education requirement. A ten-hour exam tests the candidates' ability to apply their financial planning knowledge to client situations.[3]

❏ Certified Investment Management Analyst (CIMA)—The CIMA offers an intense educational focus on asset allocation, manager search and selection, investment policy, and performance measurement. The program begins with a self-study Level 1 program and exam. The Level 2 materials and exam can be completed either by attending a one-week class held at a leading business school or online.[4]

❏ Chartered Life Underwriter (CLU)—The CLU is conferred only upon successful completion of a ten-part course that covers fundamentals of economics, finance, taxation, investments, and other areas of risk management as they apply to life insurance. The course of study can be completed through home study or by attending courses at a branch of the American Society of Chartered Life Underwriters or at an affiliated college or university.[5]

❏ Certified Public Accountant (CPA)—One of the world's leading licensing exams, the CPA examination serves to protect the public interest by helping to ensure that only qualified individuals become licensed as certified public accountants. CPA examinations are offered throughout the year, and requirements vary by state.[6]

❏ Certified Trust and Financial Advisor (CTFA)—To earn the CTFA credential, candidates must meet the experience, education, ethics, and examination requirements determined to be competency measures for personal trust professionals. Applicants must take a personal training program approved by the Institute of Certified Bankers (ICB) for precertification.[7]

In addition to passing one or more exams, there may be requirements such as signing an ethics statement, demonstrating particular types of

experience, and providing professional references. Some of the profes-
sional-designation certification programs also have a continuing-education
requirement. Unfortunately, none of them adequately train the beginning
professional in the area of tax-aware of investing, but weaknesses in curriculum are being addressed. Several supplemental education initiatives are under way to improve the curriculum and testing to enhance the capabilities of
the taxable-account practitioner. One initiative—the May 2004 launching
of the Investor Education Collaborative by Charlotte B. Beyer and Susan
Remmer Ryzewic—is extremely promising, as the principals involved have
extensive hands-on experience in education for the ultra-affluent.[8] In the
meantime, these five programs serve the needs of practitioners who focus
on the high-net-worth family or individual market:

❑ American Bankers Association (ABA) Private Wealth Management
School—The school introduces seasoned relationship managers to
unique consultative sales approaches for delivering financial services to
wealthy clients. During a six-day resident session, students receive in-
termediate-level instruction on building the skills necessary to become
a more competent and proactive adviser. Recognized practitioners and
industry experts assemble at the Duke University Fuqua School of
Business to serve as faculty and counsel to students. Two modules are
offered over consecutive years.[9]

❑ Institute for Private Investors (IPI)/Wharton School Private Wealth
Management Program—Through class lectures and interactive case-
work, participants can increase their depth of knowledge in key areas
of wealth management. As part of the core curriculum, the program
places participants within a fictitious family with worldwide businesses
and investments. During a six-day resident session, they make decisions that will affect the family's wealth for future generations.[10]

❑ Investment Management Consultants Association (IMCA) Wealth
Management Certificate Program—This program teaches the tools
and techniques for creating and implementing strategic solutions to
the complex challenges associated with wealthy clients. The curriculum
is divided into three phases reflecting the natural life cycle of wealth.
Students study assigned materials, complete online quizzes, and then
attend a full day seminar. It culminates with a two-day symposium.[11]

❑ New York University Certificate in Wealth Management—This
course is designed to enhance the relationship between advisers and
high-net-worth clients to achieve desired goals. The curriculum includes core courses plus electives that address investment management,
alternative investments, and wealth transition and transfer.[12]

❑ American Academy of Financial Management Chartered Wealth
Manager—The five-day program offers a core group of courses

focused on skills for high-net-worth consulting. Prerequisites include a recognized degree, a professional certification, and five years of related industry experience.[13]

Schooling, certification, and supplemental education provide the foundation of knowledge, but tax-aware investing as an art form is still relatively new. Moreover, as will become obvious in the following chapters, the curriculum of the programs noted above usually do not cover the application of tax-aware principles to security selection, portfolio management, asset allocation, and location, as they simply lack faculty who are qualified to teach it. Additionally, one must be careful about using the terms "wealth management" and "high-net-worth client." These terms were previously reserved for clients with liquid financial assets above $100 million. With the "retailization" of the investment management industry, these terms are often used by overzealous marketers and financial planners that reflect any opportunity where there are investable assets, no matter what the magnitude. Therefore, the tax-aware practitioner should seek every opportunity for self-improvement through avenues that will allow for continual improvement of the practitioner's skill.

Inquisitiveness

The tax-aware practitioner knows that many markets and individual securities are inefficiently priced when taxes are considered. A great deal of truly outstanding work has been done in the modern era of investing to develop well-known theories, such as the efficient market hypothesis and capital asset pricing equation, but in most cases the impact of taxes was not part of the process. Therefore, arbitrage opportunities are often available for the tax-aware practitioner who is willing to question the traditional wisdom that was developed for tax-exempt accounts. Moreover, many of these concepts are simple and require no more than a "back of the envelope" explanation. For example, before 2003, the tax rate on dividends in the United States was almost twice the rate for securities sold with gains held twelve months or more. Let's create a scenario of two common stocks that have the long-term potential to produce a total rate of return, dividends plus appreciation, of 10 percent per year. As **FIGURE 4.1** shows, the results are similar for the stocks of the two companies (A and B), with the exception of how much of their earnings they pay to shareholders in dividends.

Investors who are considering the two securities for a tax-exempt account should be indifferent to whether to hold stock A or B, as they end up with the same amount of dollars at the end of each year. However, let's see what happens if we start with a $100 purchase of both stocks and sell them after one-, five-, and ten-year periods with dividends subject to a tax

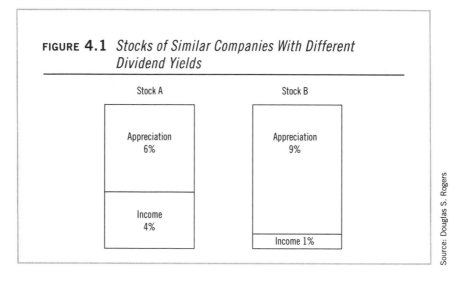

FIGURE **4.1** *Stocks of Similar Companies With Different Dividend Yields*

of 39.6 percent and long-term capitals taxed at 20 percent, which was the case not too many years ago (see **FIGURE 4.2**).

Again, we started with $100 invested in each stock. Dividends are taxed each year at 39.6 percent and the dollar amount of the "tax haircut" is deducted. For the one-year scenario, we assume the holding period is just less than the amount of time required to qualify for the more favorable tax rate on long-term capital gains. Therefore, both dividends and appreciation for the one-year scenario are subject to a tax rate of 39.6 percent. In this case, regardless of whether investors hold stock A or stock B in a taxable account, they end up with $106.04 after paying federal taxes. As time increases, we uncover the potential of an arbitrage opportunity created by just having a rudimentary understanding of the tax code for individuals. Stock A has 3 percent (4 percent dividend yield of stock A versus 1 percent

FIGURE **4.2** *Terminal Dollar Value of Two Stocks With Different Dividend Yields*

(39.6% Tax on Ordinary Income and 20.0% Tax on Long-Term Capital Gains)

YEARS	STOCK A	STOCK B
1	$106.04	$106.04
5	$142.69	$147.27
10	$206.62	$222.04

dividend yield of stock B) more of the total return attributable to dividends, which are subject to the higher tax rate of 39.6 percent. Plus, the tax on dividends is paid annually, whereas the tax on capital gains at the lower rate is not paid until the sale at the end of holding period. In this example, an individual investor subject to the highest federal tax rates would be better off holding stock B instead of the high-dividend-paying stock A by $4.58 and $15.42 over the five- and ten-year periods, respectively. One may counter that this arbitrage opportunity for longer periods no longer exists since the federal tax rates on dividends and long-terms gains are now equal. That is true, but the opportunity existed for years and not enough investors understood its potential or, more important, took advantage of it. Additionally, this example highlights the value of being familiar with the history of the tax rates and recent legislation, as the tax on dividends will return to regular tax rates on ordinary income, currently 35 percent, in 2009 unless there is additional legislation. So if the opportunity is not available today, we need to be aware of how we might be able to take advantage of a particular tax-driven scenario in the future.

Are there opportunities for tax-advantaged alternatives today? Yes, for example, listed options are subject to a 60/40 blend of the long-term capital gain and ordinary income tax rates even if they are held less than a year. If the holding period is short and the market is likely to rally, consider a qualified option or future contract, instead of holding a mutual fund, and pocket the substantial tax savings. The point here is that tax-aware practitioners look for these opportunities and take advantage of them when they make sense.

To obtain an understanding of concepts like those shown in the two examples above, the tax-aware practitioner will benefit from attending conferences and keeping abreast of the latest developments in the industry. This can be done by attending one or several national conferences sponsored by the following organizations:

- ❏ American Bankers Association
- ❏ Chartered Financial Analysts Institute (formerly AIMR)
- ❏ Family Office Exchange (FOX)
- ❏ Financial Planning Association (FPA)
- ❏ Financial Research Associates (FRI)
- ❏ Ibbotson Associates
- ❏ Information Management Network (IMN)
- ❏ Institute of Certified Bankers (ICB)
- ❏ Institute for Private Investors
- ❏ *Institutional Investor*
- ❏ *Investment Advisor*
- ❏ National Association of Personal Financial Advisors (NAPFA)

❑ New York University Institute on Family Wealth Management
❑ NMS Management
❑ Nuclear Decommissioning Trust (NDT)

Regional and local programs are also are also offered by the CFA, FPA, and NAPFA organizations and their local chapters. The New York Society of Security Analysts (NYSSA), a local chapter of the CFA Institute, has access to so much talent it consistently produces high-caliber programs on a par with the finest national organizations. Additionally, *Financial Planning* publishes annually an extensive list of broker-dealer programs that may be of interest. The key here is to build an association with organizations and individuals that best suit the needs of the clients you serve and to stay in tune with innovative developments.

Patience

To accomplish superior results with taxable accounts takes time and patience! Someone who has a day trader's mentality and wants to be a successful tax-aware practitioner will have to attain the self-discipline necessary. There are no shortcuts here, and that is why it is so difficult to educate individuals on the benefits of tax-aware investment management when for years they may have been subject to a transaction-oriented arrangement. A 1 to 2 percent enhancement in performance is not out of the question when applying tax-aware principles and concepts.[14] This increment may initially seem insignificant to some individuals, but the long-term benefit of tax-aware investment management is meaningful, as highlighted in **FIGURE 4.3**.

We will start with a portfolio of $10,000. Obviously, most client taxable portfolios are much larger, but this amount is used for the sake of simplicity. For an initial $10,000 investment, the benefit of tax-aware management in the first year is $100 to $200 and may at first appear to be hardly worth the effort. However, as the investment horizon increases and the benefit compounds, the total dollar benefit becomes more meaningful. Note that with a 2 percent annual benefit, assets double in value in slightly more than thirty-five years. That may seem like a long time, but it is certainly not an unreasonable one for young professionals just out of college entering the workforce who are establishing a savings plan or for long-term trusts. Moreover, this is not just an exercise for the wealthy. Failing to achieve optimal results most likely will not disrupt the lifestyle of wealthy people, but it could mean the difference between enjoying retirement and having to work for a few additional years for average individual investors. To analyze a specific situation, simply divide the size of the client portfolio by $10,000 and multiply the result by the level of benefit from the table. For example, if you have a $1 million portfolio, and the level of benefit

FIGURE **4.3** *Dollar Benefit of Tax-Aware Investment Management (Beginning With $10,000)*

YEARS	LEVEL OF BENEFIT	
	1%	2%
1	$100	$200
10	$1,046	$2,190
20	$2,202	$4,859
30	$3,478	$8,114
40	$4,889	$12,080
50	$6,446	$16,916

Note: At 2% growth, the principal amount doubles in slightly more than 35 years.

Source: Douglas S. Rogers

you estimate is 2 percent over forty years, multiply 100 ($1,000,000 / $10,000) by $12,080 to arrive at an estimated benefit of $1,208,000. Remember, for taxable accounts, compounding tax-free is a beautiful thing. Some professionals even consider it the equivalent of getting a tax-free loan from the government!

Passion

Tax-aware practitioners are passionate about their craft. This passion builds over time, because they realize they are "doing the right thing." Many will take the time to share their wisdom and knowledge to further the body of knowledge. A risk inherent with writing any text relating to taxes is that after someone has labored for hours to complete it, a major change in the tax code can render it obsolete. Therefore, it is important to identify sources of information that explain concepts and methods in addition to those that suggest a particular strategy that may come about or change with the dynamics of the tax code. Another challenge for research on tax-aware investing is that information on pretax returns for securities and asset classes is far more readily available than information on after-tax returns. Perhaps the greatest challenge for education relating to taxable accounts in general is trying to obtain funding, because the group that benefits the most from the process is typically wealthy individuals. As one well-known practitioner in the industry put it, "If you ask a wealthy individual or charitable organization to fund a charitable cause for the less-privileged in a distant land they can relate to the need, but asking them to fund an effort to teach those who are already considered to be privileged simply does not resonate with them." The point here is that those of us in the industry and our clients are already doing well, so limited resources should be shared with those that have the greatest need. Many journals are supported by the certification programs mentioned earlier. What follows is a list of the best-known journals and periodicals.

- ❏ *Advisor*
- ❏ *American Bankers Association Trusts and Investments*
- ❏ *Wealth Manager*
- ❏ *Financial Analysts Journal*
- ❏ *Financial Planning*
- ❏ *Financial Services Review*
- ❏ *Investment Advisor*
- ❏ *Journal of Accountancy*
- ❏ *Journal of Financial Planning*
- ❏ *Journal of Investing*
- ❏ *Journal of Investment Consulting*
- ❏ *Journal of Portfolio Management*
- ❏ *Journal of Wealth Management*
- ❏ *Monitor*
- ❏ *Private Asset Management*
- ❏ *Trusts & Estates*

The most prestigious journal within academic circles is *Financial Services Review,* edited by Conrad S. Ciccotello of Georgia State University. The one most focused on tax-aware investment management issues currently is *Journal of Wealth Management.* Its editor, Jean C. Brunel, an influential author and speaker in the ultra-affluent market, has been able to attract noteworthy submissions from many of the well-known practitioners you will likely encounter at national and regional conferences.

The following three books should be in the library of anyone attempting to understand taxable-account investing and are recommended for the professional ability of their authors.

- ❏ *Integrated Wealth Management,* by Jean L. P. Brunel (Institutional Investor Books)— Presents the new paradigm of wealth management for ultra-affluent clients.
- ❏ *Wall Street Secrets for Tax-Efficient Investing,* by Robert N. Gordon with Jan M. Rosen (Bloomberg Press)—Offers a working knowledge of little-known accepted methods to efficiently conduct taxable transactions.

❏ *J. K. Lasser Pro Integrating Investments and the Tax Code,* by William Reichenstein and William Jennings (John Wiley)—Explains the modeling of a saving vehicle's tax structure and discusses related investment implications.

Each of the books serves a distinct purpose or particular level of wealth, as noted above. *Tax-Aware Investment Management: The Essential Guide* is intended to complement them and round out the body of knowledge especially so those involved in the day-to-day management of taxable accounts can make better-informed investment decisions.

The tax-aware practitioner must realize that not everyone agrees with this concept, as some put the motive for profit before the client. There is still a lot of time and effort invested in the "sins of the past," and many clients will be reluctant to change until they are made aware of a more compelling strategy or product. Passion causes persistence, and although the process may be long and gradual, the concepts of tax-aware investment management are gaining ground, and enhancements in products, methods, and technology are following at a rapid pace. The fun of being a tax-aware practitioner is in implementing a strategy that works to the advantage of all concerned and, during or at the end of the process, seeing solid evidence that you have added value well in excess of the fee that is charged.

The body of knowledge pertaining to tax-aware investment management continues to expand, but to realize the full potential of the process we need to codify sound methods and principles. Additionally, we must convince others that people entering the industry need access to education to overcome the steep and long learning curve typically associated with taxable accounts. Future tax-aware practitioners also need to be empowered with software solutions that are only now beginning to address the need for tailored solutions across multiple accounts. Fortunately, for taxable investors or clients, the future for tax-aware investment management is promising and is limited only by the imagination and the willingness to devote sufficient resources to achieve desired solutions.

Chapter Notes

1. Zvi Bodie, Alex Kane, and Alan J. Marcus, *Investments,* 5th ed. (Boston, McGraw-Hill, 2002).

2. CFA Institute, http://www.cfainstitute.org (accessed July 27, 2004).

3. Certified Financial Planner Board of Standards, http://www.cfp.net (accessed July 27, 2004).

4. Investment Management Consultants Association, "Certify Your Profession-alism," http://imca.org (accessed July 27, 2004).

5. California State University, Northridge, "A Guide to Professional Certification Programs," http://www.csun.edu (accessed July 27, 2004).

6. The Uniform CPA Examination, http://www.cpa-exam.org (accessed July 27, 2004).

7. Institute of Certified Bankers, "Certified Trust and Financial Advisor (CTFA)," http://www.aba.com (accessed July 27, 2004).

8. Institute for Private Investors, press release, May 26, 2004, http://www.memberlink.net (accessed July 27, 2004).

9. American Bankers Association, "ABA Private Management School," http://www.aba.com (accessed July 27, 2004).

10. Institute for Private Investors, "Memberlink—2004 Private Wealth Management Program," http://www.memberlink.net (accessed July 27, 2004).

11. Investment Management Consultants Association, "Wealth Management Certificate Program," http://imca.org (accessed July 27, 2004).

12. New York University, "Certificate in Wealth Management," http://www.scps.nyu.edu/department/certificate.jsp?certId=851 (accessed December 27, 2004).

13. Institute for International Research, "Chartered Wealth Manager," http://www.iirme.com/cwm/ (accessed December 27, 2004).

14. J. Richard Joyner, "Tax-Efficient Investing: Can It Add 250 Basis Points to Your Returns?" *Journal of Investment Consulting* vol. 6, no. 1 (Summer 2003): 82–89.

CHAPTER **5**

Creating the Triumvirate of Qualified Professionals

All the Congress, all the accountants and tax lawyers, all the judges, and a convention of wizards all cannot tell for sure what the income tax law says.

—WALTER B. WRISTON

To achieve optimal results in investment management when taxes come into play requires three distinct skill sets. This applies whether you are offering advice to an individual investor, high-net-worth family, property and casualty insurance company, nuclear decommissioning trust, voluntary employee beneficiary association, or any other type of taxable account. The three skill sets are: investment management, tax, and regulatory or estate matters (see **FIGURE 5.1**). All taxable accounts require the investment management and tax skill sets. The factor that is different for taxable accounts is whether regulatory or estate matters influence decisions. Individuals and high-net-worth families need to account for the impact of estate taxes, whereas taxable corporate entities must address ongoing regulatory matters.

Each of the skill sets and elements is important separately, but if one or more is eliminated or overshadowed, the client will receive a less than optimal solution. The different requisite skills should complement one another and work in unison. Every attempt should be made to avoid conflict or operating as separate units.

The complexity of the assignment will dictate the level of skill or qualification necessary to achieve a satisfactory outcome. For example, a financial planner with an accounting and legal background operating

45

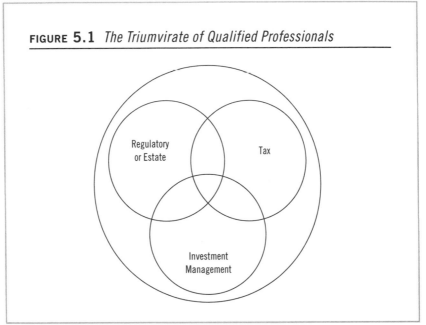

FIGURE **5.1** *The Triumvirate of Qualified Professionals*

Source: Douglas S. Rogers

separately may be able to provide outstanding service and advice to an individual investor if the firm is able to prepare the necessary documents for wills, et cetera. However, the process for property and casualty insurance companies typically incorporates sophisticated asset/liability modeling, custom portfolios, extensive involvement with the firm's financial staff, and coordination with highly specialized lawyers and accountants who assist in guiding the firm through the maze of federal and state regulatory requirements. The one aspect that permeates throughout the "qualified triumvirate" of skills is the impact of taxes. This feature adds another layer of complexity to the traditional tax-exempt account and makes tax-aware investment management challenging. It is also why qualified practitioners who are recognized for their expertise in this arena can demand a premium for their services.

To avoid costly errors, it is best to bring these skill sets together and establish a plan before funding takes place. High-net-worth individuals often acquire substantial liquid financial assets through the sale of a private company. In these cases, it is critical that the family establish the qualified triumvirate before discussing the sale of the asset with investment bankers. There is one distinction between the value-added proposition of the tax and estate elements and that of the investment management process. The savings or value added from the tax and estate elements can often be accomplished in a short period of time and involve substantial sums, whereas the investment process typically takes an extended period of time to produce gradual, meaningful results. In the case of a high-net-worth family, having the proper estate structure in place before the sale of a business may save millions of dollars. While the estate attorney and accountant may lead the discussion during this phase of the engagement, the financial adviser needs to be present and prepared to offer a professional opinion on whether the return assumptions are reasonable and whether the evolution of the estate plan or ultimate structure will lead to a viable long-term portfolio mix.

Very simply, actions ought not be taken for tax savings alone, as they may result in a situation that will force a costly solution in the future that far outweighs the initial benefits. An example is using taxable bonds in a trust, in lieu of tax-exempt or municipal bonds, as a wealth transfer strategy, because the parents pay the tax bill. At first this may seem like a sound idea, because the tax adviser and estate attorney recommend transferring as much wealth as possible out of the parents' estate so that at death the dollar amount of the estate tax will be minimal or subject to less than the maximum tax rate. First, tax-exempt bonds typically do not trade at a discount equal to the maximum federal tax rate, so the client ends up paying unnecessary taxes on a portion of the return. More important, this approach does not take into account alternative options that can be achieved using higher-yielding equity portfolios, purposely taking long-term gains, and raising the cost basis of the equity portfolio, which will likely prove far more beneficial over time especially after the death of the parents. Without bringing in tax-aware investment strategy analysis in the planning process, the wealth transfer strategy may actually benefit the government far more than the tax-paying client. Another example is placing an international equity manager in a taxable investment entity versus a tax-exempt one solely to recapture the dividend withholding tax. The recapture may be a benefit, but it is typically a minor one in the overall scheme of manager location. This tax nuance of international equities is worth considering, but the rate at which capital gains are realized is generally a more significant factor in the decision to place the manager in a taxable or tax-exempt investment entity. Equally important, the financial adviser should not try to force a premature asset allocation plan or the funding of managers. Patience by the financial adviser during the initial planning stages is critical. Even though yields may be paltry during this time, it is prudent to maintain a liquid posture until all parties involved agree on critical elements of the plan. This will avoid potentially costly and embarrassing situations later.

Clients often underestimate the importance of and time required to develop a comprehensive plan or investment policy statement. During this critical development period, the financial adviser needs to keep the client focused and engaged in the process. Every attempt should be made to address and eliminate distractions, especially when the client gets off track and begins discussing the various attributes of specific managers and funds. Having the client work closely with the qualified triumvirate to finalize the plan is critical, as the tax-aware positioning of asset classes can add as much or more value than the identification of the right managers or funds. If prepared properly, the final document will serve as a blueprint or business plan. Many professionals open their meetings by reviewing this document, as it reinforces core values and directs behavior to achieve common goals and objectives.

Members of the qualified triumvirate offer professional advice they believe will offer the greatest value. In doing so, they will gradually position themselves in relative importance in the eyes of the client. This interaction ultimately leads to one professional achieving the lofty position of "trusted adviser." This is perhaps the most overused term in the financial services industry today, yet its importance cannot be denied. Becoming the trusted adviser provides two distinct advantages over other advisers in the process. First, the trusted adviser is the one that the client will usually go to first when he or she has a question, a problem to be solved, or even a personal issue to vet. Second, through this advantageous positioning, the trusted adviser has significant influence over the flow of additional services and products. There is no one rule as to which of the professionals involved should serve as the trusted adviser. It simply depends on the financial situ-

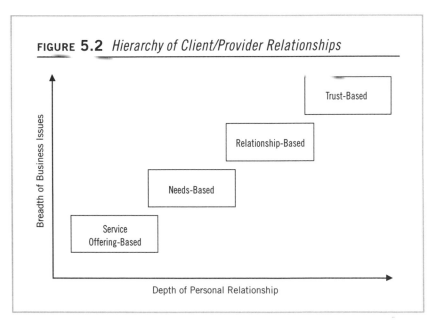

FIGURE 5.2 *Hierarchy of Client/Provider Relationships*

Source: David H. Maister, *The Trusted Advisor* (New York: Touchstone, 2001), 9–10

ation and personal chemistry between the client and each professional. While all parties may naively believe they serve as the trusted adviser, the true designation is ultimately awarded to the professional that earns the client's trust with the most sensitive matters.

Unfortunately, the term "trusted adviser" may be used as a marketing gimmick without understanding the true meaning and significance of the designation. David H. Maister outlines in his book, *The Trusted Advisor,* the hierarchy of client/provider relationships, shown in **FIGURE 5.2**.[1] He then lists the various characteristics of the relationship levels in a table (see **FIGURE 5.3**).

As Figure 5.2 suggests, establishing trust stands at the pinnacle, above providing education, solving problems, and generating ideas. Trust is not something that is immediately achieved; it grows over time. Moreover, it cannot be achieved solely within the physical confines of the service organization, as interaction with the client is mandatory. It may also cross the fine line from developing a professional relationship to a long-lasting friendship. From an ethical standpoint, developing trust can best be achieved by "doing what is right for the client," which may involve offering solutions that forgo immediate profits in order to develop a mutually rewarding, long-term relationship.

Why is the concept of the trusted adviser so important to tax-aware investment management? For the simple reason that if the adviser does

Source: David H. Maister, *The Trusted Advisor* (New York: Touchstone, 2001), 9–10

FIGURE 5.3 *Characteristics of Relationship Levels*

	FOCUS ON	ENERGY SPENT ON	CLIENT RECEIVES	INDICATIONS OF SUCCESS
Service-Based	Answer, expertise, input	Explaining	Information	Timely, high-quality responses
Needs-Based	Business problem	Problem solving	Solutions	Problems resolved
Relationship-Based	Client organization	Providing insights	Ideas	Repeat business
Trust-Based	Client individual	Understanding the client	Safe haven for hard issues	Varied— e.g., creative pricing

not believe in the philosophy or is not aligned with providers and platforms that embrace tax-aware investment, then it will be a struggle at best to achieve a favorable solution. Even if the investment adviser is not the "trusted adviser," optimal results can still be accomplished, but the other members of the qualified triumvirate have to believe in the tax-aware practitioner's approach and be willing to support it when questioned by the client. This is why it is so important to develop relationships with preferred providers and take the time to share the benefits of the tax-aware process.

The ability to achieve a tax-aware solution is influenced not only by the expertise of the professionals of the qualified triumvirate but also by the characteristics of the financial services platform. There are two primary types of platforms or service arrangements: discretionary and nondiscretionary. Under a discretionary arrangement the financial adviser can make decisions on the client's behalf, whereas in a nondiscretionary platform the ultimate decision rests with the client. Discretionary platforms usually work best with clients who are migrating from a retail broker, and where the skill set of the qualified triumvirate is usually contained within the same organization. Discretionary platforms lend themselves better to standardization and the ability to offer proprietary, internal products. The firms that serve this niche may offer commingled products that serve particular client risk profiles. It is also easier to show prospects potential results, as the outcomes are more uniform.

More knowledgeable and hands-on type clients typically prefer nondiscretionary platforms, giving them access to "best of breed" service providers. Each solution of a nondiscretionary platform is ultimately approved or driven by the client. The client is offered several manager or fund options within each asset class and chooses a custom solution. As a result, the returns of individual clients may vary widely. It is also more difficult for prospects to grasp the provider's ability to add value, since the ultimate mix of assets and managers/funds was decided by each client.

Perhaps the easiest feature to understand about the nondiscretionary platform is fees, which typically consist of custodian, manager, and adviser fees. Adviser fees typically include reporting services. Additionally, advisers typically negotiate with outside managers on behalf of all their clients en masse to obtain a more favorable arrangement than if clients approached the managers on their own. The ability to accomplish this differs with the asset class and with each manager on the adviser's recommended list, but the savings may be sufficient where the adviser ultimately becomes a profit center, rather than a cost of doing business. On the other hand, the pricing of nondiscretionary platforms can be confusing, as fees are typically bundled together, and it is often difficult to determine the cost of any one service or product. This is especially true when discounts are offered for using internal products, such as trading through the firm's broker-dealer, which may create potential layers of hidden costs.

Like marriages, relationships between clients and their providers do not always last until death. When clients have security positions with substantial unrealized gains, the decision to end the relationship can be costly. Therefore, it is important for the investor seeking taxable-account services to consider not only the inconvenience but especially the financial consequences if it becomes necessary for any reason to terminate a relationship. With a nondiscretionary platform, the advisory, custodial, and manager/fund services are usually modular and can be replaced separately. Replacing a particular element may require time to select another provider and attention to detail to transfer the responsibility, but if the transition is conducted with new providers that appreciate and understand tax-aware investment management, the time and disruption can be minimal. A transfer of "assets in kind" of existing security positions to new managers without selling will allow the new team to do what is best for the client. If done properly, it may take tax-aware portfolio managers a year or more to make the transition to their model portfolio. However, with the discretionary platform, especially when propriety products are involved, clients will be forced to liquidate all the holdings and begin anew if the relationship is terminated. Nondiscretionary platforms can be a good fit for certain client profiles. However, investors that choose them need to have a much higher degree of confidence in the soundness of their decision making than investors selecting discretionary platforms.

With the proliferation of high-net-worth individuals, as a result of wealth created during the latter half of the 1990s, the number of firms employing nondiscretionary service platforms also proliferated. The primary reason is that it takes an extremely experienced investment professional to carry the sophisticated relationship required for a discretionary platform, and the supply is limited. This situation gets even more challenging when the client desires exposure to alternative investments. Therefore, many firms have no choice in what platform they offer. As a result, individuals seeking an independent discretionary platform will likely discover their niche is served by only a small number of firms.

The potential of a particular platform to achieve a tax-aware solution depends on the ability to satisfy the four critical elements of tax-aware investing:

1 Utilizing after-tax assumptions in the asset allocation process
2 Allocating asset classes and managers/funds according to the characteristics of each investment entity
3 Positioning tax-aware equity managers
4 Identifying tax-aware managers/funds

The first three elements pertain to process and the fourth to product. Having all four elements in place is optimal, but not all platforms can achieve this. Accomplishing the first three requires educating the financial services providers, which many platforms have not yet embraced, but this situation is gradually improving. If the limitations of a platform are such that it cannot deliver tax-aware managers and funds, then *caveat emptor,* or buyer beware. The key for the investor is to evaluate the four essential elements to determine if the financial services provider is capable of satisfying or exceeding his or her expectation.

There is a saying in the financial planning community that "individuals are willing to pay for their health, but not for their wealth." There is a lot of truth to this statement, as some individuals just cannot get over the fact that a person offering them financial advice needs to be financially rewarded for that service. There will always be some individuals who, for whatever reason, will not pay for advice, so the only way they can be served is when fees are embedded in the portfolio strategies recommended. This aspect segments the financial planning community into fee-based versus product-based providers. It is extremely difficult to create optimal tax-aware solutions in the product-based segment. Unfortunately, many of the desirable products available in the marketplace today are low-fee in nature and do not offer a way for product-based providers to be compensated. It is a sad fact that the investor seeking the product-based route may unfortunately end up paying an opportunity cost that far exceeds the cost of a fee-based planner who offers a tax-aware menu of managers and mutual funds.

Fee arrangements have an impact on the ability of service providers to align their interests with the client. The following discussion will allow investors to gain a basic understanding of the positive elements and concerns of the most common fee arrangements. First, there is the hourly charge, which is common with accountants and estate attorneys. Hourly fees are easy for many clients to accept, because you are only charged for services utilized. Hourly fees are typically higher during the inception of the relationship, as there is more work necessary to develop an effective financial plan. Second, there are clients who prefer retainer fees over hourly fees. They believe this arrangement to be superior, since the charge is based on addressing the needs of the relationship. Clients who prefer the retainer fee structure feel it facilitates communication, since they do not feel compelled to limit the interaction to avoid excessive charges. Additionally, they feel there is no need for the providers to inundate them with additional ideas, as might a retail broker. The third type of fee arrangement is to charge a percentage of the overall assets under management or supervision. This is the most common approach by financial services providers, which may offer a sliding scale to achieve a volume discount. Advocates of this approach believe that the service providers are rewarded as the client's wealth increases. Skeptics of this arrangement believe it causes the providers to offer more high-return, high-risk options. For example, the portfolio mix could be more heavily oriented toward equities than necessary, since historically they have provided higher returns than fixed income securities. The fourth type of fee arrangement is one based on performance. The manager must achieve a return above a designated hurdle rate before the incentive or performance fee kicks in. Plus, there may be a high-water mark to make sure the manager is only paid the performance fees when previous share or unit values are exceeded. It is encouraging that there are now managers willing to accept assignments where the performance fee is based on exceeding a hurdle rate calculated after taxes. The fifth and last area is hidden fees. These illustrate why it so important for prospects to ask the right questions to gain an understanding of all fees involved. This gray area may include items such as marketing fees, soft dollar commissions, or trading through the firm's broker-dealer. The importance of this last area cannot be underestimated, because costs—like taxes—influence the net result. No fee arrangement is perfect for all situations, and the low-cost solution may not be the one that can deliver optimal after-tax results. The investor very simply needs to determine if the fee arrangement offered will motivate the providers to achieve an optimal tax-aware solution.

Investors or prospects who are seeking financial service providers and wish to develop a qualified triumvirate of professionals, should consider these questions:

- ❑ Can the skills required of the qualified triumvirate be satisfied by one professional/firm, or does my situation necessitate multiple "best of breed" specialists?
- ❑ Can I devote the time necessary to achieve desired results?
- ❑ Is my trusted adviser capable of supporting a tax-aware approach?
- ❑ Will the financial services platform I am considering be able to deliver a tax-aware solution?
- ❑ How costly will the transition to another provider be if I later decide to terminate the relationship?
- ❑ To what degree can my financial services provider deliver the four key elements of tax-aware investment management?
- ❑ Do I really understand the fee arrangements of the potential providers' services and products and how they affect the ability to deliver a tax-aware approach?

Tax-aware investment management requires long-lasting relationships to achieve favorable results. Therefore, providers that offer the qualified triumvirate of necessary skills with servicing platforms and fee arrangements and can ultimately obtain the client's trust will be the ones most likely to succeed.

Chapter Notes

1. David H. Maister, *The Trusted Advisor* (New York: Touchstone, 2001), 9–10.

PART **TWO**

After-Tax Reporting and Measures of Tax Efficiency

All taxes are a drag on economic growth. It's only a question of degree.

—Alan Greenspan

CHAPTER 6

Mutual Fund After-Tax Reporting

It's not what you make, it's what you keep.

—Anonymous

The after-tax reporting standards proposed by the Securities and Exchange Commission (SEC) were signed into law as the last official act of the Clinton administration. Since early 2001, after-tax returns have been required in the risk/return summary of the prospectus, with the exception of money market funds and those marketed solely to tax-exempt accounts.[1] This legislation has had a profound impact on tax-aware investment management by ensuring that the impact of taxes on investment returns would reach the millions of individual investors who hold mutual funds.

The pain taxable mutual fund shareholders experienced during the latter half of the 1990s created the demand for after-tax reporting, as **FIGURE 6.1** from the Investment Company Institute (ICI) highlights.[2] Figure 6.1

As mentioned in chapter 1, Congress addressed the concern of fund shareholders in March of 2000. Concurrently, the SEC issued a proposal for public comment. It received input from professional organizations such as the Association for Investment Management and Research (AIMR), which adopted after-tax reporting standards for separate accounts in 1994, along with several hundred responses from individual mutual fund investors. As expected, AIMR and mutual fund shareholders were extremely supportive of the SEC initiative. Interestingly enough, the greatest num-

Source: Investment Company Institute, 2004 Mutual Fund Fact Book (www.ici.org). Reprinted with permission.

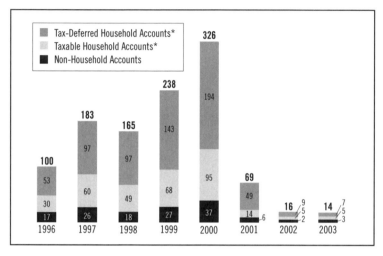

FIGURE **6.1** *Capital Gain Distributions Paid by Mutual Funds, 1996–2003 (billions of dollars)*

*Households are defined to exclude mutual fund assets attributed to business corporations, financial institutions, nonprofit organizations, fiduciaries, and other institutional investors.

Note:
Components may not add to the total because of rounding.

ber of comments came from visitors to the Motley Fool website. The website's education initiative was certainly not foolish with regard to tax-aware investment management, and visitors were encouraged to respond to the SEC in support of the proposal. However, several professional organizations lobbied to overturn the standards even after they were signed into law by President Clinton. In spite of these challenges, U.S. Securities and Exchange Commission, Final Rule: Disclosure of Mutual Fund After-Tax Returns, Section II.D, came about on April 16, 2001. Readers can obtain a copy of the mutual fund after-tax standards by visiting the SEC's website (www.sec.gov). This document should certainly be part of the library of any professional who interacts with taxable investors holding mutual funds.

A performance display from an actual fund report for the Vanguard Tax-Managed Growth and Income Fund for periods ending June 30, 2004, will highlight several key points about the standards (see **FIGURE 6.2**). It has an enviable record of not having made any capital gains distributions since its inception in 1994.[3] This fund was selected for illustrative purposes, not as an endorsement of the product.

FIGURE **6.2** *Sample Display of Mutual Fund After-Tax Return Reporting*

Vanguard Tax-Managed Growth and Income Fund
Average Annual Total Returns*

	PERIODS ENDED JUNE 30, 2004		
	ONE YEAR	FIVE YEARS	SINCE INCEPTION**
Return Before Taxes	17.86%	−2.16%	11.06%
Return After Taxes on Distributions	17.58	−2.56	10.76
Return After Taxes on Distributions and Sales of Fund Shares	11.95	−2.04	9.77

*All fund returns are adjusted to reflect fees. Each of the Vanguard Tax-Managed Funds assesses a 2 percent fee on redemption of shares held in the fund for less than one year and a 1 percent fee on redemptions of shares held in the fund for at least one year but less than five years.
**Inception date is September 6, 1994.

The figure shows the two different methods required by the SEC for presenting after-tax returns in a logical progression that builds on the before-tax returns. The first row, "Return Before Taxes," is the same information required for displaying pretax returns and includes the impact of fees. The second row, "Return After Taxes on Distributions," takes into account only the taxes on income and capital gains distributions. As mentioned in chapter 3, this is known as the pre-liquidation methodology for calculating after-tax returns. The third row, "Return After Taxes on Distributions and Sales of Fund Shares," is known as the post-liquidation calculation methodology.

Both calculation methodologies provide useful information. Together they allow the taxable mutual fund investor to make better-informed investment decisions. There are cases where one calculation methodology or type of after-tax return is more appropriate than the other. For example, the pre-liquidation after-tax return information is appropriate for individuals who will take advantage of the step-up in basis at death. For someone who is rebalancing a client's asset allocation, the post-liquidation methodology is more appropriate, because it takes into account the impact of the client's unrealized capital gain or loss position on the after-tax return when fund shares are sold.

The SEC requires the highest federal tax rates to be applied when calculating after-tax returns. Although this may not represent the tax profile of the average investor, it does provide the most conservative scenario. If your own tax situation or that of your clients is different, check the website of your mutual fund provider, as some firms have created online calculators that allow investors to apply their personal tax profile to analyze historical after-tax results.

In the "One Year" column, the highest federal tax rate is applied even though the fund would qualify for the more favorable long-term capital gains rate if held for one more day. This was one of the more controversial elements of the after-tax proposal, as many professionals within the fund industry thought it was unrealistic. However, the SEC felt strongly this was necessary, since the average holding period for mutual funds had fallen significantly during the 1990s. This requirement highlights the concept that if you don't hold a fund for more than a year it is impossible to take advantage of the benefit of the lower rate for long-term capital gains, currently 15 percent.

Another key point is that after-tax returns can be greater than pretax returns for information shown in the row "Return After Taxes on Distributions and Sales of Fund Shares" calculated by the post-liquidation methodology. If the fund is sold when the market value is below cost, a credit is given to the after-tax return, because like the AIMR standards for separate accounts, the SEC standard for mutual funds assumes the loss can be used to offset a gain in another fund or portfolio or be applied in the future. For example, if a fund is held less than a year, the 35 percent federal tax rate applies. Therefore, if the before-tax return is –10 percent with no dividend distributions, the "Return After Taxes on Distributions and Sales of Fund Shares" would be only –6.5 percent (10% × [1 – 35%]). An example of this situation is in the column marked "Five Years" in **FIGURE 6.2**. All the returns are negative, but the "Return After Taxes on Distributions and Sales of Fund Shares" (–2.04 percent) is greater than the "Return After Taxes on Distributions" (–2.56 percent) and "Return Before Taxes" (–2.16 percent). Although the differences in this example are quite small, they would be much larger if the display had been taken from the spring of 2003, when large-capitalization stocks on average had been subject to three years of negative returns.

While the SEC after-tax standards provide mutual fund investors with meaningful information, two additional items should be considered to make truly informed investment decisions. The first pertains primarily to equity funds, whereas the second applies to bond funds. Even though

it was an AIMR Subcommittee recommendation, the SEC ultimately decided not to require the percentage of unrealized gains or losses in the
performance display.[4] With taxable accounts—in contrast to the tax-
exempt account arena—what the fund has done in the past in fact can
and does have a significant impact on future after-tax returns. To highlight this point, recall that investors in the latter 1990s were concerned
about how to avoid equity funds with substantial unrealized capital gains
positions, which reached 50 percent of total assets or more for large-
capitalization, growth-oriented style funds. For example, the Stagecoach
Equity Fund Index–A Fund had an unrealized gain position of 70 percent![5] Some practitioners even thought funds with large unrealized capital gains positions should have included a warning label, similar to the
one on a pack of cigarettes, stating that investing in them could result in
detrimental tax consequences. The situation became such a concern in
1999 that some fund groups contemplated opening vintage year index
funds for their taxable investors. By the spring of 2003 the pendulum
had swung to the opposite direction, and after three years of losses there
was an opportunity to purchase funds with substantial embedded unrealized losses. While the percentage of unrealized capital gains embedded in
a fund is limited to 100 percent of assets, the percentage of losses can be
greater than 100 percent. This occurs when fund managers sell shares and
losses cannot be passed through to shareholders, because of the accounting convention that funds must apply. If the redemptions are significant
and the manager must sell shares below cost, the amount of losses in
dollars can exceed the remaining assets in the fund. As of June 30, 2004,
there were approximately 5,900 mutual funds on Morningstar Principia
that showed a negative percentage of unrealized capital gains with a few
close to –1,000 percent![6] Advisers can add meaningful value for their clients by considering the percentage of unrealized capital gains of possible
fund alternatives when they make purchase recommendations for the taxable portion of assets. Given two funds that are equal in every dimension
except the unrealized capital gains position, the tax-aware investor will
always choose the one with the least amount of unrealized gains or greatest amount of unrealized losses. As we will see later in this chapter, the
accounting convention lends itself to arbitrage opportunities, or what
some may consider a "free lunch."

Fortunately for the taxable investor, information pertaining to the
percentage of unrealized capital gains or losses can be obtained from a
Morningstar Investment Detail Report (again using the Vanguard Tax-
Managed Growth and Income Fund as an example).[7] As **FIGURE 6.3**
shows, this particular fund had an internal +6 percent unrealized capital
gains position. This percentage changes with the market value of securi-

FIGURE 6.3 *Example of Morningstar Principia Display Mutual Fund After-Tax Return Information*

TAX ANALYSIS	TAX-ADJ RTN%	% RANK CAT	TAX-COST RATIO	% RANK CAT
3 Yr (estimated)	2.78	35	0.46	36
5 Yr (estimated)	−2.72	43	0.44	23
10 Yr (estimated)	11.50	7	0.53	8
Potential Capital Gain Exposure: 6% of assets				

*All fund returns are adjusted to reflect fees. Each of the Vanguard Tax-Managed Funds assesses a 2 percent fee on redemption of shares held in the fund for less than one year and a 1 percent fee on redemptions of shares held in the fund for at least one year but less than five years.
**Inception date is September 6, 1994.

Source: Morningstar

FIGURE 6.4 *Sample Display of Mutual Fund After-Tax Return Reporting*

1994	1995	1996	1997	1998	1999
9.77	13.16	15.89	20.88	26.55	31.81
−1.70*	37.53	23.03	33.31	28.67	21.12
	0.00	0.09	−0.04	0.10	0.08
	−0.24	0.58	0.46	1.65	0.21
0.00	2.58	2.14	1.77	1.40	1.19
	34.95	20.89	31.54	27.27	19.93
	12	28	13	15	37
0.09	0.25	0.28	0.28	0.29	0.31
0.00	0.00	0.00	0.00	0.00	0.00
0.20	0.20	0.20	0.17	0.19	0.19
2.82	2.37	2.04	1.62	1.32	1.11
	6	7	2	4	4
31	98	235	579	1,352	2,240

* Inception date is September 6, 1994.

ties held in the portfolio and shareholder purchase and redemption activity. Figure 6.3 also shows the after-tax returns, tax-cost ratios, and relative ranking information Morningstar provides its subscribers for three-, five- and ten-year periods. An explanation of the information provided in the four columns follows:

   1 *Tax-Adjusted Return Percentage*—This is Morningstar's calculation that follows the SEC guidance for return after taxes on distributions, or pre-liquidation after-tax returns. It should be noted that after-tax returns also include the impact of loads, when appropriate.

   2 *Percentile Rank Category*—Morningstar gives the fund's relative percentile ranking within its peer group. Figure 6.3 shows that for the past ten years, the Vanguard Tax-Managed Growth and Income Fund was ranked at 7, which means six out of 100 funds had superior results.

   3 *Tax-Cost Ratio*—In this column, Morningstar employs a proprietary measure to calculate the amount of return that would have been lost each year to payment of taxes. For the past ten years this

2000	2001	2002	2003	12-04	HISTORY
28.66	24.93	19.15	24.23	26.36	NAV
−9.03	−11.93	−21.95	28.53	10.83	Total Return %
0.07	−0.05	0.14	−0.14	−0.04	+/− S&P 500
−1.24	0.52	−0.30	−1.36	−0.57	+/− Russ 1000
0.94	1.05	1.31	1.79	1.95	Income Return %
−9.97	−12.98	−23.26	26.74	8.88	Capital Return %
63	44	42	29	35	Total Rtn % Rank Cat
0.30	0.30	0.33	0.34	0.47	Income $
0.00	0.00	0.00	0.00	0.00	Capital Gains $
0.19	0.17	0.17	0.17		Expense Ratio %
0.96	1.44	1.44	1.63		Income Ratio %
5	5	9	5		Turnover Rate %
2,427	1,606	1,077	1,321	1,395	Net Assets $mil

fund would have lost 0.53 percent on average each year to the payment of taxes.

4 *Percentile Rank Category*—Morningstar also gives a relative percentile ranking on the tax-cost ratio. In this example, the fund has a ranking of 8 based on the tax-cost ratio over the past ten-year period of analysis.

A bit of experience and several pieces of information are required to make sage decisions when recommending mutual funds for taxable investors or for personal investment. In addition to return-related information, it is also helpful to review the history of income and capital gains distributions plus expenses.

Fortunately, the Morningstar Investment Detail Report provides this information, as well (see **FIGURE 6.4**).[8] Reviewing the calculation-only information, one immediately wonders, why isn't the tax-cost ratio relative percentile ranking for the Vanguard Tax-Managed Growth and Income Fund higher than 23 for the five-year period of analysis? The 23 percentile ranking is good, but one might expect the measure to be higher, especially since only a small percentage of stock funds truly focus on tax management. The tax-cost ratio is driven by three factors: capital gains distributions from trading activity, the amount of income or dividends, and the expense ratio. As mentioned earlier, the Morningstar report shows this fund has never made a capital gains distribution, as evident by the row marked "Capital Gains $," so this is not a contributing factor. Therefore, the amount of taxes must be a result of the amount of net taxable dividends generated by the portfolio. From the figure, you can also see the fund's "Income Ratio %" for 2003 was +1.63 percent. Additionally, the fund has had a low "Expense Ratio %" of only 0.17 percent for the past three years. Therefore, in 2003 it would have had a gross income or dividend yield before fees of +1.80 percent (1.63 percent + 0.17 percent). In this case, the portfolio replicates the composition of the Standard & Poor's 500 stock index. To lower the tax-cost ratio and improve the relative ranking, Vanguard could remove the 1 percent redemption fee, manage a portfolio that pays dividends equal to or less than its fees of +0.17 percent, or increase the management fee. To take any of these measures would not make sense. So the relative ranking of 23 percent for the five-year period is about as high a score as Vanguard is likely to achieve. This simple example demonstrates that it often takes several pieces of information to make sound, tax-aware investment decisions.

The other factor pertains to tax-exempt or municipal bonds. Unless there is a change in the tax code for individuals, more and more investors will be subject to the alternative minimum tax (AMT) (see **FIGURE 6.5**).[9]

Source: Congressman Jim Saxton, Chairman, Joint Economic Committee, *The Alternative Minimum Tax for Individuals: A Growing Burden, Congressional Budget Office 2001*, U.S. Congress, May 2001.

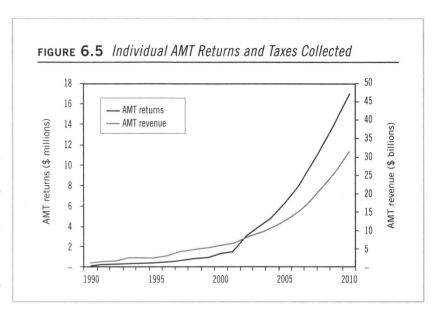

FIGURE **6.5** *Individual AMT Returns and Taxes Collected*

Most investors do not realize that funds holding less than 20 percent of private activity bonds issued after 1986 subject to the AMT are permitted to call themselves tax-exempt bond funds, whereas funds holding greater than 20 percent of AMT issues are classified as municipal bond funds. For individuals subject to the AMT, private activity bonds are taxed at a rate of 26 percent or 28 percent, depending on the amount of alternative minimum taxable income (AMTI).[10] Tax-aware advisers establish procedures to avoid placing clients subject to the AMT in municipal or tax-exempt bond funds with AMT exposure. To deal with this challenge, it is essential to periodically call fund complexes to obtain their exposure to private activity bonds subject to the AMT.

Although the title of this chapter emphasizes after-tax reporting, we cannot simply ignore the impact the accounting convention for mutual fund investing has on the actual after-tax results investors may achieve, which can benefit certain taxable shareholders and disadvantage others. Unlike separate accounts, mutual funds cannot pass losses through to investors. Furthermore, they can only take advantage of a loss by using it to offset a realized gain for a period up to eight years, whereas with a separate account an individual can use them indefinitely.

When investors purchase shares in a mutual fund, they establish their cost basis. The following example illustrates how the timing of a purchase can result in quite different tax consequences when a distribution of capital gains is made. Let's assume a mutual fund is created on January 1 with a $10,000 purchase of shares by our first investor, and in each of the next

FIGURE **6.6** *Mutual Fund Shareholder Accounting Example*

MONTH	INVESTOR	MONTHLY INVESTMENT	ENDING VALUE	SHARES	VALUE
January	1	$10,000.00	$10.00	1,000.00	$10.10
February	2	$10,000.00	$10.10	990.10	$10.20
March	3	$10,000.00	$10.20	980.30	$10.30
April	4	$10,000.00	$10.30	970.59	$10.41
May	5	$10,000.00	$10.41	960.98	$10.51
June	6	$10,000.00	$10.51	951.47	$10.62
July	7	$10,000.00	$10.62	942.05	$10.72
August	8	$10,000.00	$10.72	932.72	$10.83
September	9	$10,000.00	$10.83	923.48	$10.94
October	10	$10,000.00	$10.94	914.34	$11.05
Total	**10**	**$100,000.00**		**9,566.02**	

Source: Douglas S. Rogers

nine months a new investor purchases $10,000 of shares. Additionally, the fund appreciates 1 percent each month (see **FIGURE 6.6**).

At the end of ten months, the fund has ten investors who have contributed a total of $100,000. The net asset value of the fund is $11.05. After ten months of consistent appreciation, the fund has a total value $105,704.52 (9,566.02 shares × $11.05). The fund has increased in value beyond the contributions of shareholders by $5,704.52 ($105,704.52 − $100,000). On November 1, the directors of the fund announce that all shareholders of record on that day will receive a capital gains distribution of $5,704.52, or 100 percent of the profit earned since January 1. Since there are now 9,556.02 shares outstanding, a capital gains distribution of $0.59 ($5,704.52 / 9,556.02 shares) will be made to each share.

The last column in **FIGURE 6.7** shows the dollar amount of the capital gains distribution made to each of the ten shareholders. Note the difference between the columns marked "Profit" and "Capital Gains Distribution" for investors 1 and 10. Shareholder 1 has made a profit of $1,050, taking into account the current closing price of the fund, but only has to pay taxes on $590 in capital gains, whereas shareholder 10 has a profit of

FIGURE **6.7** *Mutual Fund Example: Profit vs. Capital Gains Distributions*

INVESTOR	DOLLAR INVESTMENT	SHARES	MARKET VALUE	PROFIT	CAPITAL GAINS DISTRIBUTION
1	$10,000.00	1000.00	$11,050.00	$1,050.00	$590.00
2	$10,000.00	990.10	$10,940.61	$940.61	$584.16
3	$10,000.00	980.30	$10,832.32	$832.32	$578.38
4	$10,000.00	970.59	$10,725.02	$725.02	$572.65
5	$10,000.00	960.98	$10,618.83	$618.83	$566.98
6	$10,000.00	951.47	$10,513.74	$513.74	$561.37
7	$10,000.00	942.05	$10,409.65	$409.65	$555.81
8	$10,000.00	932.72	$10,306.56	$306.56	$550.30
9	$10,000.00	923.48	$10,204.45	$204.45	$544.85
10	$10,000.00	914.34	$10,103.46	$103.46	$539.46

only $103.46 and has to pay taxes on $539.46 in capital gains. When you compare the two columns, no investor has a profit exactly equal to the capital gains distribution. This example is fairly straightforward, but investors typically make investments over many years and most funds have both income and capital gains distributions.

How dramatic can this injustice between shareholders be? To answer this question we need to look back to 1987. During the "correction of 1987," stocks rose significantly during the summer and early fall, but then they hemorrhaged in the third week of October. Many mutual funds have October 31 as their fiscal year-end. Therefore, there were cases where individual investors purchased shares in equity mutual funds, saw their investment drop 20 percent or so in value, and then got hit with a sizable capital gains distribution. Fortunately, the market gradually rebounded, but many of those investors were forced to sell shares at unfavorable prices to cover their tax bill the following year.

Congress has attempted to rectify this situation, but though well-intentioned, the solution often disregards the basic failure of managers to take taxes into account when managing their funds. For example, Congressman Jim Saxton has proposed legislation (H.R. 168) that would allow each individual an annual deduction from capital gains distributions.[11] Also, Congressman Paul Ryan has introduced legislation (H.R. 1989) that would require individuals to pay taxes on capital gains only when they sell fund shares.[12] Both proposals are intended to make things easier for mutual fund investors. However, what is often ignored is that these bills would only exacerbate the problem of portfolio managers ignoring the impact of taxes. Moreover, as we will discover in chapter 9, there are already free market solutions that have solved this issue. Unfortunately, tax-aware solutions do not vote and the shareholders who use them still represent a small portion of the market. If Congress really wants to provide investors with a meaningful change, it should change the accounting convention for mutual funds to allow losses to flow through to investors. It may take several years, if ever, for a fund manager to take advantage of the loss position, whereas individual investors may be able to apply them immediately since they typically hold multiple funds and portfolios where gains can be taken.

The actual after-tax returns for individuals who invest in dollar-cost averaging programs or reinvest fund distributions can be quite different, depending on what accounting convention they personally apply. There are three primary accounting conventions that investors and their advisers should be concerned with:

❏ First in, first out
❏ Specific lot identification
❏ Average cost

The IRS allows investors latitude in choosing their preferred method. The average cost method is typically the default method used by custodians. Therefore, if you desire to apply one of the first two conventions, you need to make an election before transactions are accounted for by the average cost method. The particular accounting convention applied can have a significant impact on the amount of taxes that will be paid in any year. It will not change the dollar amount of capital gains, but it can change or shift the tax liability considerably. This can be seen in the following example, using monthly prices from the Vanguard 500 Index Fund in 2003.[13] The investor starts with an initial purchase in January of $3,000 to satisfy the account minimum and makes additional purchases in each of the next seven months for a total investment of $10,000 (see **FIGURE 6.8**).

During this time frame, the market bottomed in the spring and rallied strongly for the remainder of the year. Even though the investor intended to have a long-term investment horizon, in December he ran into a situation that forced him to sell thirty shares at the price of $102.67. He will be

FIGURE **6.8** *Mutual Fund Accounting Convention Example*

MONTH	PURCHASE	DOLLAR INVESTMENT	PURCHASE PRICE	SHARES	ENDING VALUE	PROFIT/ LOSS
January	1	$3,000.00	$79.02	37.97	$3,897.87	$897.87
February	2	$1,000.00	$77.82	12.85	$1,319.33	$319.33
March	3	$1,000.00	$78.27	12.78	$1,311.74	$311.74
April	4	$1,000.00	$84.73	11.80	$1,211.73	$211.73
May	5	$1,000.00	$89.19	11.21	$1,151.14	$151.14
June	6	$1,000.00	$90.02	11.11	$1,140.52	$140.52
July	7	$1,000.00	$91.59	10.92	$1,120.97	$120.97
August	8	$1,000.00	$93.36	10.71	$1,099.72	$99.72
December	10	$10,000.00	102.67	119.34	$12,253.03	$2,253.03

Source: Douglas S. Rogers

required to pay taxes on the transaction at the federal short-term capital gains rate of 35 percent. As **FIGURE 6.9** shows, the three different accounting conventions result in tax obligations ranging from $326.93 to $709.85.

First in, first out (FIFO) accounting is mechanical in nature and probably satisfactory for fixed income funds where appreciation is usually not a significant part of the total return. As Figure 6.9 shows, thirty shares were used to establish the cost basis from the first purchase. If more than 37.97 shares—the number of shares acquired in the initial purchase, or tax lot—were sold, it would be necessary to examine the second-oldest purchase and continue the process until shares equaling the amount of the sale transaction were accounted for.

Specific lot identification requires a bit of extra work, but the benefit can be well worth the effort. As Figure 6.9 shows, the first lot chosen was the one with the highest cost basis, followed by the lot with the next-highest cost basis, and so on until a total of 30 shares is reached. Therefore, only 8.37 of the total 11.11 shares in tax lot 6 are used. The remaining 2.74 shares will be accounted for during a future sale of shares. This method requires accurate accounting records. The example above is quite simple and did not include any reinvestment of distributions. To ensure that they are keeping adequate records and adhering to proper procedures, taxable investors and their advisers should adopt the

FIGURE 6.9 *Mutual Fund Accounting Convention Example*

	LOT	SHARES	PURCHASE PRICE	FIRST IN FIRST OUT	SPECIFIC LOT IDENTIFICATION	AVERAGE BASIS
Shares Sold				30.00	30.00	30.00
Price				$102.67	$102.67	$102.67
Total Value				$3,080.10	$3,080.10	$3,080.10
Cost	1	30.00	$79.02	$2,370.60		
	8	10.71	$93.36		$1,000.00	
	7	10.92	$91.59		$1,000.00	
	6	8.37	$90.02		$753.52	
	All	30.00	$83.79			$2,513.70
Total Cost				$2,370.60	$2,753.52	$2,513.70
Gain/Loss				$709.50	$326.58	$566.40
Tax Rate				35.0%	35.0%	35.0%
Tax Due				$709.85	$326.93	$566.75

Source: Douglas S. Rogers

format shown in IRS Publication 564, *Mutual Fund Distributions* (see **FIGURE 6.10**).[14]

High in, first out (HIFO) is another accounting convention that may encountered with separate account management, with slightly less onerous requirements than specific lot identification. FIFO often yields a result equal or similar to specific lot identification, but the latter strategy offers more freedom of choice.

Average cost is simply calculated by taking the total amount of funds used to purchase shares and dividing by the total number of shares. Again, this is the default method used by most custodians. In this example, the tax obligation using average cost fell between those using the FIFO and specific lot identification conventions, but this may not always be the case.

Our example focuses only on 2003. However, the future is important as well: in this case, the next sale will most likely cause some or all or the remaining purchases or tax lots to qualify for the more favorable rate on

FIGURE **6.10** *Sample Mutual Fund Accounting Format*

| MUTUAL FUND | ACQUIRED[1] | | | ADJUSTMENT TO BASIS PER SHARE | ADJUSTED[2] BASIS PER SHARE | SOLD OR REDEEMED | |
	DATE	NUMBER OF SHARES	COST PER SHARE			DATE	NUMBER OF SHARES

1 Include share received from reinvestment of distributions.
2 Cost plus or minus adjustments

long-term capital gains. The FIFO method will most likely prove even more costly, as it would have expended most of the oldest lot with the greatest amount of appreciation per share to be taxed at 35 percent and a smaller amount of capital gains now remains in the portfolio. This example demonstrates that it may be worth the additional time and expense to use an accounting convention other than average cost for the particular type of fund and the size of the investment.

The tax act of 2003 may go down in history as "the tax break the average individual never received!"[15] Mutual funds can save shareholders taxes by applying the income they receive from dividends to offset fund expenses. Prior to 2003, this worked to the advantage of the average shareholder, as it doesn't make sense to distribute a dividend and pay a 38.6 percent (the maximum federal rate at the time) tax on it when it can be avoided. However, when the tax on qualified dividends was reduced to 15 percent, many holders of actively managed equity mutual funds received almost none of the tax break. For example, the fee on the average actively managed domestic stock is currently 1.5 percent and the average dividend yield is only 1.6 percent. Since only 0.1 percent of taxable dividends are distributed, there is very little income left, if any, after the fund uses it to offset expenses. The groups of shareholders receiving almost all of the benefit of the favorable tax legislation are those invested in low-fee index-oriented mutual or exchange-traded funds. For a shareholder in a fund with a fee of 0.2 percent, the lower tax on dividends resulted in an enhancement in after-tax return of 0.33 percent ([1.6% – 0.2%] × [38.5% – 15.0%]) annually versus 0.02 percent ([1.6% – 1.5%] × [38.5% – 15.0%]), or almost nothing for the average actively managed equity fund. Once again, this example shows how important fees and a basic understanding of the tax code can be. When this legislation came about, the author was interviewed by a major financial services magazine and made this his number one point. Do you think it was included when the story went to press? Of course not, because low-fee funds don't support advertising budgets! This occurrence supports the premise that tax-aware products are bought by informed investors and not sold through expensive marketing and advertising efforts. Once again, education proves to be paramount in tax-aware investing.

Mutual fund tax information is reported to the shareholder on Form 1099 DIV, which is shown in **FIGURE 6.11** for 2003. As with all IRS forms, the format of Form 1099-DIV may change from year to year, depending on changes in the tax code.

The most critical information that an investor will encounter is addressed in the following sections of the form:

1a Total ordinary dividends—includes ordinary income and short-term capital gains.

1b Qualified dividends—dividends that qualify for the more favorable rate on long-term capital gains.

2a Total capital gains distributions— long-term capital gains.

2d Unrecaptured Section 1250 gains—attributable to depreciable real estate investments.

3 Nontaxable distributions—distributions that are not taxable, but the cost basis must be reduced by this amount.

6 Foreign taxes paid—an investor may be able to take a deduction for this amount.

Sections 1 through 2a apply to most funds, whereas sections 2d and 3 apply to real estate investment trusts and section 6 applies to international stock funds. One of the problems with mutual fund tax reporting is that short-term capital gains are lumped in with taxable income. Therefore, if an investor has short-term losses that could be used to offset the short-term gains from the fund holding, there is no way to obtain the information.[16]

FIGURE 6.11 *Sample IRS Form 1099-DIV*

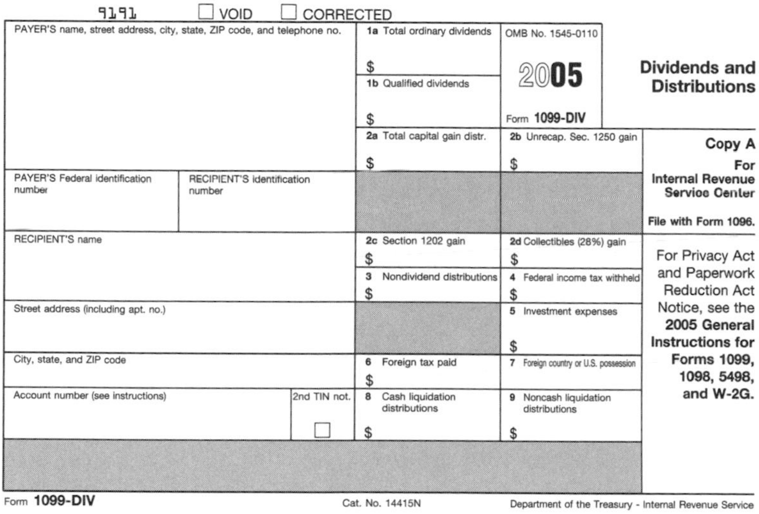
9191 ☐ VOID ☐ CORRECTED

PAYER'S name, street address, city, state, ZIP code, and telephone no.

1a Total ordinary dividends $

1b Qualified dividends $

OMB No. 1545-0110

2005

Form 1099-DIV

Dividends and Distributions

2a Total capital gain distr. $

2b Unrecap. Sec. 1250 gain $

Copy A For Internal Revenue Service Center

File with Form 1096.

PAYER'S Federal identification number

RECIPIENT'S identification number

RECIPIENT'S name

2c Section 1202 gain $

2d Collectibles (28%) gain $

3 Nondividend distributions $

4 Federal income tax withheld $

Street address (including apt. no.)

5 Investment expenses $

City, state, and ZIP code

6 Foreign tax paid $

7 Foreign country or U.S. possession

Account number (see instructions)

2nd TIN not. ☐

8 Cash liquidation distributions $

9 Noncash liquidation distributions $

For Privacy Act and Paperwork Reduction Act Notice, see the **2005 General Instructions for Forms 1099, 1098, 5498, and W-2G.**

Form **1099-DIV** Cat. No. 14415N Department of the Treasury - Internal Revenue Service

Source: Internal Revenue Service

All too often, the investor pays taxes on the distribution when reported on Form 1099-DIV and then again when shares are sold. Thus, the investor may inadvertently pay taxes on the same amount of capital gains twice! This happens more frequently than most people realize, because many fund shareholders do not understand the accounting involved and fail to keep good records. This brings us to the following rules of thumb for mutual fund investors:

- ❑ Be sure to check when the fund's fiscal year ends and the amount of income and capital gains distributions anticipated before making an investment, so you will not end up paying taxes on a significant amount of capital gains you did not earn.
- ❑ Keep in mind that when new investors make contributions to a fund in a rising market, taxable gains are likely to be distributed to a greater number of shareholders, which can enhance after-tax returns. On the other hand, when investors sell shares in a declining market, the portfolio manager may be forced to take gains, to the detriment of the dwindling number of remaining shareholders.
- ❑ Consider whether specific lot identification or FIFO is worth the time and effort to achieve a potentially more desirable result than the average cost convention of accounting for gains and losses.
- ❑ Keep good records of mutual fund purchases, reinvestment of dis-

tributions, and sales of fund shares to avoid inadvertently paying taxes twice.

The SEC's requirement that mutual funds provide after-tax returns has been far more valuable than investors realize. The display format is relatively simple and provides useful information that not only allows investors to make more informed decisions but also serves as a way to educate them on the benefit of longer holding periods. With the SEC's after-tax standards, there is now a foundation of information to build on. Over time, modifications can be made to address issues such as those the author has noted to improve on what is already extremely valuable information. Since more and more investors are becoming comfortable with the SEC's after-tax standards, they are beginning to ask providers in other niches of the taxable marketplace, "If my mutual fund can provide after-tax returns, why can't I receive them in this platform?" Providers that are responding to this call are already beginning to distinguish themselves. As a result, they are attracting the more discriminating and knowledgeable tax-aware investors.

Chapter Notes

1. Securities and Exchange Commission, "Final Rule: Disclosure of Mutual Fund After-Tax Returns (S7-09-00)," April 16, 2001, 7.

2. Investment Company Institute, *Mutual Fund Fact Book 2004* (Washington, D.C.: ICI, 2004), 29.

3. Vanguard Group, *Vanguard Tax-Managed Funds Semiannual Report,* June 30, 2004, 19.

4. AIMR letter to U.S. Securities and Exchange Commission, Re: Proposed Rule for Disclosure of Mutual Fund After-Tax Returns (File Reference No. S7-09-00), June 29, 2000, 2.

5. Anne Granfield and James M. Cash, "Crash Taxes," *Forbes,* June 14, 1999, 370–372.

6. Morningstar Principia, December 31, 2004.

7. Morningstar Principia, Vanguard Tax-Managed Growth and Income Fund, July 2004.

8. Morningstar Principia, Vanguard Tax-Managed Growth and Income Fund, December 31, 2004.

9. Congressman Jim Saxton, Chairman, Joint Economic Committee, *The Alternative Minimum Tax for Individuals: A Growing Burden, Congressional Budget Office 2001,* U.S. Congress, May 2001.

10. CCH Tax Law Editors, *2004 U.S. Master Tax Guide* (Chicago: CCH, 2003), ¶ 1401, p. 449.

11. Chairman Jim Saxton, *The Taxation of Mutual Fund Investors: Performance, Saving and Investment, Joint Economic Committee,* U.S. Congress, April 2001.

12. Investment Company Institute, "Bill to Help Mutual Fund Investors Earns Strong ICI Endorsement," May 7, 2003, http://www.ici.org (accessed October 18, 2004).

13. Vanguard 500 Index Fund, http://finance.yahoo.com (accessed October 17, 2004).

14. IRS Publication 564, *Mutual Fund Distributions,* http://www.irs.gov/pub lications/p564/ar02.html (accessed October 17, 2004).

15. Jack C. Bogle in discussion with the author, September 2, 2004.

16. Gary I. Gastineau, *The Exchange-Traded Funds Manual* (New York: John Wiley, 2002), 99–100.

CHAPTER 7

Separate Account After-Tax Reporting

The incidence of taxation depends upon the substance of a transaction.

—HUGO L. BLACK

T he first formal attempt to create uniform standards for after-tax reporting was initiated by Lee N. Price. His firm, Rosenberg Capital Management (RCM), was serving nuclear decommissioning trust (NDT) clients and they requested after-tax returns for manager comparison purposes and to satisfy regulatory requirements. Price approached the Association for Investment Management and Research, which formed a Taxable Portfolios Subcommittee chaired by Price and Robert E. Pruyne.[1] The subcommittee consisted of working professionals having extensive experience with taxable accounts.[2] Its recommendations were adopted and can be found in the *AIMR Performance Presentation Standards Handbook.*[3] Only about a half dozen firms that were serving more-demanding NDT clients adopted the standards. Vendors of portfolio accounting software were slow to respond, as they were unwilling to commit the resources necessary to modify their tax-exempt-account-oriented portfolio accounting systems until there was a catalyst to do so. The catalyst proved to be the Securities and Exchange Commission's after-tax standards, as the retail portion of the market now had better information than the more sophisticated and demanding, separate account segment of the market.

The AIMR Subcommittee for After-Tax Return Reporting was reconstituted in the spring of 2000, first to respond to the SEC proposal and then to review the existing after-tax standards for separate accounts. A blue-ribbon panel of experts in various related fields volunteered considerable time and effort to recommend revisions to the existing AIMR after-tax standards.[4] Lee Price was again a significant contributor to this process and as a result should be forever known as the "father of after-tax reporting." The AIMR board adopted the modifications to the after-tax standards on February 8, 2003. Following this action, the Investment Performance Council (IPC) then endorsed the modifications on March 6, 2003. While efforts by the SEC (in regard to mutual funds) and AIMR (in regard to separate accounts) have paved the way for after-tax standards in the United States, it is hoped that the IPC will soon respond with a global initiative so that other countries can adopt appropriate after-tax standards with relative ease based on their respective tax codes. Thus far, Australia and Canada have shown interest.

After-tax standards for separate account reporting composites are optional, as not all firms manage taxable accounts. The revisions to the existing AIMR after-tax standards took effect January 1, 2005. Firms focused on serving the needs of taxable investors have taken action and have aligned themselves with service providers to allow them to provide after-tax returns for individual accounts as well as for composite construction for use in marketing presentations. **FIGURE 7.1** is from the after-tax provisions of the AIMR Performance Presentation Standards.[5]

To be in compliance with the AIMR standards for after-tax reporting, five rows of information beyond what is required for before-tax reporting must be provided. These rows are shaded in the "required" section of the template.

There are also three additional rows of "recommended" information that may be provided if a firm believes it can add value beyond the mandatory elements. The first item, adjusting for nondiscretionary capital gains, is intended not to penalize the manager for a requested distribution from an account that is beyond the manager's control. This type of request frequently happens with high-net-worth family accounts when there is a need to pay taxes or fund a major purchase, such as buying a second home. When the portfolio manager responds to a request to liquidate funds of this nature, despite attempts to minimize the impact of taxes, inevitably some gains will be realized. Since this measure can only work to the advantage of the firm, it is possible for the manager to "game" the situation by classifying certain gains as nondiscretionary that perhaps are not. In all instances, the portfolio manager should work to the benefit of the client and include only those gains that are the result of specific requests. For a detailed discussion on this topic, see "Calcula-

FIGURE **7.1** *Sample AIMR-PPS Compliant Presentation for an After-Tax Composite*

XYZ U.S. Equities After-Tax Composite

	2004	2005	2006	2007	2008
REQUIRED (IF COMPLIANT WITH AIMR-PPS STANDARDS AND SHOWING AFTER-TAX PERFORMANCE)					
After-Tax Total Return (%)	21.99	31.03	25.02	22.02	−6.17
After-Tax Composite Dispersion (%)	3.1	5.1	3.7	3.2	2.4
Before-Tax Total Return (%)	24.31	34.02	27.33	24.03	−8.44
Before-Tax Benchmark Total Return (%)	22.95	33.35	28.58	21.04	−9.01
Before-Tax Composite Dispersion (%)	2.9	3.3	2.6	1.8	1.5
% of Unrealized Capital Gains to Composite Assets	9	25	37	43	19
% of Taxable Portfolios Included in Both the U.S. Equities After-Tax & Before-Tax Composites	75	78	81	79	82
Dollar-Weighted Anticipated Tax Rate	44.2	44.3	44.5	44.1	43.9
Number of Portfolios	26	32	38	45	48
Total Assets at End of Period (U.S. $millions)	165	235	344	445	420
Percentage of Firm Assets	33	36	39	43	37
Total Firm Assets (U.S. $millions)	500	653	882	1,035	1,135
RECOMMENDED					
After-Tax Return Adjusted for Non-Discretionary Capital Gains (%)	21.99	31.07	25.25	24.12	−5.99
After-Tax Benchmark Return (%)	21.78	32.05	27.78	20.21	−9.37
Percentage Benefit from Tax Loss Harvesting	0.00	0.00	0.00	0.00	3.51

tion and Reporting of After-Tax Performance" by Lee N. Price[6] and the "Interpretative Guidance" section of the AIMR Standards.[7]

The next recommended item of information is the after-tax benchmark return. Currently, there is no central depository for after-tax returns on the most common physical benchmarks or indices where the tax ramifications on individual security positions are taken into account. Unfortunately, standard practices do not exist for constructing benchmarks, and some of the methods used by providers make the calculation of after-tax returns a daunting, if not impossible, task. Just a few of the items of concern are availability of data, reconstitution of the indices, and treatment of dividends. For fixed income benchmarks, pricing issues, the large number of securities, and amortization and accretion of fixed income securities make calculating after-tax returns a most challenging task.

Practitioners need to be careful with the use of after-tax benchmark information. For example, they should not link information when after-tax returns are calculated according to the post-liquidation methodology, as the inception date of the portfolio and benchmark will likely have a significant impact on the gains and losses that will ultimately be realized. Fortunately, after-tax returns calculated by the pre-liquidation methodology are not affected by the level of the markets at the inception date of measurement. Until a database for the physical benchmarks can be created and maintained, most practitioners are using after-tax returns from passive portfolios of index and exchange-traded funds (ETFs) for comparative purposes. A benefit of using mutual funds and ETFs is that the frequency of distributions is usually no greater than monthly, so far less effort is needed to collect the information necessary to calculate the after-tax return. The information can be extracted straight from the fund's prospectus, but the source of information should be properly footnoted. Perhaps the most compelling reason to use after-tax returns from funds for comparison is that mutual funds and ETFs are in fact investable alternatives for investors. As a result, this method is gaining in popularity with tax-aware managers. However, when managers who do not consider taxes in the security selection process compare their results with an index mutual fund, they quickly discover how difficult it is to outperform this proxy on an after-tax basis, as the articles by Arnott and Jeffrey and by Dickson and Shoven concluded a decade ago. Since many managers are even less competitive on a relative basis than with before-tax results, most firms continue to avoid developing a process to offer after-tax returns to prospects and clients . Those readers wishing greater detail with regard to after-tax benchmarks should seek articles by Jeffrey L. Minck (1998), David M. Stein (1999), and James M. Poterba (1999).[8] One issue that requires special treatment is significant cash flows. Innovative solutions have been suggested, like "shadow portfolios" by Ron L. Surz, where the benchmark experiences flows similar to the client portfolio's.[9]

The last item of recommended information is the percentage benefit from tax-loss harvesting. It should be noted that tax-loss harvesting is typically most prolific and valuable in declining markets and at the inception of a long-term relationship. Therefore, the benefit displayed may vary significantly among client portfolios with different inception dates, so this information should be used only as a guide. The degree of the tax-loss harvesting benefit may not be replicable for future investors, as the direction of the market may not create a similar opportunistic environment. Firms with strategies that rely heavily on tax-loss harvesting should accompany this row of information with a footnote explaining the concept, as this can be a major source of tax alpha for tax-aware managers. Alpha is the incremental return for a given level of risk taken by the manager. If he takes the same level of market risk (beta) as the Standard & Poor's 500 stock index and outperforms it by 2 percent, then this is considered to be his alpha. By generating losses that can be used to offset gains in other portfolios, the manager generates what is referred to as tax alpha. At the same time, a manager could have a before-tax alpha less than, equal to, or greater then 0 percent that comes from such traditional sources of incremental value as sector allocation and security selection. Obviously, the ideal is for a manager to have a positive alpha both before and after taxes. This is the ultimate goal, and more separate account managers are joining a select group of elite practitioners that are accomplishing both, as will be discussed in chapter 12.

One of the concerns of the investment management industry was the possibility that the additional cost of calculating after-tax returns for client reporting and marketing could only be absorbed by larger, more profitable firms. Interestingly enough, one of the first firms, if not the first, to conquer the task of preparing composite information according to the AIMR after-tax standards was Gratry & Associates, a small boutique in Cleveland, Ohio, specializing in international American depositary receipt (ADR) portfolios. By monitoring the activity of the AIMR Subcommittee and working closely with their providers, Gratry was able to achieve this accomplishment almost immediately following the announcement of the proposed revisions and more than a year and a half before the January 1, 2005, implementation date. To Gratry, having the capability to share its after-tax performance results was extremely important, as the firm has a history of adding incremental value for its clients through tax-loss harvesting, in addition to what is achieved from country positioning, sector allocation, and security selection.

With the enhancement in trade management systems over the past decade, firms managing tax-exempt accounts have been able to achieve extremely low variability or dispersion of individual account returns. If the firm is considering the impact of taxes during the buy-and-sell decision process, dispersion with taxable account returns should naturally be greater. Significantly higher dispersion may in fact reinforce that the firm is adhering to a philosophy of managing each taxable account according to its own unique objective. The firm should evaluate the key factors it believes differentiates its taxable accounts results and develop after-tax return composites that reflect the major differences. Therefore, a firm may have multiple taxable-account composites for a given portfolio strategy but only one composite for tax-exempt accounts. If sufficient time and effort is put into developing the composites, dispersion of the after-tax returns will most likely become less of a concern. The following is a list of factors a firm might consider when constructing composites when reporting after-tax returns:

- ❏ The type of taxable account—for example, individual or high-net-worth family, nuclear decommissioning trust, voluntary employee beneficiary association, or property and casualty insurance company
- ❏ The clients' anticipated or maximum federal tax rate
- ❏ The clients' state of residence for tax purposes and the respective tax rate
- ❏ Vintage year or year of the inception of the relationship
- ❏ Accounts starting with a cash portfolio versus existing holdings or a concentrated position
- ❏ Accounts that treat expenses differently, such as mutual funds and trusts versus taxable separate accounts

The type of taxable account can have a significant impact on portfolio management decisions. For example, the methodology employed to effectively manage property and casualty insurance company portfolios periodically emphasizes realizing capital gains for annual financial reporting purposes.

The federal tax rate to which individual investors are subject to has a greater influence on security selection for fixed income accounts in the United States, because we have both taxable and tax-exempt bonds. At low-enough federal tax rates, clients may be better off holding a portion or the entire portfolio in taxable bonds, as their after-tax yields may be greater than what is offered from similar effective maturity tax-exempt bonds. Fixed income portfolios that take into account the client's tax profile and adjust the allocation to taxable and tax-exempt bonds depending on their after-tax return potential are referred to as "crossover" portfolios. Additionally, the percentage of tax-exempt bonds held from the client's state of residence for tax purposes in the portfolio might be quite different for a client in a high-tax state like New York, compared with Texas where the residents are not subject to a state income tax.

The vintage year is especially important for equity portfolio strategies that emphasize tax-loss harvesting. Obviously, for the first three years of the relationship, the opportunities to add value from this process would have been far greater for accounts beginning in 2000, as compared with those initiated in 1996.

Some firms have made the decision to include only accounts that start with 100 percent cash in their composites, as they believe this is the way to ensure the accounts represent their discretionary management process. The firm is likely to inherit portfolios with substantial unrealized capital gains, which are likely to produce after-tax results inconsistent with the discretionary composite. It may take months or years before some of these portfolios mirror the discretionary portfolio. They should be monitored and moved to the discretionary when they achieve a satisfactory level of consistency.

The last element pertaining to creating composites is how expenses are treated. Unlike mutual funds, as discussed in chapter 6, most stand-alone separate accounts cannot offset income with expenses. Therefore, they will have lower after-tax returns when compared with mutual fund and trust portfolios, where income may be offset with expenses. To accommodate these differences, it is recommended that the after-tax returns be adjusted for the tax benefit of the offset. For example, if a mutual fund is being placed in a composite of equity-strategy separate accounts for individual investors and it charges the industry average 1.5 percent fee, it would be proper to increase the annual after-tax returns of the mutual fund by approximately by 0.23 percent (1.5% fee × 15% tax rate applicable to qualified dividends), or the firm might decide to maintain the accounts as separate composites. In such cases, a disclosure should be made stating why the after-tax return would be different if the strategy were held in a stand-alone separate account arrangement.

The list of items to consider certainly need not be limited to those listed here and in other AIMR documents. The key is not to limit the composites to some preconceived number but rather to come up with the number of composites necessary to allow practitioners to effectively communicate the results of their taxable accounts according to their unique circumstances with clients, prospects, and interested third parties.

There are three main points that should be understood with the revisions to the AIMR after-tax reporting standards. Previously, application of the clients' maximum federal tax on ordinary income, currently 35 percent, was mandatory when calculating after-tax returns. The revised after-tax standards favor the application of the clients' "anticipated" tax rate. This was done for several reasons. First, for most strategies it is simply part of a professional's duty to ascertain from the client what types and level of taxation need to be considered in order to make sound investment decisions. Second, as mentioned earlier, a fixed income manager may elect to purchase a taxable bond if the initial after-tax yield to maturity is greater than the return from a tax-exempt bond of similar effective maturity. In these instances, applying the maximum federal tax rate for the client type would result in after-tax returns that would not reflect the manager's ability to add value. Third, firms that were calculating after-tax returns discovered that their performance measurement professionals were actually calculating and maintaining two separate after-tax returns for each account, and the amount of work required to do this was simply overwhelming. After-tax returns using the maximum federal tax rate were being used for composite purposes, yet clients were provided information using the preferred "anticipated" tax rates, which were more in line with their actual experience. Since there is a deduction at the federal level for the payment of state and local taxes, the anticipated tax rate is less than or equal to the sum when more than one rate is considered. The formula to calculate the anticipated tax rate is:

$$TR_{anticipated} = TR_{federal} + (TR_{state} \times [1 - TR_{federal}])$$
$$+ (TR_{local} \times [1 - TR_{federal}]),$$

where TR stands for tax rate. If the client is subject to a 35 percent federal tax rate, 10 percent state tax rate, and a 2 percent local tax rate, then the anticipated tax rate is equal to 42.8 percent as shown below:

$$35\% + (10\% \times [1 - 35\%]) + (2\% \times [1 - 35\%]), \text{ or}$$
$$35\% + (10\% \times 0.65) + (2\% \times 0.65), \text{ or}$$
$$35\% + 6.5\% + 1.3\% = 42.8\%$$

These rates should be maintained for each client portfolio in the composite. In reality, the client's actual tax rate will be a combination of the anticipated tax rates for ordinary income, short-term capital gains, qualified dividends, and long-term capital gains. To come up with this more precise weighted rate would be extremely time-consuming. Besides, the tax information for separate accounts is lot-specific. Therefore, use of the anticipated tax rate based on the rate of ordinary income at least gives the reviewer of the composite information a framework as to how investment decisions may have been affected by the level of taxation. There are legitimate cases, like wrap relationships, where the client does not have access to this information. In these instances, using the maximum federal tax is acceptable and should be encouraged.

Advocates of using the maximum federal rates claim that use of the anticipated tax does not facilitate comparing after-tax results of multiple managers. This implies a level of accuracy that is simply not obtainable or reasonable, as additional information is required to make sound decisions. Even before-tax reporting is an estimate of performance, but the case is far more so with after-tax results.

The second key feature of the revised after-tax standards is that AIMR instituted a specific method for the treatment of taxes. This lends itself to a form of branding, and under the Global Investment Performance Standards (GIPS) a firm can put on a client's quarterly performance report that "the after-tax returns have been calculated in a manner consistent with the AIMR after-tax reporting standards," or words to this effect. This is notable because many firms view the quarterly performance report as their most important communication tool. While firms may only use the pre-liquidation after-tax returns for composite construction, the firm's clients are likely to ask for both. Therefore, firms should look for this capability when selecting software vendors.

The third key element of the AIMR after-tax reporting standards is that the Subcommittee was careful to ensure they were consistent with the SEC standards for mutual funds, except where modification was warranted. The one major difference is that the SEC standards require reporting of returns after taxes on distributions and sale of fund shares—known as the post-liquidation calculation methodology—whereas the AIMR standard does not. The post-liquidation methodology does in fact provide extremely meaningful information for a single separate account or individual mutual fund. Unlike the SEC's after-tax standards, which allow individual investors to make better-informed investment decisions on specific funds, the AIMR standards were originally developed with an emphasis presenting results from a composite of accounts managed according to a distinct style, such as domestic large-capitalization growth equity portfolios. With performance composites, accounts are continually being added or dropped. Unfortunately, the flow of account information in composites distorts post-liquidation after-tax returns to the point they cannot be relied on to provide relevant information. If the composite legitimately consists of only one account, a firm could certainly provide this additional information if it might be helpful to prospects. This does not mean other methods of calculating after-tax returns should be ignored, but if supplemental information is provided it should be marked as such and the pre-liquidation returns must be shown prominently. One such case is a fixed income practitioner that applies the "full-liquidation" method, in which the complete tax impact is calculated for the unit of measurement, currently monthly. This method is more appropriate for fixed income portfolios and usually results in the most conservative after-tax return. Since property and casualty insurance companies typically have a majority of their assets allocated to fixed income, their advisers will often support use of the full-liquidation methodology. However, this fails to account for the benefit of compounding tax-free by extending the holding period, which is extremely important with equity portfolios. Readers desiring to read more about various after-tax calculation methodologies should refer to Lee N. Price (1995).[10]

In both the SEC and AIMR after-tax reporting standards, the tax impact is accounted for when the taxable event takes place, rather than at the end of a period. A system that utilizes the client's data from Form 1040 and end-of-year custodial records may in fact provide extremely accurate after-tax return information, but it is inconsistent with the AIMR standard. The rationale behind the AIMR after-tax standards is to capture the portfolio manager or firm's decision to take the client's tax profile into account at the time of the transaction, versus establishing an extremely accurate accounting report. If the latter was the objective, then a high-net-worth individual account that has a taxable event in January would not, in many cases, see an after-tax return until perhaps twenty-one or more months later, as many families do not finalize their taxes until the following fall. Application of this rationale also makes it much easier for the firm when a retroactive tax bill occurs, which happened in 2003. Even though the bill was passed near midyear, the lower tax rate on qualified dividends of 15 percent was retroactive to the beginning of the year. Applying this approach again ensured that the after-tax returns captured how portfolio managers were accounting for taxes, as until the bill was passed they had to operate under the assumption that the existing higher rate on ordinary income would apply. Moreover, performance-measurement professionals were not burdened with the task of recalculating six months of previous returns for accounts subject to the change in the tax code.

Significant cash flows require attention with tax-exempt accounts, but even more so with taxable accounts. Constructing composites that take into account the various factors noted above will give prospects more meaningful information, but equally important, portfolio managers can apply the information more effectively in the day-to-day management of their taxable accounts in their quest to produce superior results.

The key to after-tax performance is that it is an art form, rather than a science. It is simply foolish to think you can compare one return against another and come to a valid conclusion without analyzing additional information affecting day-to-day tax management. The tax-aware practitioner needs to be cognizant of the market environment in which the portfolio manager was operating to understand how tax consequences have been managed and to draw meaningful conclusions.

FIGURES 7.2, 7.3, and 7.4, courtesy of Parametric Portfolio Associates, show how a firm can distinguish itself through after-tax reporting. These

FIGURE **7.2** *Portfolio Performance—Income Statement*

Parametric Portfolio Associates Sample Quarterly Performance Report

	FOURTH QUARTER	YEAR TO DATE	SINCE INCEPTION (10/23/1998) CUMULATIVE	ANNUALIZED
Pretax Performance				
Portfolio	11.7%	28.2%	13.3%	2.4%
Benchmark	12.2%	28.7%	11.9%	2.2%
After-Tax Performance				
Portfolio	11.6%	29.4%	23.4%	4.1%
Benchmark	12.1%	28.4%	8.5%	1.6%

exhibits are part of the quarterly communiqué that Parametric sends each of its separate account clients. The Portfolio Performance section of the communiqué starts with pretax and after-tax comparative results against an appropriate benchmark for the current quarter, year-to-date, and since inception of the account (Figure 7.2). This can be viewed as the income statement of the report. In the column labeled "year to date," you can see that the portfolio lagged the performance of the S&P 500 by 0.5 percent before taxes, but it outperformed on an after-tax basis by 1.0 percent. This highlights the potential of a tax-loss harvesting strategy, which is paramount to the success of Parametric and other firms focused on this niche of the market. Note that the "since inception" annualized value-added from the process is +2.5 percent (4.1 percent after-tax return for Parametric as compared to 1.6 percent for the S&P 500). This example is for periods ending December 31, 2003. It should be noted that Parametric is one of the few firms that attempts to calculate the actual after-tax return for a comparative benchmark portfolio of securities. To do this properly requires running benchmark portfolios for the different inception dates for all accounts under management.

The Portfolio Value section highlights the balance sheet of the account from a tax accounting perspective (Figure 7.3 on the following page). As shown, the portfolio has less than 0.2 percent in unrealized losses. This tells the client two things. First, Parametric has been diligent in tax-loss harvesting. Second, unless some of the holdings fall significantly in price

FIGURE **7.3** *Portfolio Value—Balance Sheet*

Parametric Portfolio Associates Sample Quarterly Performance Report

	AT 12/21/03
Market Value	$3,366,382
Cost Basis	$2,283,892
Unrealized Gains	
Short Term	$152,440
Long Term	$934,995
Unrealized Losses	
Short Term	$660
Long Term	$4,286

Source: Parametric Portfolio Associates

FIGURE **7.4** *Income and Realized Gains—Cash Flow Statement*

Parametric Portfolio Associates Sample Quarterly Performance Report

INVESTMENT FLOWS	FOURTH QUARTER	YEAR TO DATE	CUMULATIONS
Dividend Income	$13,751	$49,402	$196,860
Net Realized Gains			
Short Term	0	–$73,784	–$555,053
Long Term	0	–$26,458	–$287,224

Source: Parametric Portfolio Associates

during the months ahead there will be less opportunity to add value through tax-loss harvesting in subsequent periods.

The Income and Realized Gains section of the communiqué serves as the cash flow statement of the report (Figure 7.4). The Parametric format addresses the three key areas essential to tax planning for a common stock portfolio: dividend income and net realized short- and long-term capital gains. By tracking the "year to date" column, members of the qualified triumvirate serving the client are able to make better-informed decisions as to how the net losses can be most effectively utilized. Additional information can be provided to highlight the critical portfolio characteristics that reflect the particular type of strategy. For a firm like Parametric that hopes to reduce tracking error to a defined benchmark, items such as the number of securities in the portfolio and sector weightings are important. Other firms may wish to focus on characteristics such as dividend yield and valuation metrics to emphasize a particular style or orientation. To develop a client performance report of this quality requires a significant commitment of resources on the part of the firm, but like Gratry with its after-tax composite information, Parametric thought it was worth the effort to highlight the value of its process and demonstrate its distinctive competence with the one document that is most important to its clients.

After-tax returns should be a source of pride for a firm. Therefore, firms that understand the value-added proposition from tax-aware investment management are the ones most likely to provide after-tax returns. Service providers responding to the needs of firms can be segmented into the following categories:

❑ *Portfolio accounting stand-alone systems*
—IDS
—Osprey
—Shaw
—Sungard

❑ *Separate account supplemental systems*
—iKindi
—Meradia
—Price Performance Systems

❑ *Systems development and support*
—Accounting firms with AIMR auditing practices
—Cutter Associates
—Meradia
—Osprey
—Tower Group

These are providers the author is aware of as of the summer of 2005. The list does not represent an endorsement of any firm. There may certainly be other well-qualified providers available, and additional firms are likely to offer similar services in the future.

Stand-alone systems are the calculation and reporting engine for the asset management firm. Supplemental systems work in conjunction with information provided from the stand-alone system or custodial reports. Price Performance Systems offers an equity-oriented product, whereas iKindi has undertaken the challenging task of providing the ability to calculate after-tax returns for fixed income, taking into account amortization and accretion of premiums and discounts.

There are various providers of systems support. The key to establishing an after-tax reporting capability is to ensure all key decision makers are included in the process. If the planning is done with care, the firm will most likely avoid costly mistakes and solutions that do not satisfy the needs of clients and investment professionals. Any firm considering entering the realm of taxable account investing today would be foolish to entertain a proposal from a software vendor that does not already offer an after-tax reporting capability consistent with the AIMR provisions. It is difficult enough to become AIMR compliant with before-tax returns and having to recalculate historical returns or reconstruct composites, but to do so for after-tax returns may be almost an insurmountable task, especially with fixed income accounts.

As mentioned in chapter 6, firms desiring to include after-tax benchmarks returns in their composite displays are encouraged to utilize after-tax returns from an appropriate index-oriented mutual or exchange-traded fund. Meaningful offerings are now available for traditional asset classes—with the exception of municipal bonds, for which a competing mutual fund product of similar duration and quality should be sufficient. Another alterative is to use a taxable bond mutual fund and just apply the average historical spread between it and a municipal bond benchmark. Depending on the average historical term (cash equivalents, short, intermediate, or long) the spread to be applied may range from 70 percent for shorter-term benchmarks to 85 percent for longer-term benchmarks. For example, let's say your municipal bond product is intermediate term and after analyzing the spread between appropriate Lehman bond indices you decide to multiply returns of the Barclays Government/Credit ETF by 0.80. Although it will not track the municipal bond market perfectly, clients will appreciate that you are attempting to measure and communicate the importance of taxes on investment returns!

The challenges of creating an after-tax reporting capability are magnified for consulting firms, especially those with high-net-worth clients. Unfortunately, this niche has been served by providers with pension-consulting software that does not consider taxes. If the system calculates returns by security position versus transaction information it needs to be replaced by one that can provide an after-tax reporting capability consistent with the AIMR methodology. Tax-lot accounting and transaction-based information are simply a must, and there are no shortcuts or alternatives to them. The typical source of information is the custodial statement. The property and casualty insurance consulting industry is able to obtain the same information from a small number of providers of statutory information.[11] This makes the process much more efficient. Therefore, consulting firms in general can benefit if they limit their clients to a select few sources of account information. Efficient data feeds are critical so that the reconciliation process focuses on exceptions rather than every piece of data. Also, having all the information in one database lends itself to the use of third-party providers to achieve consistent pricing, portfolio characteristics, et cetera. Once the calculations are made, a custom report writer can create a product to respond to various client needs. One way to simplify the entire process is to establish an industry HTML format for security transaction information, an idea that was proposed to the author by Jay Whipple III, the founder of Security APL and Osprey, well-known providers of portfolio accounting software and solutions. This would alleviate the challenges of applying various accounting conventions and matching sales with specific tax lots.

At this juncture, firms are still spending inordinate amounts of time and effort choosing a portfolio accounting system to calculate after-tax returns. Firms embarking on this decision should read articles prepared by Douglas S. Rogers and Lee N. Price (2002), John D. Simpson (2003), and Douglas S. Rogers (2000, 2003).[12] If the firm desires an AIMR-compliant solution, the system must include these critical elements:

❏ The ability to incorporate the impact of taxes as outlined by AIMR for the modified Dietz, daily valuation, or modified BAI methods
❏ Tax-lot accounting that captures the amount and date of every transaction
❏ The impact of each and every transaction
❏ Maintenance of the information, including such items as the amortization and accretion of fixed income securities purchased at a level other than par
❏ Information that captures the tax parameters of the types of taxable clients that will be entered into the system
❏ Ability to distinguish between various types of securities, such as taxable bonds versus tax-exempt bonds or government bonds exempt from state taxes versus others
❏ The ability of the software provider to keep up with changes in the tax code for the client type you are servicing

There is one "last frontier" in the area of after-tax analysis and reporting that has yet to be solved: after-tax performance attribution. Utilizing current attribution software on taxable accounts is almost a useless, and in some cases a detrimental, exercise, because none of the existing systems take into account the capital gain/loss position of a security. For example, a particular security that a portfolio owned may have lagged the performance of its peers in the same industry, and the industry in turn may have also lagged the overall performance of the benchmark. Therefore, one might have naively concluded that the manager's security selection and sector allocation was negative for the period. However, the security may have had a substantial short-term unrealized capital gain position, and selling the position would have been detrimental to the client. Resolving this quandary can potentially integrate attribution with the portfolio decision-making process. By doing this properly, the performance measurement professional would become part of a forward-looking value-added proposition rather than just providing backward-looking information to explain past events and activity.[13]

Since Lee Price first responded to clients' requests in the early 1990s, substantial progress has been made to master the art of after-tax reporting. We now have accepted after-tax reporting calculation methodologies and standards that enable both taxable mutual fund investors and separate account investors to make better-informed investment decisions. Fortunately, there are a select group of software providers that proved that the standards can be successfully implemented, given the desire and resources. It takes a meaningful commitment of resources to achieve an after-tax reporting capability, but even small boutique firms have accomplished it. Therefore, there is no longer a valid excuse for investment managers not to offer this capability. Firms that embrace after-tax reporting initially will most likely be those that will benefit by communicating their results according to an accepted format, allowing others to evaluate and confirm their value-added proposition in ways never before possible.

Chapter Notes

1. Much of the discussion on separate account after-tax reporting has been taken directly or summarized from the author's article with Sean W. Egan, "Evaluating and Classifying Taxable Account Managers," *Journal of Wealth Management* (Fall 2004): 49–62.

2. The first AIMR Subcommittee for After-Tax Reporting consisted of co-chairs Lee N. Price and Robert E. Pruyne and Scott R. Abernethy, Michael S. Caccese, Robert H. Jeffrey, Catherine M. O'Connor, John R. O'Toole, and Douglas S. Rogers.

3. Association for Investment Management and Research, *AIMR Performance Presentation Standards Handbook,* 2d ed. (Charlottesville, Va.: AIMR, 1997).

4. The AIMR Subcommittee for After-Tax Reporting reconstituted in 2000 was chaired by Douglas S. Rogers. Members included Jennifer P. Cahill, Thomas F. Drumm, Paul J. Jungquist, Sean S. Keogh, Daniel W. Koors, David A. Krause, James Poterba, Neil E. Riddles, David M. Stein, Ronald J. Surz, and Cecilia S. Wong. Lee N. Price served as an observer.

5. AIMR Performance Presentation Standards (AIMR-PPS)—Amended and Restated as the AIMR-PPS Standards, the U.S. and Canadian version of GIPS and Interpretive Guidance on the AIMR-PPS After-Tax Provisions Contained in Section 9, February 8, 2003, 23.

6. Lee N. Price, "Calculation and Reporting of After-Tax Performance," *Journal of Portfolio Management* (Winter 1996): 6–13.

7. AIMR Performance Presentation Standards (AIMR-PPS)—Amended and Restated as the AIMR-PPS Standards, the U.S. and Canadian version of GIPS and Interpretive Guidance on the AIMR-PPS After-Tax Provisions Contained in Section 9.G., February 8, 2003, 25–26.

8. Jeffrey L. Minck, "Tax-Adjusted Equity Benchmarks," *Journal of Private Portfolio Management* (Summer 1998): 41–50; James M. Poterba, "After-Tax Performance Evaluation," *AIMR Conference Proceedings: Investment Counseling for Private Clients* (Charlottesville, Va.: AIMR, 1999), 92-105; David M. Stein, Brian Langstraat, and Premkumar Narasimhan, "Reporting After-Tax Returns: A Pragmatic Approach," *Journal of Private Portfolio Management* (Spring 1999), 10–21.

9. Ron L. Surz, in discussions with the author during speaking engagements and the AIMR Subcommittee for After-Tax Reporting where the subject of shadow portfolios has been raised.

10. Lee N. Price, presentation on after-tax return calculation methodologies, 1995.

11. Peter N. Gunder, director–insurance consulting, for Cardinal Investment Advisors, in discussion with the author, August 3, 2004.

12. Douglas S. Rogers and Lee N. Price, "Challenges With Developing Portfolio Accounting Software for After-Tax Reporting," *Journal of Performance Measurement* (Supplement 2002): 12–18; John D. Simpson, "Searching for a System to Meet Your After-Tax Performance Reporting Needs," *Journal of Performance Measurement* (Supplement 2003): 22–28; Douglas S. Rogers, "The Challenges of After-Tax Performance Reporting," *Journal of Performance Measurement* (Spring 2000): 10–15; Douglas S. Rogers, "The State of After-Tax Reporting." *Monitor* (November/December 2003): 26–27.

13. Douglas S. Rogers, "A Call to Arms! The Next Frontier for Taxable Accounts—After-Tax Return Performance Attribution, *Journal of Performance Measurement* vol. 9, no. 3 (Spring 2005): 43–46.

CHAPTER 8

Measures of Tax Efficiency

A citizen can hardly distinguish between a tax and a fine, except that the fine is generally much lighter.

—G. K. CHESTERTON

There are four key calculations that practitioners may encounter for measuring the tax efficiency of the portfolio management process:

❑ Accountant's ratio = \$ amount of long-term capital gains realized / \$ amount of total capital gains realized

❑ Capture ratio = R_{at} / R_{bt}, where R equals the return after-tax and R_{bt} equals the return before-tax

❑ Relative wealth measure[1] = $([R_{at} - R_{bt}] / [1 + R_{bt}]) \times 1,000$

❑ Morningstar tax-cost ratio[2] = $(1 - [(1 + R_{at}) / (1 + R_{bt})]) \times 100$

This chapter examines the characteristics of each and how they can be applied to allow investors and advisers to make better tax-aware decisions.[3]

Accountant's ratio: This ratio is applied to see if the portfolio manager is taking advantage of the lower tax on long- versus short-term capital gains. The difference between the two tax rates is currently 20 percent. Obviously, the higher the percentage of the accountant's ratio the better, with the ideal being 100 percent. The ratio is best used for discussions within the firm, as it has several weaknesses. First, there is no direct linkage between this measure and the actual after-tax returns. Second, it does not take into account the offsetting of realized gains and

95

Source: Douglas S. Rogers

FIGURE **8.1** *Challenges with the Capture Ratio*

RETURN		
BEFORE-TAX	AFTER-TAX	CAPTURE RATIO
10.0%	9.0%	90.0%
10.0%	11.0%	110.0%
2.0%	1.0%	50.0%
−1.0%	1.0%	−100.0%
−8.0%	−6.0%	75.0%

losses. Third, it can't differentiate between "good" and "bad" turnover, as we discussed in chapter 3. However, even with its weaknesses, some firms have found it useful to communicate to their clients a commitment to tax-aware principles.

Capture ratio: This measure is certainly the easiest to understand and was widely accepted by the consulting community almost without question until 2000. When the before-tax return is 10 percent and the after-tax return is 8 percent, the manager has "captured" 80 percent of the before-tax return. Its simplicity is what makes the capture ratio so attractive when communicating tax efficiency. Unfortunately, the usefulness of the capture ratio diminishes when returns are other than the ideal upward-sloping, smooth shape or what is called the "hockey stick market"—and when the magnitude of returns deviates significantly from average annual historical returns.

The first two rows in **FIGURE 8.1** make sense, but the results in the last three rows are difficult to explain to clients and have little or no relevance.

Relative wealth measure: The relative wealth measure was developed by members of the AIMR Subcommittee for After-Tax Reporting. Their effort was in direct response to the frustration with the weakness of the capture ratio. An equation was proposed and simplified to the current form. Rather than calling it a ratio, the Subcommittee decided to label it more appropriately as a measure. The relative wealth measure is a range bound by a rough estimate of the maximum tax rate applicable to the client portfolio. For example, if the client is subject to the 35 percent federal maximum tax rate on ordinary income and the portfolio realized a maximum amount of short-term capital gains, the relative wealth measure is roughly −35, but more precisely it is −31.8. On the other hand, if the

Source: Douglas S. Rogers

FIGURE **8.2** *Comparison of Relative Wealth Measure and Tax-Cost Ratio*

RETURN		AIMR SUBCOMMITTEE RELATIVE WEALTH MEASURE	MORNINGSTAR TAX-COST RATIO
BEFORE-TAX	AFTER-TAX		
0.100	0.090	−9.091	0.9091
−0.100	−0.110	−11.111	1.1111
0.080	0.100	18.519	−1.8519
−0.100	−0.080	22.222	−2.2222

portfolio harvested the maximum amount of losses, the measure would be +35, or +31.8 to be exact. If there is no net tax liability or credit, then the measure is 0.

The beauty of the relative wealth measure is that it delivers reasonable results regardless of the direction or magnitude of the market. Therefore, it overcomes the major shortcoming of the capture ratio and has served to advance the understanding of tax efficiency. However, it is a bit challenging to explain to clients when they encounter it for the first time.

Morningstar tax-cost ratio: This ratio was created after the relative wealth measure and provides a meaningful improvement over other ratios and measures. As shown in the four examples in **FIGURE 8.2**, the Morningstar tax-cost ratio is a derivation of the AIMR subcommittee's relative wealth measure.

The series of numbers is the same in each calculation. The differences are the placement of the decimal point and whether the result is positive or negative. As you can see, the relative wealth measure has a negative sign when the result is detrimental to the taxpayer, whereas the tax-cost ratio is positive. Morningstar intended the ratio to be a "percentage of an investor's assets that are lost to taxes," or the difference between the before-tax and after-tax return.[4] Thus, the positive sign of the output of the equation makes sense. This methodology is easier to explain to clients and, therefore, well suited to more retail-oriented mutual fund investors. Don Phillips shared a story about receiving a call from a disgruntled investor when Morningstar launched the tax-cost ratio. The investor's concern was that our country was in a pension-funding crisis and future market returns would most likely be lower than in the late 1990s. Now that the

FIGURE **8.3** *Information Required to Analyze After-Tax Capability*

MUTUAL FUND	BEFORE-TAX	RETURNS AFTER-TAX DISTRIBUTIONS	DIST & SALE	TAX-COST RATIO	UNREALIZED CAPITAL GAINS
PIMCO PEA Value A	8.26%	6.77%	6.42%	2.67	14%
Dodge & Cox Stock	8.23%	7.61%	7.22%	1.73	20%

Source: Morningstar, Douglas S. Rogers

mutual fund investors have this information, the concerned individual felt it would only heighten the awareness of the magnitude of the problem.[5] Fortunately, for the rest of investors who do wish to be informed, the educational value of the tax-cost ratio has been extremely powerful, and mutual fund investors now have a reliable way of analyzing the impact of taxes on before-tax returns.

The problem with all the ratios and measures adopted thus far is that none of them have been able to find a way to account fairly for the impact of the internal unrealized capital gains position. Therefore, to analyze managers properly, it is essential to incorporate before- and after-tax returns, a measure of tax efficiency, and the percentage of un-realized capital gains.

The two large-cap value funds in **FIGURE 8.3** have similar outstanding before-tax performance for the five years ending June 30, 2004.[6] The Dodge & Cox Stock Fund has been the more tax-efficient of the two funds, as evident by the lower tax-cost ratio. Therefore, you would expect the after-tax performance of the Dodge & Cox Stock Fund to be superior to the PIMCO PEA Value A Fund. In this case, the difference is 0.84 percent annually when only taxes on distributions are accounted for. Since PIMCO PEA Value A has 6 percent less capital gains outstanding, the difference in after-tax performance narrows to 0.80 percent using the sale-of-fund-shares methodology.

Another piece of information that can be valuable when trying to anticipate future tax efficiency is the trend in the fund's net purchase and redemption activity, as shown in **FIGURE 8.4** for the Dodge & Cox Stock Fund and PIMCO PEA Value A Fund. This is calculated by multiplying the beginning year-end asset value (row 2) by the fund's total rate of return (row 3) plus 1 for the year (row 4). Then subtract this result (row 5) from the current end-of-year assets (row 1) to find the net purchase and redemption activity (row 6).

FIGURE **8.4** *Estimating Purchase and Redemption Activity*

	DODGE & COX STOCK	PIMCO PEA VALUE A
1. Assets end 2003 (millions)	$34,156	$484
2. Asset beginning 2003 (millions)	$29,437	$237
3. 2003 Return	32.34%	43.99%
4. 1 + 2003 Return	1.3234	1.4399
5. Return-based assets	$38,957	$341
6 Net purchase (+)/redemption (–) activity	–$4,801	$143

This quick calculation should have raised a flag for the Dodge & Cox Fund. Upon further investigation you would have discovered that this fund is closed to new investors. As discussed in chapter 6, the most advantageous position for a shareholder to be in is that of an early investor in a fund that is continuing grow, as the capital gains are distributed to a greater number of investors. Since there is no cash flow from new investors, existing taxable shareholders should anticipate experiencing a higher-than-normal period of gains realization until the fund reopens. This case is certainly not of the magnitude achieved during the spring of 2000, when growth funds had 50 percent unrealized capital gains positions and sales and net redemption activity resulted in capital gains distributions equaling 15 to 20 percent of fund assets.

The question tax-aware practitioners should ask is: What are reasonable measures of tax efficiency for tax-aware products or portfolios? **FIGURE 8.5** provides reasonable measures of tax efficiency for both separate account and mutual fund products. The ratios and measures can change significantly, depending on the market environment. The information provided is what should be expected with average historical returns over a ten-year period. As we will see in chapter 9, year-to-year tax efficiency can swing dramatically. What is important is that the practitioner be familiar with the strengths and weaknesses of each tax-efficiency measure and know when and how to apply them. The relative wealth measure, even though a bit complex, is best suited for separate accounts, whereas the tax-cost ratio works quite well when returns after distributions are reported for mutual funds. With these measures and techniques, investors and investment professionals can analyze after-tax results more effectively than ever before.

FIGURE 8.5 *Efficiency Ratios and Measures for Tax-Aware Products*

| ASSET CLASS | SEPARATE ACCOUNT | | MUTUAL FUND | |
	CAPTURE RATIO	RELATIVE WEALTH MEASURE	CAPTURE RATIO	TAX-COST RATIO
Tax-Aware Core Equity	113%	10.2	98%	0.18
Large-Cap Index	96%	−3.6	96%	0.36
Active Large-Cap Growth	94%	−5.5	92%	0.55
Active Large-Cap Value	90%	−9.1	88%	1.09
Active Small-Cap Growth	88%	−10.9	86%	1.27
Active Small-Cap Value	86%	−12.7	84%	1.45
Active International	92%	−5.5	90%	0.91
Active International with Currency Overlay	85%	−13.6	83%	1.55
Tax-Aware Municipal Bond	105%	4.5	99%	0.09

Source: Morningstar

Chapter Notes

1. AIMR Performance Presentation Standards (AIMR-PPS)—Amended and Restated as the AIMR-PPS Standards, the U.S. and Canadian version of GIPS and Interpretive Guidance on the AIMR-PPS After-Tax Provisions contained in Section 9.G., February 8, 2003, 32–33.

2. "Morningstar's Tax Cost Ratio Tool," Morningstar.com, http://news.morning star.com/doc/article/0,1,833313,00.html (accessed October 23, 2004), 1–4.

3. Much of the discussion on measures of after-tax reporting has been taken directly or summarized from the author's article with Sean W. Egan, "Evaluating and Classifying Taxable Account Managers," *Journal of Wealth Management* (Fall 2004): 49–62.

4. "Morningstar's Tax Cost Ratio Tool," Morningstar.com, http://news.morningstar .com/doc/article/0,1,833313,00.html (accessed October 23, 2004), 1.

5. Don Phillips, in discussion with the author, October 14, 2001.

6. Morningstar Principia, June 30, 2004.

PART THREE

Tax-Aware Portfolio Management

In case you didn't know, ethanol is made by mixing corn with your tax dollars.

—Paul A. Gigot

CHAPTER 9

Outperforming the Index Fund

I'm putting all my money in taxes—it's the only sure thing to go up.

—Anonymous

T hus far, we have demonstrated through various studies and examples that it is difficult to outperform an index fund on an after-tax basis. We should note, however, that not all index funds are created equal, nor have they all been tax-efficient with low fees. For example, in 1997 the Galaxy II Small Company Index Fund and MainStay Institutional EAFE Index Fund had capital gains distributions equal to 34.4 percent and 25.4 percent of their assets, respectively, and some index funds charge fees close to those of actively managed products.[1] Chapter 3 described how Charles Schwab funded two working papers by John Shoven and Joel Dickson of Stanford University to support the Schwab 1000 Index Fund, which since its inception has never made a capital gains distribution. The purpose of the first working paper was to demonstrate the comparative value of a tax-aware product, whereas the purpose of the second was to explain techniques that could be employed to achieve the lofty goal of managing a fund without capital gains distributions. Shoven and Dickson identified the following principles as critical to avoiding capital gains distributions:

1 When you have to take gains, sell the highest-cost-basis shares first.
2 Realize capital losses to offset future capital gain liabilities.

3 Establish rules to overcome limitations created by the wash sale rule.

The first element was enhanced through the application of high in, first out (HIFO) accounting, versus first in, first out (FIFO) or average cost accounting. Dickson and Shoven recognized that a buy-and-hold approach to portfolio management would not be sufficient to obtain the desired goal. Therefore, they determined it was necessary to take losses when they were available and noted that as early as 1983, George M. Constantinides of the University of Chicago demonstrated that securities with greater price volatility offer more potential for the "tax-loss harvesting" trade.[2] Lastly, the wash sale rule created a challenge, because to get credit for a loss you had to ensure you did not purchase the same security again within thirty days. If flows come into the fund and certain securities cannot be purchased, then the characteristics of the portfolio might deviate from the actual index. Therefore, rules had to be established for when a security should be sold, how much of the position to sell, and what the minimum index weight to hold is. By modeling this process, they discovered they could potentially add another 0.85 to 0.95 percent in incremental return, or tax alpha, beyond the before-tax returns of the index.[3]

Launched in 1991, the Schwab 1000 Index Fund was already building an enviable record of achievement when Dickson and Shoven began their research. At the beginning of their second working paper, they acknowledged the contribution of George U. "Gus" Sauter, chief investment officer at Vanguard Investments for "providing us with key data and insight into the management of Vanguard's 500 Index Fund." So it is no coincidence that Vanguard founder Jack Bogle took note of their conclusions. For at least eight years prior to that time Bogle had been encouraged on more than one occasion by Tad Jeffrey to run a tax-aware fund similar to the Windsor II Fund, but he just couldn't be convinced it could be done successfully over a long period of time with an active approach.[4] Since Bogle had his heart and soul tied to passive investing, this was certainly no surprise. It was the work of Dickson and Shoven in 1993 that finally convinced him that his position on applying an index-based portfolio was the proper approach and that the process could be done without harming Vanguard's reputation. Shortly thereafter, in September of 1994, Vanguard launched a series of tax-managed funds. With the success of Google, one has to wonder if the Stanford team of Dickson and Shoven now look back and wish they had personally cashed in on the practical value of "A Stock Index Mutual Fund Without Net Capital Gains Realization" rather than sharing their findings with the public. In Dickson's case, he would soon put his knowledge to use: after completing his doctorate, he spent a short stint at the Federal Reserve analyzing the mutual fund industry, and then Bogle made one of his many astute business decisions by hiring him to assist Gus Sauter with operation of Vanguard's index and tax-managed funds.[5]

By adhering to and building on the three principles outlined by Dickson and Shoven, the Schwab 1000 Index Fund and Vanguard Tax-Managed Funds collectively boast well over a half century of operating without distributing capital gains. As Bogle has said, "they have been outstanding for their shareholders, but a marketing disappointment."[6] These are certainly the products that should have virtually eliminated high-cost variable-annuity products. The Schwab and Vanguard tax-managed products offer a tax-deferral mechanism similar to a variable annuity but with significantly less cost and daily liquidity. More important, if held more than a year, the appreciated amount of the tax-managed products are taxed at the federal rate for long-term capital gains rather than the much higher ordinary income tax rate for variable annuities. So why, in some years, are more than $50 billion of variable annuities issued? For the simple reason that annuities are "sold" to investors who do not realize there is a vastly superior alternative, whereas tax-managed products are "bought" mostly by self-educated tax-aware investors. Once again, the key is education, because if investors understood the tax ramifications of various investment alternatives, they would likely make quite different purchase decisions.

Tax-managed mutual funds may have redemption fees that are waived after a designated period. This feature is intended to attract only those investors with long time horizons or to deter others who frequently redeem shares. The Vanguard tax-managed series employs a 2 percent redemption the first year and 1 percent for the next four years. Bogle believes that although the feature was needed and perhaps ahead of its time, it has been detrimental to the growth of the products, as he knows there are sizable amounts of taxable assets in their S&P 500 Index Fund even though the Tax-Managed Growth & Income Fund has more potential to achieve superior after-tax returns.

At the time Dickson and Shoven were working on their papers there emerged another tax-efficient product: the exchange-traded fund (ETF). The largest and most recognizable ETF is the Standard & Poor's Depository Receipt (SPDR), which appeared in January 1993. However, the idea of trading a portfolio as a share began with index participation shares (IPS), which began trading on the American and Philadelphia stock exchanges in 1989. These products were originally designed for institutions that sought a vehicle with intraday liquidity to increase or decrease significant market exposure in a cost-effective manner. Like so many items in tax-aware investing, the innovation required a catalyst to attract sufficient attention. This market was pretty much dormant until investors embraced

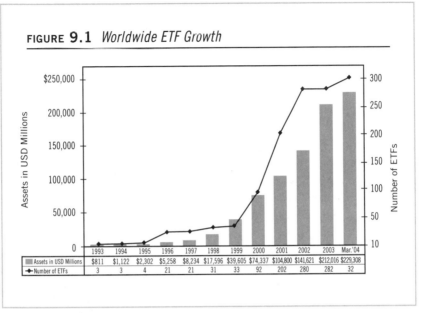

FIGURE **9.1** *Worldwide ETF Growth*

the "QQQ" that replicates the technology-laden Nasdaq-100 Index in the spring of 2000. As **FIGURE 9.1** shows, the worldwide market for ETFs has grown steadily from less than $1 billion in 1993 to more than $200 billion today with approximately 300 different offerings.[7]

Along the way, investment professionals began to recognize a unique feature of ETFs that wasn't being touted. Through an in-kind transfer of shares, which was originally done to allocate expenses, ETFs can achieve a level of tax efficiency that rivals the tax-managed funds.

There are two types of markets for ETFs: a primary market of "authorized participants" and a secondary market of individual investors. ETFs are created when an authorized participant sends in a basket of securities to fund a "creation unit." A creation unit is usually a block of 50,000 shares. Unlike mutual funds, there is no exchange of cash with the authorized participant, just an exchange of securities for shares in the ETF. When he wants to redeem his shares, the authorized participant will exchange his ETF shares for securities. This is known as the in-kind transfer. When a smaller investor wishes to buy shares, he does so through a broker by purchasing them through an exchange. In this case, he pays cash for the shares and receives cash when he sells. However, his transaction does not have a tax impact on the underlying securities. This process is illustrated in a schematic provided by Barclays Global Fund Advisors (see **FIGURE 9.2**).

This process is quite different from buying and selling shares of a traditional open-end mutual fund, in which case the portfolio manager of the

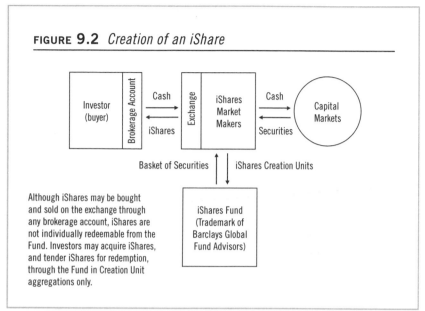

FIGURE **9.2** *Creation of an iShare*

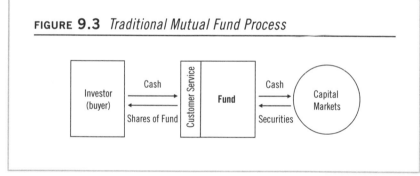

FIGURE **9.3** *Traditional Mutual Fund Process*

fund buys and sells securities to satisfy daily net purchase and redemption activity (see **FIGURE 9.3**). If the security is sold at a level other than the current cost or book value, then a taxable event occurs. Therefore, from a tax standpoint, the open-end mutual fund is very susceptible to daily shareholder purchase and redemption activity.

When an authorized participant redeems shares, it does not cause a taxable event for other ETF shareholders, because there is simply an exchange of securities for the ETF shares. Afterward, the authorized participant can do whatever he desires with the basket of securities, but again it has no tax impact on the ETF. Better yet, when a creation unit is redeemed, the manager of the ETF does not have to give back the original shares. Since he can choose which shares to distribute through the application of specific lot identification accounting, he will most likely distribute the shares with the lowest cost basis. This causes the average cost of the securities comprising the portfolio of the ETF to trend upward over time. In essence, the in-kind transfer is a substitute for the tax-loss harvesting trade, that is, the ETF manager lowers the amount of embedded capital gains in the fund through the in-kind transfer, whereas the mutual fund manager takes losses when available to offset gains.

Like index funds, ETFs have very low expense ratios. Unless the buyer is an authorized participant, ETFs are purchased in the secondary market through a broker, who receives a commission. Since ETFs are traded intraday, the underlying securities need to be somewhat liquid. Although there are more than 100 ETFs available to investors and new ETFs are being launched almost weekly, the structure is not suitable for all asset classes. Unfortunately, as a result of challenges with liquidity and pricing, none of the providers have been willing to undertake a municipal bond ETF, even though there is tremendous demand for such a product.

Some advisers are fans of ETFs, while others prefer tax-managed open-end mutual funds. Unfortunately, neither ETFs nor tax-managed funds are the right choice or perfect solution for all situations. Therefore, tax-aware advisers need to be aware of the tax consequences of each so that they can offer their clients sage advice.

FIGURE 9.4 builds on a schematic utilized by Gary Gastineau in *The Exchange-Traded Funds Manual* to compare a typical mutual fund, ETF, and a holder, which is a portfolio of stocks.[8] The evaluation system of the figure is the same, but it is limited to a comparison of a tax-managed and exchange-traded funds. The fields have been expanded and subdivided into three major areas: tax efficiency, operational, and estate.

Tax efficiency: Both tax-managed mutual funds and ETFs benefit the taxable investor by taking advantage of specific-lot-identification accounting and offsetting fund expenses with taxable income. The key difference in how tax-managed mutual funds and ETFs attempt to achieve tax efficiency is their reliance on the internal tax-loss harvesting trade versus the in-kind transfer. Both types of funds can sell depreciated securities, harvest the loss, and apply it against gains in the future. However, ETFs typically achieve better tax efficiency from exchanging low-cost-basis for high-cost-basis shares. Perhaps the greatest advantage ETFs have over tax-managed funds is how the in-kind transfer can handle items like index reconstitution, deferral of short-term gains, and stocks acquired in mergers. With these advantages, ETFs offer a more tax-efficient solution for taxable investors who want to obtain exposure to small- and middle-capitalization domestic equities.

FIGURE **9.4** *Comparing Tax-Managed and Exchange-Traded Funds*

	TAX-MANAGED	EXCHANGE-TRADED
Tax Efficiency		
Ability to Deduct Expenses	+	+
Specific Lot Identification or HIFO Accounting	+	+
Apply Tax-Loss Harvesting Trade	+	+
Tax Benefit From In-Kind Transfer of Shares	–	+
Tax Consequences of Index Reconstitution	–	+
Deferral of Short-Term Gains	–	+
Tax Impact of Stocks Acquired for Cash in Mergers	–	+
Operational		
Intraday Liquidity	–	+
Additional Commission Cost	+	–
Bid/Ask Spread	+	0
Low Fee	+/0	+/0
Redemption Fee	+/–	+
Shareholder Contributions	+	0
Shareholder Withdrawals	–	+
Diversification Rules	–	–
Estate		
Gift Appreciated Shares to Charity	0	0
Step-Up of Basis at Death	+	+

+ Best
0 OK
– Worst

Source: Gary Gastineau, Douglas S. Rogers

Operational: The ETF can be bought and sold intraday, but unless investors are authorized participants creating and redeeming ETF shares, they must pay a broker's commission on the transactions. The investor may pay a slight premium for this additional liquidity in terms of a bid/ask spread, but these differences are small with high-volume products. Mutual fund shareholders benefit when they invest early in a fund and future capital gains are distributed across a greater number of investors. However, ETF investors benefit with redemptions when the manager exchanges out of low-cost basis shares. Both tax-managed funds and ETFs offer investors reasonable or low fees, with some ETFs charging fees less than 0.10 percent annually. ETFs typically do not have redemption fees. Redemption fees can be both a positive and negative for the investor in a tax-managed fund. The negative side is investors may have to pay them if they redeem their shares earlier than anticipated. However, redemption fees assist in driving away hot money that leads to capital gains generation. Also, the redemption fees are left in the fund, which can boost fund performance. ETFs are not immune to capital gains distributions. There are times when they simply have to sell a security and cannot avoid taking a gain. For example, country-specific funds may not be able to avoid a capital gains distribution if a certain holding exceeds the limit set by various regulatory diversification rules and has to be sold. Perhaps the best-known examples are the iShares MSCI Canada and Sweden ETFs, which each had distributions of more than 18 percent of assets in 2000.[9] In the Canada ETF, Nortel became more than 25 percent of the capitalization of the portfolio. As Nortel continued to increase in size relative to other stocks in the Canada portfolio, the manager was forced to sell. Fortunately, this situation is primarily limited to the country-specific funds, but it highlights that advisers need to be informed of how gains can be generated with ETFs so they can avoid potentially embarrassing situations with their clients.

Estate: Tax-managed funds and ETFs are pretty much equal when it comes to charitable giving and taking advantage of the step-up in cost basis at death.

The information in Figure 9.4 enables advisers to check a client's personal situation of before recommending a tax-managed or exchange-traded fund. Unless they are dealing with the same size and type of client with identical circumstances, one product may be more suitable in some instances than the other. Additionally, managers of these products are always looking for ways to refine their processes and enhance performance. Therefore, it is recommended advisers maintain a similar checklist that incorporates the most recent developments.

FIGURE 9.5 shows ten years of before- and after-tax performance for the Vanguard Tax-Managed Growth and Income Fund, ETF SPDR, and

Source: Morningstar Principia, January 2005

FIGURE **9.5** *Before- and After-Tax Returns of Similar Tax-Managed and Exchange-Traded Funds*
(For the 10-Year Period Ending December 31, 2004)

EXCHANGE-TRADED OR MUTUAL FUND	BEFORE-TAX	AFTER-TAX	
		DISTRIBUTIONS	DISTRIBUTIONS & SALE OF SHARES
Vanguard Tax-Managed G & I	12.09%	11.51%	10.48%
SPDR Trust Series 1	11.88%	11.23%	10.21%
Vanguard 500 Index	12.00%	11.32%	10.34%

Vanguard 500 Index Fund. These three funds were chosen for this comparison exercise because they all use the S&P 500 stock index to construct the underlying portfolio of stocks.

From this limited amount of information come three conclusions. First, it is readily apparent that the differences in performance between the three funds are extremely small. Second, each of the funds has an extraordinarily high level of tax efficiency, as the Morningstar ten-year tax-cost ratios range from only 0.52 to 0.63. Therefore, all of the managers of the funds have done an outstanding job of executing their strategy in a tax-aware manner.

Over extended periods of time, there are two key factors that dictate whether the mutual fund or ETF format is better for managing the unrealized gain position. Manageable redemption activity benefits the remaining shareholders of the exchange-traded fund, whereas reasonable price volatility of individual securities benefits the tax-managed mutual fund. Extremes in either case may result in a cascade of redemption activity that could force the sale or distribution of shares, with a meaningful capital gain distribution to follow.

The results shown thus far are all net of fees, which is customary with mutual and exchange-traded funds. Now let's examine the results on a gross of fee basis to the actual return of the S&P 500 (see **FIGURE 9.6**).

Note that all three funds have achieved gross before-tax returns close to the S&P 500 stock index. Two of the funds have actually exceeded the results of the benchmark by a small margin. Many practitioners call funds and accounts of this nature "passive" investments or portfolios. Therefore, the third and perhaps the primary teaching point of this exercise is that tax-aware investing is anything but passive! In fact, there may be more

FIGURE **9.6** *Before- and After-Tax Returns of Similar Tax-Managed and Exchange-Traded Funds (For the 10-Year Period Ending December 31, 2004)*

EXCHANGE-TRADED OR MUTUAL FUND	BEFORE-TAX	STATED FEE	GROSS BEFORE-TAX
Vanguard Tax-Managed G & I	12.09%	0.17%	12.26%
SPDR Trust Series 1	11.88%	0.12%	12.00%
Vanguard 500 Index	12.00%	0.18%	12.18%
Benchmark: S&P 500 Stock Index			**12.07%**

Source: Morningstar Principia, January 2005

trading activity in these portfolios than in the typical "actively" managed fund. The difference here is that it is informed trading activity that works to the benefit of the taxable investor.

There are a number of techniques that are valuable in managing index-based portfolios. These include :

❑ Cost-efficient trading that includes electronic crossing networks
❑ Purchasing derivatives when they are initially cheaper than the underlying stocks
❑ Pledging securities of the portfolio for security lending
❑ Purchasing stocks before they are added to the index
❑ Taking advantage of an imbalance in a particular security

Anything the manager can do that leads to superior results without taking on undue risk should be encouraged.

The last point is that ETFs have lagged the performance of their mutual fund tax-managed peers with similar portfolios by a very slight margin before tax but have done quite well after tax. One of the reasons for the minor differential in before-tax returns of the SPDR Trust Series 1 is that it has not been allowed to reinvest the dividends it receives from its portfolio holdings: the cash must be held in a money market fund. Additionally, shares cannot be put out for securities lending. Early ETFs, like the SPDR, were registered as unit trusts, whereas newer ETFs are registered as open-end mutual funds and do not face this disadvantage. This weakness is known and has been shared with the SEC. In the meantime, some brokerage houses have established cost-effective dividend reinvestment plans to minimize this impact.[10] Hopefully, a positive resolution to this challenge will be provided soon. Another feature that may have benefited tax-managed funds during this period is the redemption fee. While most investors in tax-managed products plan to stay with a fund for five years or more, unforeseen personal events can occur that force them to sell shares. Also, redemption activity in the Vanguard Tax-Managed Funds increased during the bear market of 2000 to 2001, but it was still far below the industry average. Investors that redeemed shares during their first year would have received 98 percent of their net asset value, and those that were in the one-to-five-year range received 99 percent. The dollars of the 1 to 2 percent redemption fees remained with the fund and had a small but favorable impact on performance.

Do the results of these three funds mean tax-aware investors should not own ETFs? Absolutely not: ETFs are an innovative solution that tax-aware investors can add to their arsenal of weapons, and there are many cases where they in fact offer the optimal tax-efficient solution. Moreover, it has only been since about 2000 that the managers of ETFs have come to fully recognize how important the tax advantage of the in-kind transfer is to their taxable investors. Now investors and advisers need to determine when it is best to apply them. Barclays has been extremely proactive in the market by offering investment seminars that emphasize general education on ETFs rather than emphasizing how their products may be superior to the competition. As a result, more advisers are beginning to understand the tax benefits of ETFs and applying them in innovative ways. Most important, once investors become comfortable using tax-efficient products and see the favorable result when their taxes are due, they are reluctant to revert to using less tax-efficient mutual funds and separate account products and managers.

Mutual funds that include terms such as "tax-managed," "tax-aware," or "tax-efficient" in their titles are required to include after-tax returns in their advertising materials, whereas it is optional for others.[11] However, this does not guarantee an investor will receive a tax-efficient outcome. There are two noteworthy historical examples of shareholders who, unfortunately, did not receive tax-efficient outcomes.[12] The first example involves the Bernstein Tax-Managed International Fund. This initially successful fund attracted a meaningful amount of assets and developed a substantial unrealized capital gains position. Then the prices for international stocks began to fall, and along with this development came shareholder redemptions. Although the manager attempted to minimize the capital gains distributions, there was only such much he could do. Eventually he was forced to sell shares with embedded gains. This example highlights how shareholder activity beyond the control of the manager can influence the after-tax returns of shareholders who remain in the fund. The other instance is the Standish Small

Capitalization Tax-Managed Equity Fund. In this case, the team managing the fund sold large positions in technology and biotechnology shares in the spring of 2000, and soon thereafter departed for another employer.[13] Standish's compliance personnel were naturally concerned that there would be significant redemptions as a result of the departure and that not distributing the capital gains would be unfair to shareholders that remained in the fund. They decided to announce a capital gain distribution rather than to wait and see if the rest of the fiscal year would offer the potential to sell some shares at losses to reduce the magnitude of the distribution. With the market decline in 2000, the distribution came to more than 19 percent of the fund's asset value at year-end.[14] These two examples have been pretty much forgotten by investors, but at the time they drew a lot of negative attention to the emerging niche of tax-aware mutual funds. These examples are mentioned as illustrations of the potential challenges in delivering on a tax-aware goal, despite what a particular fund title may imply.

It will be interesting to monitor how index, tax-managed, and exchange-traded funds will manage the reconstruction of the S&P 500, MidCap 400, SmallCap 600, and REIT Composite indices for full float adjustment. Previously, Standard & Poor's derived the percentage for the allocation by taking into account the total shares outstanding versus the available float in the marketplace. These percentages can differ significantly if a controlling family or a company's treasury function is holding a significant stake. Therefore, the amount of shares of a particular company available to investors as measured by the outstanding float can be quite different than what was previously portrayed by index funds. Standard & Poor's announced the methodology and analysis of the adjustment for float on September 28, 2004, thus giving market participants knowledge of what will eventually take place and when. The S&P plan is for the indices to be half float-adjusted on March 18, 2005. The example given in the announcement is: "a company with an 80% float factor will be adjusted to a 90% factor—half way from 100% to 80%." On September 16, 2005, all S&P indices are to be fully float-adjusted.[15] For some stocks, the shift will be dramatic, such as Wal-Mart Stores, which adjusted to a half-float factor of 0.80 on March 18, 2005, and was scheduled to adjust to a full float factor of 0.60 on September 16, 2005 (see **FIGURE 9.7**).[16]

This procedure will result in a reduction in the outstanding float of approximately 20 percent of the stocks in the S&P 500. To avoid generating substantial capital gains from this exercise is going to take careful planning and coordination on the part of the fund managers.

Managers of exchange-traded and tax-managed funds realize today more than ever how important maintaining their reputations and records for tax efficiency are to future success. Evolving risk-management tools

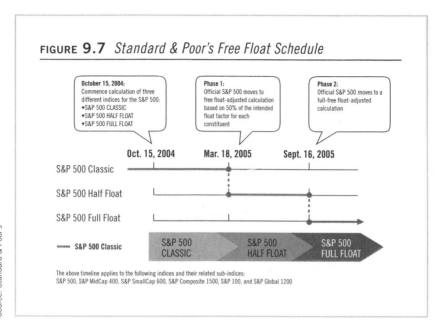

FIGURE **9.7** *Standard & Poor's Free Float Schedule*

allow managers to stress-test portfolios to determine the potential for gains in adverse markets. As a result, managers are better prepared for challenging situations than ever before. Although it would be foolish to say investors seeking a tax-efficient fund solution will not encounter another instance of a sizable capital gains distribution, the experiences of the past and the growing body of knowledge pertaining to tax-aware investing should result in attractive fund products that have a high probability of outperforming the underlying index of securities on an after-tax basis.

Chapter Notes

1. Aaron Lucchetti, "Index Funds Aren't Always Tax Efficient," *Wall Street Journal*, July 28, 2000.

2. George M. Constantinides, "Capital Market Equilibrium With Personal Tax," *Econometrica* 51, 611–636.

3. Joel M. Dickson and John B. Shoven, "A Stock Index Mutual Fund Without Net Capital Gains Realizations," NBER Working Paper No. 4717, April 1994, 1–26.

4. Robert H. Jeffrey to John C. Bogle, May 29, 1985, and July 6, 1990.

5. Joel Dickson, in discussion with author, September 21, 2004.

6. Jack Bogle, in discussion with author, September 2, 2004.

7. "Meeting Investment Challenges With ETFs," Forbes Special Advertising Section, http://www.federalreserve.gov/releases (accessed October 30, 2004).

8. Gary L. Gastineau, *The Exchange-Traded Funds Manual* (New York: John Wiley & Sons, 2002).

9. Dawn Smith, "An Education in ETFs," http://www.smartmoney.com (accessed October 30, 2004).

10. Karen Damato, "For Index Funds, the Devil Is in the Detail," *Wall Street Journal,* September 7, 2004.

11. Securities and Exchange Commission, "Final Rule: Disclosure of Mutual Fund After-Tax Returns (S7-09-00)," news release, April 16, 2001, 11.

12. Danny Hakim, "In Gloom, a Beacon: Tax-Savings Funds," *New York Times,* February 25, 2001.

13. Aaron Lucchetti, "Standish Fund Payout to Carry Tax Bite," *Wall Street Journal,* August 22, 2000.

14. Danny Hakim, "In Gloom, a Beacon: Tax-Savings Funds," *New York Times,* February 25, 2001.

15. Standard & Poor's, "Standard & Poor's Announces Float Adjustment Schedule for S&P 500 and Affiliated Indices," http://www.standardandpoors.com (accessed September 15, 2004).

16. Standard & Poor's, "S&P 500 Investable Weight Factors," news release, September 17, 2004; Standard & Poor's, "Standard & Poor's Announces Float Adjustment Schedule for S&P 500 and Affiliated Schedules," news release, August 12, 2004.

CHAPTER **10**

Quantitative Tax-Aware Portfolio Management and Concentrated Stock

Tax issues are fun. Getting to love them may take a bit of effort, but the same is true for Beethoven's string of quartets, and think of how much pleasure they give if one does make the effort.

—PETER L. FABER

In this chapter, we introduce the concept of the quantitative tax-aware (QTA) portfolio strategy and compare it with other methods of diversifying a concentrated stock position. The QTA investment strategy is similar to what a tax-managed mutual fund manager may employ with tax-loss harvesting. Unlike losses realized in mutual funds, losses in separate accounts can be used to offset a client's gains in other portfolios and are not subject to the eight-year carryforward limitation that applies to mutual fund losses. Therefore, this strategy is ideally suited for combining with tax-inefficient, high-alpha-generating strategies or for use as a tax-efficient mechanism to transition concentrated stock positions to diversified portfolios. As a result, tax-inefficient active management strategies should be reviewed in conjunction with other concentrated-stock diversification strategies such as exchange funds, collars, and prepaid variable forwards.

FIGURE 10.1 illustrates the impact of tax-loss harvesting over time with a portfolio funded all in cash. It shows a First Quadrant Monte Carlo simulation of 500 observations, taking into account an average annual yield of 1.44 percent and total return of 7.92 percent with 15 percent annual stock volatility and a 35 percent marginal tax rate. Individual stock volatility was 31 percent. Obviously, the results may change with different

117

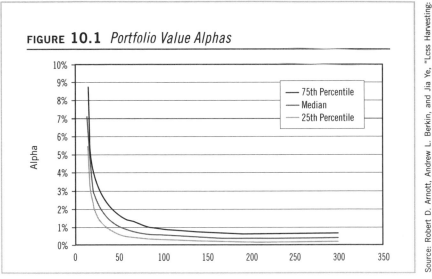

FIGURE **10.1** *Portfolio Value Alphas*

Source: Robert D. Arnott, Andrew L. Berkin, and Jia Ye, "Loss Harvesting: What's It Worth to the Taxable Investor?" *Journal of Wealth Management* (Spring 2001): 10–18.

assumptions, but the parameters applied here are very typical of what one would apply today.

The key point is the tax alpha is far greater at the inception of the relationship than when the portfolio becomes seasoned. However, even after twenty-five years, there are still opportunities for losses that produce a tax alpha of about 0.5 percent a year.[1] Unfortunately, there will always be surprises like Enron and MCI, but at least tax-loss harvesting extracts economic value from deteriorating situations. At current levels of taxes, the estimated average annual alpha for the first ten years is approximately 1.3 percent, whereas it had been about 1.5 percent before the long-term capital gains tax was reduced from 20 percent to 15 percent and tax on qualified dividends from 38.6 percent to 15 percent.

Separate account portfolios that emphasize tax-loss harvesting have been around for only about a dozen years. In 1992, Parametric Portfolio Associates received a call from CTC Consulting in Portland, Oregon. CTC had a large family client in the Northwest for about a decade, and both CTC and the client had become disgruntled with the lack of attention their active equity managers were paying to the impact of taxes. Parametric was in the custom index business, but until this time it had not taken on a taxable account. The inquiry caught the attention of the firm's chief investment officer, Mark England, and he assigned portfolio manager Brian Langstraat to assist him with this special project. They listened carefully to comments from the client and CTC consultants Ralph Rittenour and Nancy Jacob.

Parametric first ran the strategies with a typical before-tax approach according to value or growth mandates by capitalization. The taxable turnover in large-capitalization stock indices was running less than 5 percent a year and was attributed primarily to mergers and acquisitions that were consummated by a cash transaction rather than an exchange of shares. Therefore, the index approach by itself was a vast improvement over the client's previous managers' tax efficiency, or lack thereof. Parametric was beginning to analyze how it could add value by applying other than traditional approaches when the articles by Jeffrey and Arnott and Dickson and Shoven in 1993 caught its attention and, more important, that of other CTC clients. In 1995, Parametric began making tax-loss harvesting trades, and one client soon turned into three. Mark England retired, and things really picked up when Parametric hired David Stein as chief investment officer in 1996. Parametric soon found that its early lead in this new niche would have an overwhelming impact on the future of its business. Less than five years later, it found that demand for its approach would necessitate that it abandon the low-margin, tax-exempt, indexing commodity type of business for retirement plans, foundations, and endowments and focus its attention on the highly customized taxable account business, where its unique approach offered clients a true valued-added proposition.

Parametric was the early leader in what some refer to as passive investing, but is more appropriately designated as quantitative tax-aware investing (QTA). The passive nomenclature of this niche comes from the early portfolios having been managed according to the traditional form of index investing. Obviously, advocates of the efficient market hypothesis believe this is reason enough to employ a passive rather than an active approach to investing. However, shortly after his successful article with Tad Jeffrey was published, Rob Arnott brought First Quadrant into the debate. Historically, First Quadrant had managed portfolios using sophisticated mathematical modeling—known as the quantitative, or "quant," approach to investing—in its effort to provide clients with a before-tax alpha, which it has successfully done over time. Therefore, the industry soon had offerings that provided not only a tax-advantaged approach but also the option to closely track a designated index or to potentially achieve incremental return on a before-tax basis, as well. Moreover, as mentioned in chapter 9 about tax-managed and exchange-traded funds, the portfolio management techniques and trading of these strategies is anything but passive.

So how do QTA strategies work? The following is a list of key elements that the adviser and the client should understand:
- Benchmark selection
- Client criteria
- Custodian
- Fees
- Tracking error

Benchmark selection: The first step in the QTA process is to select the appropriate equity benchmark. Today, almost any equity benchmark in the world can be followed, as long as the manager can receive the underlying percentage allocations to each security. For large-capitalization core type indices, the process is pretty straightforward. When attempting to have a portfolio managed for a particular style, it is important to understand how the index provider constructs its style benchmarks. For example, the Russell style benchmarks have a 30 percent overlap, whereas the Barra indices have none. The manager will likely steer you toward the Russell indices, since they provide a greater number of securities to work with. The Morgan Stanley Capital International (MSCI) indices, now employed by Vanguard, utilize "buffer zones" for changes in capitalization assignment. For example, if there are 500 stocks in the index and a 100 stock buffer applies, the stock would have to drop below 600 before it is taken out of the index, or a stock would have to reach 400 before it is included. This feature is desirable for someone interested in a small- or mid-cap portfolio, as it tones down the amount of reconstitution that generates gains. As a general rule, QTA portfolios are typically more advantageous with value-style and large-cap portfolios. Growth index portfolios are naturally more tax-efficient, as top performers stay in the index. A stock is removed from the growth index because its relative valuation has fallen. Therefore, the amount of appreciation may be insignificant, or it may even transition at a loss. On the other hand, when a stock shifts from the value index to the growth index, it can only do so by a significant improvement in relative valuation, which is likely to result in substantial gains realization.

Client criteria: There are critical client factors that the manager needs to know before he can attempt to provide an optimal solution. Obviously, the tax profile of the client or taxable entity is essential. Informing the manager of the magnitude and timing of anticipated cash flows and withdrawals will allow him to better gauge the level of tax efficiency. The manager may suggest the flows be received just prior to anticipated reconstitution dates, as that will give him greater flexibility in shifting funds toward increasing sector and industry allocations. If the portfolio periodically receives a contribution of cash, then a higher level of tax efficiency can be perpetuated than shown in Figure 10.1. Also, if dividends are to be reinvested, that allows for a bit more flexibility in rebalancing the portfolio. The size of the portfolio dictates whether odd (less than 100 shares) or round (100-share increments) are purchased. Since the QTA manager typically batches trades, odd lot transactions are not a problem.

Portfolio construction: Today there are about a half-dozen significant players in this space. They are listed here in alphabetical order to avoid the appearance of a personal preference: Aperio Group, First Quadrant,

M&I Bank, Northern Trust Global Investments, Parametric Portfolio Associates, State Street Global Advisors, and U.S. Trust Corporation. These firms all have excellent ways of serving the taxable investor and attempt to differentiate themselves by their slightly different approaches, the clients they serve, and their product design. For example, Parametric has an outstanding reporting capability and serves an array of various client types, Northern Trust typically holds a greater number of securities in the portfolio to emphasize reduction in tracking error, First Quadrant aims to achieve a before-tax alpha, M&I Bank is known for a higher-yielding product, and U.S. Trust Corporation focuses more on custom solutions in conjunction with other securities and derivatives. Plus, some of the firms are subadvisers to mutual funds and various manager platforms.

Two situations that investors often fail to take into account are that the manager does not always take a loss when it may appear obvious from the account statement to do so and that the manager may actually take some gains. Both of these actions are taken to reduce the return or performance tracking error of the account. Investors should avoid attempting to override the manager's methodology by directing losses if possible. Those who intend to do this may be better off working with a broker rather than with one of the managers mentioned above, who employ sophisticated approaches.

Custodian: For these strategies to be effective, the custodian plays a major role. If the account size is small ($3 million or less), the client wishes to replicate the S&P 500 with 250 holdings, and trading turnover averages 15 to 35 percent a year, then there are going to be numerous individual transactions. The cost of the average commission and settlement charges dictates how far the security has to fall in price before it is economical to conduct the trade. Some custodians are more cost-effective with QTA accounts. Therefore, a client may find it economically beneficial to house the quantitative tax-aware portfolio with one custodian or platform and the remainder of assets with another. In the instances where this may occur, the client should seek references from the QTA manager of those who have established a similar arrangement.

Fees: One of the advantages of QTA portfolio strategies is fees are typically half those of active managers, depending on the size of the account, but don't expect them to be similar low-fee indexed portfolios. Again, these are really active rather than passive strategies. It is important that the adviser understand completely not only the management fee but also the custodial, commission, and settlement fees and charges. You may encounter a situation where the entire fee is bundled. Since M&I Bank, Northern Trust, State Street, and U.S. Trust Corporation have well-known custodial platforms, they can often be very competitive in their pricing, but this niche should not be looked at as a commodity business, as the returns net of fees and taxes can be meaningfully different.

Tracking error: Tracking error is the difference between the returns of a portfolio and its benchmark index. It is measured by the standard deviation of the difference in returns between the client portfolio and the benchmark. There are several factors that can contribute to tracking error for the QTA portfolio. First, the manager must determine the optimal number of stocks to hold in the portfolio. For example, a QTA portfolio that is intended to mirror the S&P 500 will typically hold one-half of the underlying securities of the index. Determining the number of securities is an art rather than a matter of following a scientific rule. Since the success of the strategy is tax-driven through the application of tax-loss harvesting, portfolio managers must ensure the thirty-day wash sale rule is not violated. Therefore, they must make sure there are securities similar in nature or substitute candidates that are not owned and available for purchase. The trick for managers is to ensure the securities they select for investment will satisfactorily represent each of the sectors, industries, and other portfolio characteristics they deem important. **FIGURE 10.2** is an example of the characteristics that Parametric includes in its quarterly report to facilitate a healthy dialogue with each client.

Modeling or analyzing the portfolio is usually done through a sophisticated risk-management software solution provided by Axioma, Barra, ITG, or Northfield. To distinguish themselves in the marketplace, QTA firms will customize the solution as a result of their internal research or work in consultation with other knowledgeable individuals. They are also interested in minimizing the differences in modern portfolio statistics, such as beta (amount of market risk the portfolio is subject to) and R-squared (amount of return that can be explained by the benchmark), between the client's custom portfolio and the designated benchmark. The firms may apply various rules when constructing a portfolio. For example, they may avoid securities with insufficient trading volume, as they make it difficult if not impossible to execute tax-loss harvesting. When rules of this nature are established, they may only influence a small amount of the overall capitalization of the index, but they can have a significant impact on performance. For example, many of these less-liquid securities priced under $5 a share had stellar performances during 2003, but if they were not held by the manager, the before-tax return of the portfolio could have fallen short of the benchmark by 1 percent or more.

The manager has to be extremely careful to avoid excessive tracking error with tax-loss harvesting. This can happen when a security is sold for a loss and it behaves quite differently in price than the substitute security. This is especially so with the top holdings in the benchmark. General

FIGURE 10.2 *Portfolio Characteristics and Five Largest Holdings*

Parametric Portfolio Associates Sample Quarterly Performance Report

	PORTFOLIO	BENCHMARK
Number of Holdings	301	500
Beta	1.0	1.0
Dividend Yield	1.60	1.62
Weighted Avg. Cap. (in millions)	$88,266	$90,008

ECONOMIC SECTOR WEIGHTS (%)	PORTFOLIO	BENCHMARK
Business Equip. & Serv.	3.3	3.2
Capital Goods	2.3	2.6
Consumer Durables	1.2	1.2
Consumer Nondurables	8.2	8.5
Consumer Services	4.4	4.9
Energy	5.4	5.8
Financial Services	20.3	20.2
Health Care	13.1	13.2
Multi-industry	4.6	4.1
Raw Materials	2.1	2.4
Retail	7.8	7.0
Shelter	1.6	1.3
Technology	17.6	17.8
Transportation	1.6	1.6
Utilities	6.4	6.3

POSITION WEIGHTS (%)	PORTFOLIO	BENCHMARK
General Electric Co.	3.1	3.0
Exxon Mobil Corp.	2.7	2.6
Mcrosoft Corp.	2.6	2.9
Pfizer Inc.	2.5	2.6
Citicorp Inc.	2.5	2.4

Source: Parametric Portfolio Associates

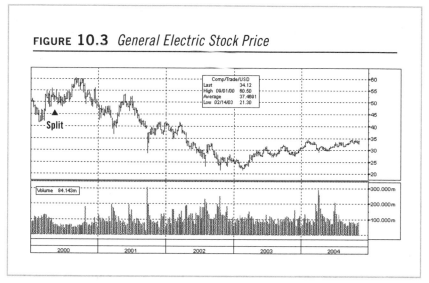

FIGURE **10.3** *General Electric Stock Price*

Comp/Trade/USD	
Last	34.12
High 09/01/00	60.50
Average	37.4691
Low 02/14/03	21.30

Volume 84.143m

Source: Bloomberg

Electric Co. (GE) was listed in the Parametric report as the largest hold-ing in the portfolio. The five-year historical price chart for GE was pulled from the Bloomberg Professional Service to show how this can happen (see **FIGURE 10.3**). Let's envision a QTA portfolio is begun after GE shares split in the middle of 2000. Later that year, the price of the security began to fall, and sometime in 2001 it would have become a candidate for tax-loss harvesting. But note that four different times between March 2001 and January 2003 when the stock dropped it quickly rebounded in price. If the entire holding of GE was sold during these times and the replace-ment lagged the upward price movement, the portfolio tracking error would have been significant. To protect against this type of adverse action, the portfolio manager typically only sells a portion of a large holding. Therefore, the differences over time are likely to average themselves out, and no one transaction should prove to be detrimental. This could be true especially if an entire holding was sold for a loss and then the company was acquired through a merger and the take-out price was substantially higher. As David Stein of Parametric says, "You can give a man a sword, but that doesn't make him a swordsman." Furthermore, if he isn't trained in the use of the sword, he may end up cutting his own throat.

To avoid excessive tracking error, the portfolio manager periodically runs an optimization in a workstation-type environment. The level of tax-loss harvesting is often dictated by the amount of projected tracking error the manager predetermines as an input variable. The output will suggest which stocks and how much of each to sell. It will also suggest replace-ment or purchase candidates and the appropriate number of shares. Then the portfolio manager reviews each suggestion to determine a final trade recommendation. He may void a particular trade and rerun the optimization if he is aware, for example, that a particular stock may be subject to a corporate action. Again, the simulation will provide him with a projected tracking error, and when he is satisfied the trades will be consummated. Since the inception date influences the initial cost basis, it is conceivable that a firm could have no two portfolios with the same holdings even if they are managed to track the same benchmark.

For QTA firms with a large number of accounts, orders are batched before a predesignated cutoff time. Various forms of trading are employed to achieve "best execution" on behalf of their clients. This may involve interaction with numerous broker-dealers and the use of electronic crossing networks. Since QTA strategies are technology-driven, their firms naturally embrace the latest solutions to enhance trading systems. As a result, the cost of trading is only pennies a share on average.

With the exception of First Quadrant, which attempts to achieve a before-tax return greater than the benchmark, positive tracking error—or a return higher than the benchmark—is a sign the manager has a weakness in its risk-control management system, and in the future it could just as likely experience negative tracking error. The importance of the before-tax tracking error of the account cannot be understated, for the simple reason that if the manager cannot deliver the before-tax return, then you may actually better off with a tax-managed mutual fund or exchange-traded fund.

In a similar fashion to what we did in chapter 9, we now compare the characteristics of a QTA separate account portfolio to a tax-managed mutual fund and ETF (see **FIGURE 10.4**). The minimum account size for QTA strategies replicating the S&P 500 typically begins at $500,000.

Tax efficiency: The major advantage of the QTA strategy is the ability to pass through losses. Additionally, individual investors can use the losses indefinitely. In most cases, specific lot identification and high in, first out accounting are available, but there are still custodians that do not offer this value-added feature. In a mutual fund, the short-term gains are lumped together with ordinary income. This should not be an issue with separate account reporting, since only if the client and his adviser make a special request should the QTA manager generate net short-term capital gains.

Operational: Where the QTA strategy stands out in this area is that the holdings are not subject to regulatory diversification rules. If so desired, the client can obtain a truly customized portfolio, which is gaining in popularity with individuals looking for socially responsible investment restrictions.

FIGURE **10.4** *Comparing Tax-Managed Funds, Exchange-Traded Funds, and Quantitative Tax-Aware Separate Account Strategies*

	TAX-MANAGED	EXCHANGE-TRADED	QTA SEPARATE ACCOUNT
Tax Efficiency			
Ability to Deduct Expenses	+	+	+/–
Specific Identification or HIFO Accounting	+	+	+/–
Apply Tax-Loss Harvesting Trade	+	+	+
Tax Benefit From In-Kind Transfer of Shares	–	+	–
Tax Consequences of Index Reconstitution	–	+	0
Deferral of Short-Term Gains	–	+	–
Tax Impact of Stocks Acquired for Cash in Mergers	–	+	–
Accrue Losses Indefinitely	0	0	+
Pass-Through Losses	–	–	+
Pass-Through of Short-Term Gains	–	–	+
Operational			
Intraday Liquidity	–	+	0
Additional Commission Cost	+	–	–
Bid/Ask Spread	+	0	–
Low Fee	+/0	+/0	0
Redemption Fee	+/–	+	+
Shareholder Contributions	+	0	0

Estate: With QTA portfolios, individual securities can be selected from the portfolio for gifting. When a request of this nature is made, the manager will typically recommend the most highly appreciated securities, which will allow him to reduce potential tracking error.

The only major concern individuals have with QTA portfolios is some people feel that after fifteen or twenty years, the portfolios may not necessarily resemble the true nature of the index and periodically adjusting them may be costly from a gains-realization perspective. This has not been a major issue thus far, but QTA strategies have yet to reach their tenth anniversary. One of the interesting twists on the QTA concept is revers-

	TAX-MANAGED	EXCHANGE-TRADED	QTA SEPARATE ACCOUNT
Shareholder Withdrawals	–	+	0
Diversification Rules	–	–	+
Ability to Manage a Custom Portfolio	–	–	+
Estate			
Gift Appreciated Shares to Charity	0	0	+
Step-Up of Basis at Death	+	+	+
Management Value Added			
Electronic Crossing Networks	+	+/+	+
Purchasing Derivatives	+	+/N/A	+/–
Overnight Lending	0	+	–
Purchasing Stocks Prior to Being Added to the Index	+	+	+
Imbalance in a Particular Security	+	+	+
Cost of Purchasing and Selling Securities	–	+	–
Adjust Portfolio for Change in Life Style	–	–	+

+ Best
0 OK
– Worst

Source: Gary Gastineau, Douglas S. Rogers

ing the tax-loss harvesting engine when you have a client in a persistent net operating loss position. In this situation, you can consistently harvest gains! The beauty of this exercise is that you don't have to worry about the wash sale rule, and you are constantly raising the cost basis of the portfolio.

QTA strategies are now entering another era of sophistication. Since the investing public has become comfortable with them, opportunities to expand their usefulness are being explored in extremely innovative ways. One rapidly growing use is the "overlay" application that is becoming more prevalent with wrap providers, which will be covered in greater detail in chapter 19. Since tax rates are historically low, firms are conducting research on whether it makes sense to sell securities that have profits to replenish the portfolio. Perhaps the most interesting method includes combining tax-loss harvesting with leverage, which has been done by Lotsoff Capital Management. To do this successfully requires sophisticated risk modeling and close coordination with a prime broker to handle the borrowing of funds properly.

Since their inception, QTA strategies have been effectively employed to reduce concentrated stock positions. Ideally, the client should have a significant amount of cash, equaling one to two times the size of the initial QTA portfolio. The process is quite simple. A QTA portfolio is set up and then periodically, usually monthly, the professional coordinating the effort determines the dollar amount of losses that can be taken and sells a corresponding of amount of the concentrated stock position. Again, the objective is to offset gains with losses, taking the various provisions for short- and long-term gains and losses into account. When the stock of the concentrated position is sold at a gain, the cash from the settlement of the transaction is transferred to the QTA portfolio. This refreshes the cost basis of the portfolio, enhancing the opportunity to harvest losses in future periods. The process continues until sufficient losses have been taken to eliminate the concentrated stock position.

First Quadrant and Lotsoff, in conjunction with Twenty-First Securities, have conducted creative derivations of this strategy. One such derivation involves a market-neutral strategy while also borrowing and taking losses on the short position. The managers may also be trying to achieve a positive alpha for both the long and short portions of the portfolio. Since, on average, the markets appreciate by 5 percent or more annually, there is greater opportunity for losses. Of course, the net benefit of the short position is influenced by the cost of borrowing. A market-neutral strategy obviously makes risk management of the portfolio far more complicated. To take the simplest case possible, consider that with a long-only S&P 500 portfolio, you would hold approximately 250 securities and use the remainder as a reserve for tax-loss harvesting. When the portfolio is both long and short, you need to have approximately 125 securities long and another 125 short, with 250 securities again serving as the tax-loss harvesting reserve. This process can expedite transitioning a concentrated position using a long-only QTA strategy, which takes approximately seven years, to a leveraged long and short QTA strategy, which takes two years or less. Obviously, this process is far more complicated than the long-only QTA strategy, but if it is done correctly the rewards are obvious.

QTA strategies are often compared with other diversification strategies. A brief discussion of each alternative follows, along with appropriate questions to assist advisers or owners of concentrated positions in determining which strategy is best suited for their specific situation.

Exchange funds: An exchange fund is a partnership in which the partners each contribute highly appreciated stock in order to achieve diversification and defer the tax liability. Eaton Vance offered its first exchange fund in 1961 and, as of the spring of 2004, has approximately $16 billion assets in this niche.[2] Other providers include the investment banks, since they often take companies public and their clients are seeking a way to diversify their concentrated stock risk without paying capital gains taxes. The investor retains his cost basis in the exchange fund shares, so this should be considered a tax deferral rather than a tax minimization option. To qualify for a tax-free exchange, the investor's stock must remain in the fund for at least seven years. For the fund to satisfy regulatory requirements, at least 20 percent of assets must be maintained in "qualifying assets," which are typically real estate investments. The investor may hold shares longer than seven years, and some funds have almost a perpetual inclination. An investor who redeems shares may be given a select group or basket of stocks or a pro rata distribution of shares held by the fund. The portfolio construction process may exclude certain types of stocks, depending on the manager's acceptance criteria. Therefore, the investor may have to check with several providers to determine if they will accept the concentrated holding. As with all portfolios, there is investment risk and a component of active management. Therefore, the exchange fund may achieve a return different from the most common stock benchmarks. In the case of Eaton Vance, it manages its exchange funds in conjunction with its Tax-Managed Growth Fund, which has a history of never having distributed any capital gains.[3] Investors and their advisers need to understand the various provisions of the fund they are considering, as there may be early-withdrawal penalties or adverse tax consequences if the seven-year holding period cannot be satisfied. Fees on exchange funds typically run about 1 percent or slightly less annually. The exchange fund may offer estate plan advantages. If the investment in the exchange fund is intended to be a gift, it is likely a meaningful discount to the face value for tax purposes can be achieved. From time to time, exchange funds have come under the scrutiny of legislators and regulators. Most recently, it is the SEC trying to determine if corporate insiders were using them to reduce their exposure without sending a signal to investors.[4]

Collars: There are many ways of constructing collars with derivatives, but the most common is the cashless collar. By selling calls and purchasing put options, the investor can bracket both the upside and downside of future returns. In this case, the proceeds from the call are used to offset the cost of the put. The trade is done in conjunction with the stock. Settlement can be done either by physically delivering stock or in cash. Physical settlement requires actually selling the investor's stock position, whereas with cash settlement cash is delivered and the investor retains control of the stock. Whether the stock closes above the strike price of the call or below the strike of the put will dictate whether stock or cash must be delivered. If the stock closes between the two strike prices and the options expire worthless, the investor can again review his various alternatives.

Prepaid variable forwards: This strategy is best suited for an investor that places high priority on protecting against a drop in the price of the concentrated stock and has a need for immediate liquidity. In this strategy, an investor sells a variable amount of his concentrated stock at a future date for cash. The investor receives a predetermined amount of cash for the future sale. The actual amount of shares the investor will have to deliver in the future is determined by an agreed-upon formula that adjusts for the change in the price of the stock. This allows the investor to receive a known range of outcomes with some potential for appreciation. The proceeds from the prepaid variable forward can also be placed in a QTA portfolio to reduce the tax impact.

Sale of the stock: One should not ignore the option of simply selling the stock. With the long-term capital gains tax at its lowest level during the post–World War II era and large government deficits looming, many investors believe it is only a matter of time before the rate is increased for wealthy individuals. Therefore, simply selling the position and paying a 15 percent tax haircut is a viable option to consider.

Factors that investors should consider when selecting a diversification strategy include:

1 Does the strategy have the potential to save tax dollars, or is it purely a deferral mechanism?
2 Is there an immediate need for cash?
3 Can the investor accept limited upside and some downside for reducing or eliminating the risk of a concentrated position?
4 How far into the future can the transaction be extended?
5 Will the capital gains generated be subject to the more favorable rates for long-term transactions?
6 Is the concentrated stock a viable candidate for the strategies being considered?
7 How will dividends be treated?
8 Will there be an impact on voting rights, and is this important to the investor?
9 What are the initial and annual costs for the strategy?
10 Can the strategy be unwound, and at what cost?
11 Is the stock restricted while maintained in a particular strategy?

12 If the investor is an employee, officer, or director of a public corporation, should a 10b5-1 plan be considered?

13 Have the strategies being analyzed been challenged by regulators in the past, and is this likely to happen in the future? If so, what is the downside with an adverse ruling, and is the investor willing to endure potential adverse consequences?

14 How attractive is the strategy when taking into account the age of the client and the step-up in basis at death?

In less than ten years, QTA strategies have established themselves as a compelling alternative to less-tax-efficient traditionally managed stock portfolios. Additionally, their application to concentrated stock positions now provides a method to achieve diversification and pay minimal capital gains tax rather than just deferring it. The next generation of QTA strategies will certainly continue to enhance risk control through the use of derivatives. However, the greatest advancement in performance will come from incorporating short sales and leverage in the mix, which are skills more closely aligned with hedge fund practitioners. Will the asset class managers and banks that have thus far dominated the QTA methodology landscape fulfill this need, or will a new set of providers emerge who are more willing to take a higher level of risk and demand a premium for their services? Regardless of who will satisfy this demand, QTA managers will become a permanent part of the taxable-account solution, barring a change in the tax code that would eliminate the benefits of tax-loss harvesting.

Chapter Notes

1. Robert D. Arnott, Andrew L. Berkin, and Jia Ye, "Loss Harvesting: What's It Worth to the Taxable Investor?" *Journal of Wealth Management* (Spring 2001): 10–18.

2. Eaton Vance internal marketing presentation, August 2004.

3. Morningstar Principia, June 30, 2004.

4. Randall Smith, "SEC Looks at How Insiders Use Exchange Funds," *Wall Street Journal,* September 7, 2004.

CHAPTER 11

Practices of Elite Tax-Aware Equity Active Managers

My father has a great expression: 'The capital-gains tax has created more millionaires than any other government policy.' The capital-gains tax tends to make investors hold longer. That is almost always the right decision.

—Chris Davis

That statement by Chris Davis has more truth than most investors would like to admit. There are times when the best thing the investor can do to maximize after-tax returns is simply not to sell positions with substantial unrealized capital gains. **FIGURE 11.1**, by Parametric Portfolio Associates, highlights the future performance the manager or investor must achieve to break even and overcome the embedded capital gain hurdle.[1]

The table shows the additional return the manager must achieve, depending on the percentage of cost relative to the market value of the security that will be sold and over what time period in years. This additional return is what all managers strive for and is known as their alpha. For example, if a manager plans to sell a security where the cost basis is 50 percent of the market value, it would require a pretax alpha, or additional annual return, of 3.5 percent for three years just to cover paying the taxes on the sale to break even. This table was prepared before the tax on long-term capital gains was lowered from 20 percent to 15 percent, but the message is clear. Managing portfolios without considering gains realization makes it extremely difficult for low-alpha-generating strategies to be competitive on an after-tax basis. Unfortunately, there are few active managers who incorporate this type of analysis with each buy and sell decision for their taxable investors.

FIGURE 11.1 *Tax Alpha Required (Per Year for Holding Time to Justify a Sale at Given Cost Basis)*

	COST BASIS				
	0	10%	20%	30%	40%
1 Yr	24.4	21.5	18.6	15.9	13.3
2 Yrs	11.6	10.2	8.9	7.7	6.5
3 Yrs	7.6	6.7	5.9	5.1	4.3
4 Yrs	5.7	5.0	4.4	3.8	3.2
5 Yrs	4.5	4.0	3.5	3.0	2.5

Active portfolio management can outperform passive investing on an after-tax basis, but it is an extremely low-probability bet when relying on traditional methods. At this juncture, nontraditional methods are those that incorporate the impact of taxes in the portfolio construction process and trading practices that are not part of the tax-exempt account industry. The hope is that these tax-aware methods will become traditional practices in the years to come, but they are currently only being employed astutely by approximately 2 percent of practitioners in 2005. It is a belief of the author that managers who employ these tax-aware methods have a greater than 50 percent chance of outperforming passive management on an after-tax basis, which is higher than the success rate of most managers before tax. This is because tax-aware methods have a much higher probability of creating alpha than the traditional methods of sector allocation and security selection.

Impressive after-tax returns that are both long-term and consistent do not happen by chance. Tax-aware investment management is truly an art form that thus far has only been mastered by a small niche of elite tax-aware practitioners.[2] They are the most proactive toward establishing and enhancing their tax management capabilities and the ones most serious about maximizing their after-tax returns. They allocate significant resources toward creating, monitoring, and maintaining their tax-management process, which shows their commitment and willingness to be successful in this area. To facilitate an understanding of what it takes to become an elite manager, we will examine a progressive list of elements. The ten elements may change with revisions to the tax code—for example, the

		COST BASIS			
50%	60%	70%	80%	90%	100%
10.9	8.5	6.2	4.1	2.0	0.0
5.3	4.2	3.1	2.0	1.0	0.0
3.5	2.8	2.0	1.3	0.7	0.0
2.6	2.1	1.5	1.0	0.5	0.0
2.1	1.6	1.2	0.8	0.4	0.0

Source: Parametric Portfolio Associates

amount of taxable income in an equity portfolio is not as important now as it was before 2003.

Elements of the Hierarchy of Tax-Aware Investing

(Equity Portfolio Management)

1 Maintaining low turnover
2 Extending the holding period beyond a year and monitoring the level of short- versus long-term capital gains
3 Adjusting the level of taxable income, when appropriate
4 Tax-loss harvesting as an end-of-year drill
5 Incorporating tax-lot accounting in decision making
6 Applying specific lot identification or high in, first out (HIFO) versus average cost or first in, first out (FIFO) accounting
7 Having qualified professionals serve taxable accounts
8 Tax-loss harvesting opportunistically throughout the year, with knowledge of the wash sale rule
9 Having analysts and portfolio managers who focus only on taxable accounts and incorporate tax implications in each buy and sell decision
10 Being committed to after-tax performance standards and reporting

The truly elite practitioners have mastered all ten elements shown above. The following discussion highlights the importance of each.

1 *Maintaining low turnover:* This is the first step or element. Low turnover is nice, but in most cases is nothing more than what comes out of the basic security selection process. All too often, it has nothing to do with attempting to enhance the after-tax returns of the portfolio strategy. Moreover, low turnover by itself does not lead to acceptable levels of tax efficiency unless it is kept below 5 percent annually. Many value managers will state their strategy is tax-efficient because they have turnover of 20 percent a year or less. However, as noted in previous chapters, this often results in tax-cost ratios well above 1.5 percent annually.

2 *Extending the holding period beyond a year and monitoring the level of short- versus long-term capital gains:* This element is very basic, but it has a meaningful impact on after-tax performance. If a manager can delay selling a security for several days or even a month so that it benefits from the lower tax rate on long-term capital gains, the delay should be encouraged. This type of activity can be monitored internally by use of the accountant's ratio, as discussed in chapter 8. Human experience should be brought into play, because if the price is likely to fall more than the amount of the tax benefit, the security should be sold. It is important to remember the process should be oriented to maximizing after-tax returns rather than minimizing the payment of tax dollars.

3 *Adjusting the level of taxable income, when appropriate:* With the change in the tax code in 2003, this feature is no longer as important as it was previously, but there are still some situations where it applies. Moreover, the lower rate on qualified dividends is scheduled to be phased out in 2009 unless additional tax legislation is enacted. Equity portfolio managers need to be careful when they purchase shares of real estate investment trusts (REITs) and foreign securities, which may not produce qualified dividends. Since REITs pay a much higher level of income than most other sectors of the market, taxable-account managers should incorporate this differential in their decision-making process. One provision of the tax act of 2003 that must remembered is that shares must held sixty days out of the 121-day period that began sixty days before the ex-dividend date for dividends to qualify for the preferential tax treatment.

4 *Tax-loss harvesting as an end-of-year drill:* There are three common ways to execute tax-loss harvesting trades. If conducted properly, these trades can add tremendous value. However, as explained below, two of the three methods may yield less than desirable results.

a. The first method is what is referred to as the "naked" trade. In this case, the manager sells the security or fund and then goes to cash for at least thirty days to avoid violating the wash sale rule. Typically the same security or fund is repurchased at that time. This leaves the investor unexposed to the desired security, sector, or asset class, thus the term "naked." This procedure is tantamount to market timing and should be avoided whenever possible. Don't be surprised if you encounter a situation where the client directs this type of activity and the asset management firm responds with a form by the compliance officer that the client has to sign, relieving the firm of any responsibility for the trade before any losses can be taken. Additionally, once it takes the losses, it will attempt to leave the proceeds in cash. This is a telltale sign the firm is incapable of adequately serving taxable accounts, contrary to their claims in marketing presentations and the like.

b. The second method is known as the "double-down" trade, a phrase from the game of blackjack. A manager employs this tactic when a security drops in price by a meaningful amount and the manager still believes in the fundamental merits of the security. As in blackjack, to execute this trade, a manager doubles the position size by purchasing an amount of shares equal to those presently owned. The manager does this because he expects the security to rebound in price so that the original purchase price can be reached or exceeded. Once this occurs, the original tax lot is sold to avoid paying taxes. This strategy represents more of a value proposition than a tax-management technique. It lacks a tax-management prospective because even if successful, a tax loss is never taken—it only delays a tax payment. Moreover, when the remaining tax lot is sold, the manager incurs a greater tax liability for the client, as the position carries a much lower cost basis than the original position. Although this strategy can be an effective trading strategy, it serves more to increase individual position risk and falls into a "value trap" and only increases the client's tax liability. This is a favorite tool of value-oriented managers and is a sign they have not given serious consideration to tax efficiency. Like the naked trade, the double-down trade is to be avoided.

c. The preferred method for executing a tax-loss harvesting trade incorporates a "pair-wise" transaction by selling one security and purchasing another that is somewhat similar or correlated. Correlation is measured in many different ways, including but not limited to buying a security in the same sector or industry, with a similar beta, or influenced by similar economic factors. An example of such a trade would be an international manager selling ING Groep, N.V., the world's largest insurer, for a loss and temporarily replacing it with AXA Group, the world's second largest insurer. The idea is that a manager is able to realize a loss for tax purposes without losing (in this example) the global insurance exposure. Of course, no other insurance company stock will be a perfect match, so individual company risk will never be entirely eliminated. There will always be the opportunity cost if ING appreciates on firm-specific news that would not necessarily affect AXA. This trade is much stronger than the two mentioned previously, as it allows the manager to recognize the realized loss, maintain the portfolio's exposure and risk profile, and return to the original security after thirty days. This method of tax-loss harvesting can lead to significant tax alpha with new accounts funded with cash, especially those in a falling market environment. Managers opposed to pair-wise trading may grouse that they cannot find suitable replacement securities. The evolution of exchange-traded funds for major markets, countries, and sectors invalidates this argument. For example, expanding on the previous example with ING, the manager has several other options available through ETFs. Instead of using AXA, which the manager might not like for a particular reason, he could use a Netherlands index fund, MSCI Europe, Australasia, and the Far East (EAFE) fund, or a global financial-sector ETF, depending on what market exposures of ING he is trying to replicate. Some managers will even use open-end mutual funds or options or futures to harvest the tax loss, as they understand this is one area where they can add tremendous value toward after-tax performance.

The tax-loss harvesting trade is paramount to tax-aware investing. If equity managers ignore this basic exercise, they should not be considered for hire, unless they can consistently deliver an alpha of at least 3 percent a year on a before-tax basis.

5 *Incorporating tax-lot accounting in decision making:* Surprisingly, in 2005 you will find some managers and custodians that do not have this capability. Tax-lot accounting is the essential element that enables managers to make trading decisions based on the cost basis or tax lots of individual security holdings. Whenever a manager buys a security, the price of that security is recorded into the portfolio accounting system. If a manager buys the same security in several different lots over time, the system will be able to record the purchase price and date of each transaction. The benefit comes at the time of sale, when the manager can use the tax-lot accounting system to identify the most advantageous tax lot or lots to sell so as to minimize realized gains when conducting a partial sale of the overall position.

6 *Applying specific lot identification or HIFO versus average cost or FIFO accounting:* As Dickson and Shoven advanced as early as 1994, the accounting convention employed has a meaningful influence on after-tax results. This feature is operational in nature. When it is present, this element is a clear sign a tax-aware culture permeates throughout the firm.

7 *Having qualified professionals serve taxable accounts:* The degradation of the account-servicing function is one of the key reasons why tax-aware investing is having difficulty gaining ground. Unfortunately, with the asset management industry changing from a boutique culture to an asset-gathering one, highly qualified servicing positions necessary to maintain a tax-aware relationship have been eliminated in droves. Many relationships have been terminated, because the economics of an asset gatherer are different than those of a boutique firm. Boutique firms typically start with a few entrepreneurs. After a successful start they pay off their initial debt and achieve a comfortable existence. They grow by providing a distinctive service. However, there comes a time when the founders of the firm would like to cash in on their success and typically sell to an asset gatherer, which pays a premium for the highly profitable operation. Unfortunately, only through rapid growth and cost cutting will the acquisition be successful, as it now has a tremendous debt load or an extremely high goal for return on capital. So following the transaction, the service positions are often eliminated or turned into sales or marketing jobs. Now individuals are compensated by gathering assets rather than by satisfying the needs of the relationship. Additionally, often a person from a tax-exempt account background is assigned the relationship. As a result, it is only a matter of time before the taxable client looks elsewhere for service.

The lack of servicing is also a major concern in open-architecture systems, which in some instances are nothing more than glorified wrap situations. While they provide access to an account strategy at a reasonable fee, they do not guarantee a meaningful relationship by a qualified servicing professional. All too often, the open-architecture system is a crutch for minimally qualified sales and servicing professionals who are only capable of presenting prospects and clients with superficial performance records. Open architecture, or access to multiple firms, is a value-added proposition when the servicing function can take the unique circumstances of the client and allocate assets to managers in a tax-aware manner, which is covered in detail in other chapters.

Tax-aware investing is about process first and long-term relationships serviced by knowledgeable individuals, but accomplishing this requires educated and experienced professionals. You know you have a winner when you hear a firm periodically pulls in all its servicing professionals for an internal conference at least annually to hear about the latest in tax, estate, or regulatory issues. Fortunately, there are still firms, both large and small, that are committed to providing their clients with this type of value-added expertise. The key point here is that firms may have excellent tax-aware products, but they have less value unless qualified individuals can interact with the taxable clients.

8 *Tax-loss harvesting opportunistically throughout the year, with knowledge of the wash sale rule:* At this level in the progression of tax-aware elements, we are getting to the point where active management can offer a true value-added proposition above and beyond what can be achieved through passive investing. This can be stated because doing it requires adherence to all the previous elements. Continuous tax-loss harvesting requires a meaningful commitment by the firm in terms of systems technology and trading. Coding of accounts for various features allows this to be done in volume. However, it requires close coordination between the investment, servicing, operational, and perhaps even the compliance functions of the firm.

These managers need to have systems in place to monitor wash sales rules to ensure they do not repurchase a security within thirty days after the sale. IRS Publication 550 states: "You cannot deduct losses when you sell or trade stock of securities at a loss and within 30 days before the sale you:

—Buy substantially identical stock or securities.

—Acquire substantially identical stock or securities in a fully taxable trade, or

—Acquire a contract or option to buy substantially identical stock or securities."[3]

The question most taxable investors have is, What constitutes a substantially identical security? Unfortunately, the Internal Revenue Service has not provided a precise definition of the term.[4] The tax-exempt fixed income community was one of first niches to apply this trade, and here is how they approach it. We will demonstrate a swap that would be considered an acceptable trade within the industry, using fictitious municipal bonds. At the beginning of 1994, the portfolio holds a New York Sewer municipal bond with a 6.0 percent coupon due May 15, 2014. The bond was purchased at par. As you may recall, there was a general increase in the level of interest rates across the yield curve of approximately 2 percent in 1994. Since the bond has a duration of approximately 10 years, it falls in price by 20 percent. You decide to sell the security to harvest the loss and wish to purchase another bond without causing a major disruption to the characteristics of the portfolio. You notice an Illinois General Obligation municipal bond available for purchase with a 5.0 percent coupon due September 15, 2013. In this example, there are several items that show the bonds are not identical: different issuer, sector or type of credit, coupon, and maturity. The bonds may have similar but not identical expected price movement to changes in interest rates, so you decide to move forward with the trade. As we discovered over the past five years, there will always be a few individuals who will push the envelope on accounting issues—even the wash sale rule. For example, they will own a mutual fund that replicates the S&P 500 stock index, sell it at a loss, and purchase an ETF that holds the exact same stocks according to the same allocation scheme. While the two vehicles may have somewhat different liquidity characteristics, they have an R-squared (percentage of return explained by another benchmark or security) of almost exactly 1, or 100 percent. In this case, you should not be surprised if someone eventually questions the trade. To be on safe ground when conducting a tax-loss harvesting trade, you should analyze if there is a meaningful amount of capital at risk when you compare the past return patterns of the sale and purchase candidates. If so, then you are probably safe. The three consequences of a wash sale are:

—You are not allowed to claim the loss on your sale.

—Your disallowed loss is added to the basis of the replacement stock.

—Your holding period for the replacement stock includes the holding period of the stock you sold.

Managers who look to harvest trades only at the end of the year are severely limiting the number of available tax-loss harvesting opportunities they can exploit. For instance, if an investment manager conducts all tax-loss harvesting trades at the end of year, he may have missed opportunities in the beginning of the year, as in 2003 when the market dropped and then rebounded. When interviewing firms, it is paramount to understand how often they review accounts for tax-loss harvesting. If it is only done quarterly or so, they will be unable to extract the true naturally occurring additional value created by market volatility.

Not all accounts need or can take advantage of tax-loss harvesting. For example, you may have clients who are in a net operating loss position and therefore have the luxury of needing to harvest gains. In such cases, the tax-loss harvesting engine can be reversed, and you don't have to worry about the wash sale rule. Better yet, when the client gets out of the net operating loss posture, his portfolio will have a cost basis close or equal to the market value of the portfolio and he can easily start taking losses. This is just another example of how knowledge of tax-aware investing—or in this case, "tax-gain harvesting" and the wash sale rule—can benefit the client.

9 *Having analysts and portfolio managers who focus only on tax-able accounts and incorporate tax implications in each buy and sell decision:* We are now getting to the pinnacle of tax-aware investing for equity managers. These managers and their firms understand that taxable-account investing should serve as a distinct separate business unit and they treat it as such. They go the extra distance to model the impact of every potential sale in their investment decisions. In certain situations, the impact of selling securities with large unrealized gains can be significant. As Figure 11.1 shows, it might take several years or more for the new security (the purchase candidate) to recapture the costs of paying the capital gains tax. These managers address this issue by using optimizers and performing break-even analysis to determine the tax impact of every potential sale. Using assumptions that are often customized to the specifics of each taxable client's portfolio, the manager considers all tax implications before making a sale. What the process entails is:

— Calculating the dollar amount of the capital gain that is likely to be realized.

— Determining how much of the price per share of the security considered for purchase must be adjusted upward for the tax impact of the potential sale.

— Recalculating the projected return of the security being considered for purchase with the upward-adjusted price.

— If the projected return of the security being considered for purchase does not clearly exceed the projected return of the security held, calculating a break-even point in years.

If the spread in projected return is still clearly in favor of the buy candidate, follow through with the trade. If not, then human experience comes back into play and you have to ask, "How much conviction do we have in our projected returns?" Some firms take the process a bit further when the projected return of the security being considered for purchase is greater than that of the sell candidate: They calculate a break-even period in years. Then they compare the break-even period with their historical average holding period, which is typically derived from the average turnover rate. If the break-even period is greater than half the average holding period, the trade is withdrawn. For example, if the historical turnover rate of a strategy is 25 percent, the firm assumes an average historical holding period of four years. If the analyst calculates a break-even period of three years for a particular buy candidate, that security would most likely be eliminated from further consideration for the immediate future. Other candidates are considered, or the trade is put on hold until there is a more favorable market environment and the transaction has superior economic value.

A portfolio manager who uses this strategy and has presented the value of its methodology at public conferences is Joanne Howard of Rosenberg Capital Management (RCM).[5] The security break-even analysis by Howard and her associates starts by analyzing the tax cost of selling the

FIGURE **11.2** *Security Break-Even Analysis*

	CURRENT INVESTMENT	NEW INVESTMENT
Company	Xerox	Cisco
Ticker	XRX	CSCO
Shares Owned/To Buy	3,900	2,413
Cost/Share	18.46	
Current Price	46.13	58.00
Current Market Value	179,888	139,970
Capital Gains Tax rate	37%	
Tax $ Paid	39,918	
After-tax Proceeds	139,970	
Assumptions		
3–5 Year Growth Rate	10.00	30.00
Current Rel. P/E	0.66	1.50
Target Rel. P/E	0.70	1.60
Conclusion:		
YEARS TO BREAK-EVEN	2	

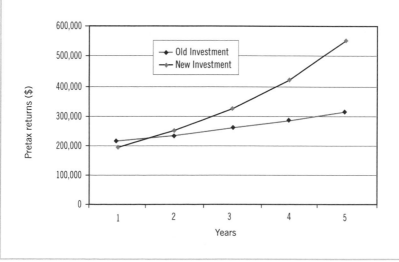

Source: Joanne Howard/Rosenberg Capital Management

existing security (see **FIGURE 11.2**). In the example, selling Xerox at the current price of $46.13 will generate a tax cost of $39,918 on the sale of a position of 3,900 shares. The tax cost is achieved by taking into account the difference in the cost basis and current market value and applying the client's tax rate of 37 percent. Obviously, this is a trade for a position held less than a year and subject to the short-term capital gains tax rate. The reason the trade is being considered is that their analyst believes Cisco has a vastly superior estimated growth rate of 30 percent, as compared with Xerox at 10 percent. However, the trade only makes sense if the current price of Cisco is low enough to overcome the tax bite or cost when Xerox is sold. In this example, the break-even or crossover point is approximately 1.7 years. Most firms that apply this type of analysis believe the break-even point for stock trades needs to be approximately two years or less to justify the trade. This is just one part of the sell decision-making process, but it is an extremely important one that quantifies the impact of taxes. If the analyst or portfolio manager feels strongly the existing holding is likely to fall precipitously in price, then the security should simply be sold. This is not the time to be tax wise and security-outlook foolish! It is this type of methodology that causes many practitioners to call tax-aware investing an art form, rather than an exact science. As simple as this type of analysis is, in the author's experience there are fewer than two dozen firms that employ this type of analysis. Firms focused on serving the needs of their taxable clients are embracing and refining this type of analysis to position themselves as elite tax-aware practitioners.

The challenge with this procedure is you need to have an efficient portfolio accounting system to keep track of the numerous tax lots across all the firm's taxable accounts of the same strategy. This example again demonstrates the value of coupling tax-aware investing concepts with technology.

We will discuss tax-aware fixed income investing in chapter 12, but Sanford C. Bernstein is one firm that has automated its analysis and trading function to the extent it can quickly determine if a block of bonds it sees offered for sale on the "Street" will add incremental value on an after-tax basis for each and every one of its individual taxable accounts, while taking into account the unique tax profile of each individual relationship. When tax-aware principles are married with technology, the results can be truly impressive. That is why this niche of investing is so exciting today, as we have only encountered the tip of the iceberg in terms of what can be done.

10 *Being committed to after-tax performance standards and reporting:* After-tax reporting is simply the icing on the cake. Firms should attempt to provide individual clients with both pre- and post-liquidation returns, as both offer useful information, depending on the needs of the client. Moreover, if firms have gone to this extreme to position themselves as elite practitioners, they should attempt to brand their report. Examples of a client report by Parametric Portfolio Associates and a sample AIMR-compliant after-tax composite report are given in chapter 7.

In years to come, further elements may be added to the list. Beecher Investors has put in place one of the more innovative initiatives. This is a firm that truly endorses tax-aware investing principles, so much so that it has instituted fees based on its after-tax results. If a manager cannot outperform an ETF or tax-managed fund—which are readily available alternatives—on an after-tax basis, then how can it justify charging a fee? It can't, so why shouldn't taxable clients insist on paying for results based on after-tax results? This is an area you will likely hear more about in the future and hopefully will become more common so that it can be added to the list of tax-aware elements in the future.

There are three additional factors managers need to consider in the management of international equity portfolios. The first is that not all foreign stocks produce qualified dividends, and U.S. domiciled accounts and funds are subject to dividend withholding taxes. Second, foreign stocks must be held sixteen days for the investor to claim a credit for the withholding taxes. The third factor involves additional taxes from currency overlay management. If possible, international managers employing currency hedging should be positioned in tax-exempt entities, since the process is inherently tax-inefficient. Unless the manager can demonstrate a meaningful alpha through a methodical process of currency management, taxable accounts are better off emphasizing managers that omit this facet of international or foreign security management.

Another method that is gaining acceptance is managing by taxable client objectives versus tax-exempt consultant demands. In the past, managers were criticized if they did not transition accounts quickly to model portfolios that resulted in minimal return dispersion between accounts. Now taxable-account managers are taking the time to properly analyze the return potential of each security they inherit in conjunction with the cost basis. This is a major change from the mindless process of immediately selling all holdings that do not conform to the new model portfolio, regardless of their cost basis. If the unrealized capital gains are substantial, tax-aware managers may take months or years before eliminating the position and will try to do so when there are losses available to minimize the tax impact. Also, even when starting with cash portfolios, some managers are only funding a portion of their taxable portfolio, as they do not want to subject new clients to rapid trading when some positions are on the

FIGURE **11.3** *Before-Fee and Tax Alpha for the Ten Years Ending December 31, 2003*

ASSET CLASS	PERCENTILE RANK FROM "TOP" 10%	25%	50%	N	BENCHMARK
Large-Cap Core	**3.80**	2.01	0.79	129	Russell 1000
Large-Cap Value	**3.25**	1.78	0.61	191	Russell 1000 Value
Large-Cap Growth	**5.29**	**4.06**	2.32	179	Russell 1000 Growth
Small-Cap Value	**5.86**	**3.76**	1.59	31	Russell 2000 Value
Small-Cap Growth	**11.38**	**9.64**	**6.93**	116	Russell 2000 Growth
International	**6.88**	**4.11**	2.03	227	MSCI EAFE
Municipal Bonds	**0.82**	**0.42**	0.17	66	Lehman Brothers Municipal

Source: Plan Sponsor Network, Sean White

cusp as sell candidates and will be eliminated in the months ahead. Each of these practices serves the client's objectives rather than catering to the whims of tax-exempt account consultants. Further insistence by clients and their advisers of managing by client objective will ultimately lead to enhanced wealth creation.

We have discussed the chances that active managers will outperform passive portfolios. To address this issue, we extract alpha-statistic information from the PSN manager database (see **FIGURE 11.3**).[6]

First, we need to determine the appropriate before-tax and before-fee hurdle for an equity manager to be competitive. We create the hurdle by determining what is required to outperform the appropriate benchmark, that is, the QTA manager's expected return. A QTA manager should outperform the benchmark on an after-tax basis by 1.3 percent per year with normal market volatility and under the current provisions of the tax code. (The outperformance was 1.5 percent under the tax code prior to 2003, when tax rates on ordinary income and capital gains were higher.) Taking into account that the average manager not adhering to tax-aware methods will likely achieve a tax-cost ratio of 1.3 percent, or lose an equal percentage that the tax-loss harvesting firm will gain, results in a return differential due taxes of 2.6 percent (1.3% + 1.3%). The difference in fees, another form of tax, for actively managed separate accounts can vary significantly but is usually in a range of 0.5 to 1 percent, depending on the asset class and size of the assignment. Using a mid-range of 0.75 percent and a 0.35 percent annual fee for QTA managers creates a fee differential of 0.4 percent. Adding the fee differential of 0.4 percent to the after-tax performance differential of 2.6 percent results in a hurdle of 3.0 percent. Again, this is the alpha, or the amount by which an equity manager needs to outperform a suitable passive benchmark before he should be considered a serious candidate to serve taxable accounts. Readers can adjust the three input variables to accommodate their own outlook for tax efficiency and fees, but this approach makes the search process a simpler task, as it eliminates many firms that simply do not have a process in place to achieve this type of result in the future. As shown for the ten years ending December 31, 2003, managers had to be in the top 10 percent of active core and value managers to outperform the 3.0 percent hurdle, or bogey. The information suggests that managers in less-efficient small-cap and international markets do have a chance to achieve attractive returns on after-tax basis, but is this information representative of the actual experience investors encountered? Unfortunately, manager databases have extreme survivor bias: managers that go out of business or stop submitting data are excluded. Additionally, marketers rarely submit data to a manager database unless the manager's initial performance is at least in the top half of managers. Also, we don't know how many of the managers shown are closed to new business, which is common with small-cap managers. With the exception of small-cap growth, none of the equity classes represented demonstrate a meaningful chance of outperforming on an after-tax basis. For the reasons mentioned, the likelihood that those managers who did outperform the 3.0 percent hurdle, will repeat in the future is far less than the information above suggests.

By applying the nontraditional tax-aware elements discussed above, elite equity managers can in fact achieve compelling after-tax results. As they become more comfortable and competent in the process of executing the elements, they discover a high probability of success. For equity managers, the alternative to a tax-aware portfolio is a concentrated portfolio of twenty securities with greater emphasis on alpha generation. Those who emphasize concentrated portfolios along with the tax-aware elements are being sought out by the most discriminating taxable-account investors and advisers. While elite managers who embrace the tax-aware elements are emerging, they are still in short supply. If taxable investors wish to ensure there are large numbers of managers who can serve their taxable-account needs, they have align themselves with advisers who can identify managers with credible processes and become less dependent on historical records of performance. Furthermore, as Tad Jeffrey suggests, long-term investors may be better off ignoring the concepts of benchmarking and tracking error and focus on factors more relevant to bottom-line after-tax results.[7] A similar issue that investors must grapple with is the approach of some managers who make large shifts to cash equivalents when they believe opportunities from stocks are less attractive. The action by itself is tax-inefficient, disrupts the overall asset allocation plan, and should be avoided unless the manager can clearly display that over long periods of time he has produced sufficient alpha to justify the process. Hopefully, the emphasis on process and on putting taxable client needs first will ultimately prove that compelling results can be achieved on both a before- and after-tax basis.

Chapter Notes

1. Parametric Portfolio Associates, "Parametric on Taxes & Investing" (internal marketing presentation), Fall 2001, 2.

2. Much of the discussion on the practices of elite practitioners has been taken directly or summarized from the author's article with Sean W. Egan, "Evaluating and Classifying Taxable Account Managers," *Journal of Wealth Management* (Fall 2004):49–62.

3. IRS Publication 550, *Investment Income and Expenses* (2003), http://www.irs.gov/publications/p550/ch04.html (accessed November 5, 2004).

4. Fairmark Press Tax Guide for Investors, http://www.fairmark.com (accessed November 5, 2004).

5. New York Society of Security Analysts Private Wealth Conference, New York, New York, July 2001.

6. Information compiled by Sean White of CTC Consulting from the PSN (Plan Sponsor Network) database, April 2003.

7. Robert H. Jeffrey, "Tax-Efficient Investing Is Easier Said Than Done," *Journal of Wealth Management* (Summer 2001): 9–15.

CHAPTER **12**

Practices of Elite Tax-Aware
Fixed Income Active Managers

*A fool and his money are soon parted. It takes creative tax laws
for the rest.*

—Bob Thaves
("Frank & Ernest")

Thus far, we have focused on equity portfolios. However, all the
tax-aware elements presented have applications with fixed income
portfolios as well. Since fixed income management is quantitative
in nature, it truly lends itself to tax-aware management. With taxable
accounts, after-tax historical results for bonds are typically about half or
even less of what they are for equities.

"Bond Management for Taxable Investors," which R. B. "Guy" Davidson III wrote in 1999, still stands as the seminal article pertaining to
tax-aware fixed income management.[1] In the article, Davidson outlines
the value of tax-loss harvesting for bond investors. As with equity portfolios, he also shows how the opportunity for tax-loss harvesting with bond
portfolios dissipates over time. When short-term losses offset short-term
gains and long-term losses offset long-term gains, he demonstrates how
tax-loss harvesting can add at least 0.5 percent and 0.8 percent annually
for periods up to ten years for ten- and twenty-year maturities, respectively
to the value of fixed income portfolios. In addition, he addresses the often-
ignored subject of taking profits with taxable bonds. When there is a drop
in interest rates, as we experienced from 1981 to 2003, many high-yield
bonds are priced at a significant premium to par value. Depending on
the outstanding life or maturity of the bond, there is a benefit in selling

the premium bond with a 10 percent-plus coupon, paying the long-term capital gains tax, and then reinvesting the proceeds in another high-yield bond with a much lower coupon at par value. This is favorable to the taxable investor, since the tax on income from the coupon of the bond for investors in the highest tax bracket is now more than twice the rate of the tax on long-term capital gains. As Davidson points out, there is a limit to the benefit of this transaction, as there are fewer proceeds to reinvest after taxes are paid. When the study was conducted in 1999, this opportunity peaked with ten-year maturities.

Bond investing is considered to be a game of inches, as compared with feet or yards in stock investing. Depending on the level of interest rates, the difference between a great fixed income manager and a good or mediocre manager may only be 0.25 to 0.75 percent annually. Additionally, as the average coupon of bonds outstanding continues to fall, it becomes more difficult for bond managers to achieve attractive absolute returns. Therefore, in a low-interest-rate environment, the enlightened or elite tax-aware fixed income manager becomes even more valuable to his clients. This chapter will address the key characteristics of tax-aware fixed income managers.

The Hierarchy of Tax-Aware Investing

(Supplemental Elements for Fixed Income Portfolios)

1 Knows that a ladder of maturities is not a tax-aware solution
2 Is willing to enhance after-tax income but not to cause detrimental consequences
3 Understands the impact of premiums and discounts
4 Avoids phantom-income situations, if possible
5 Purchases out-of-state municipal bonds when they offer superior after-tax returns
6 Purchases taxable bonds when they offer superior after-tax returns
7 Takes advantage of good things happening to municipal bonds
8 Understands that portfolios having long effective maturities offer the greatest potential
9 Can manage bond portfolios successfully for various types of taxable entities
10 Understands how to optimize portfolios for the alternative minimum tax

Each element will be examined to provide an understanding how the elite fixed income managers extract value from the bond markets on an after-tax basis.

1 *Knows that a ladder of maturities is not a tax-aware solution:* If the objective is to maximize after-tax total return, a ladder of municipal or tax-exempt bonds represents a willingness to accept mediocrity. Unfortunately, too many individuals accept them because they are informed bond ladders are not subject to price volatility as are fixed income mutual funds. All bond portfolios are subject to price sensitivity from changes in the general level of interest rates! More important, bond ladders represent a missed opportunity cost for tax-aware investors that in some cases can exceed as much as 1 percent or more in return each year. Until the SEC requires brokers to disclose the full cost of trading fixed income securities, as they do with equities, bond ladders will unfortunately continue to flourish as investors will remain unaware of the true costs of constructing and maintaining them. If you naively purchase municipal or tax-exempt bonds and hold them to maturity, you forgo tax-aware opportunities. As with equities, one of the best ways to add incremental value is through tax-loss harvesting. Unlike the case with equities, doing this effectively with bonds requires sizable, liquid positions that can be exchanged at a reasonable bid/ask spread. Moreover, there are nuances with the tax code that make tax-loss harvesting more complex for bonds, as compared with equities. The advocates of ladders cannot compete in this arena for two primary reasons. First, unless a manager trades according to best-execution provisions and passes the complete savings on to their customers, it is difficult to conduct the tax-loss harvesting trade with bond accounts. Second, as you go through the additional elements of tax-aware fixed income investing, you come to the conclusion that the experience and skill set necessary to achieve optimal fixed income results rests with a limited number of elite managers.

This discussion is oriented toward investors with sufficient assets to fund a large separate account and those professionals that manage them. However, most individuals think of a fixed income mutual fund as an alternative to a bond ladder. It is difficult to justify fixed income mutual funds when the average intermediate national municipal bond category has a twelve-month SEC yield of 3.4 percent and the average expense ratio is 1.03 percent, according to Morningstar.[2] This means the fees consume almost a quarter of the yield! This difficulty is magnified even more with money market funds, some of which have had to waive their fees to avoid having no yield. Fees matter with fixed income funds and over the long haul are a major contributor to success or lack thereof. Fees alone should eliminate the majority of fixed income mutual funds from consideration. For example, cost-competitive funds have expense ratios of 0.2 percent or less, whereas the average fund has a fee slightly greater than 1 percent. This difference of 0.8 percent alone is what differentiates a fixed income manager who is median performer from one in the top quintile. If you are with a fund group with multiple fund offerings, you can conduct the tax-loss harvesting with a phone call, which is a significant advantage over the ladder. If you take advantage of this opportunity, it can more than cover the expense ratio.

2 *Is willing to enhance after-tax income but not to cause detrimental consequences:* Taxable-bond management is different than the total-return-focused environment of tax-exempt account management. With taxable accounts, it is necessary to balance both the ability to generate meaningful income on an after-tax basis and price appreciation. Established fixed income firms, like Standish Mellon, devote significant resources to determine daily how they can achieve the highest after-tax returns for their customers without subjecting them to risks that may jeopardize principal. These firms employ state-of-the-art systems and experienced professionals with the expertise and experience to construct portfolios that generate more income than a market proxy and then to deliver more protection or appreciation, depending on their outlook for changes in the outlook for interest rates, shape of the yield curve, and relative value of various sectors they deem most compelling. Their objective is to deliver consistent, above-benchmark results without taking on unnecessary risk. They should be expected to add value, but there is a limit as to what can be accomplished within this framework. Fishermen have a saying that you can't catch a ten-pound bass if the pond is only capable producing a bass that weighs five pounds. This is so true with fixed income portfolios, as the amount of upside is limited, and investors all too often have an unrealistic expectation. When bond yields are low, you can't expect managers to add 1 percent in performance unless they are taking on additional risk. For a manager who is controlling risk, as in the case of Standish Mellon, the most investors should expect to receive in incremental return is approximately 10 percent of the current yield to maturity of the benchmark portfolio. Therefore, if municipal bonds yield 4 percent, an active manager should be able to produce a return of 4.4 percent before fees. There are too many examples of how investors have lost not 1 or 2 percent but 25 percent or more of their investment or principal from bond managers' reaching for too much yield. If additional income is being achieved beyond what is achieved by a methodology that Standish and others employ, you have to ask, "What is the additional risk I am taking, and am I being compensated for it?"

Additional income or yield can be achieved through emphasizing certain types of securities or by employing leverage. At the security level, the market offers additional income for a bond that is callable or is of lesser credit quality. Call risk arises from not participating in market apprecia-

FIGURE **12.1** *After-Tax Returns of High-Yield vs. Municipal Bond Funds Category Averages from Morningstar Principia (For Periods Ending 6-30-2003)*

MORNINGSTAR CATEGORY	ON DISTRIBUTIONS		ON DISTRIBUTIONS AND SALE OF SHARES		
	5 YEARS	10 YEARS	5 YEARS	10 YEARS	15 YEARS
High-Yield	−0.62%	1.43%	0.27%	2.08%	3.48%
Intermediate National Municipal	4.52%	5.07%	4.50%	5.03%	5.74%
High-Yield Municipal	3.49%	4.08%	3.77%	4.95%	5.81%

tion opportunities when interest rates fall or bonds are taken from you by the issuer when you have purchased them at a price greater than par. Credit risk refers to the issuer's ability to pay interest and repay principal as scheduled. What many investors fail to realize is that high yield does not necessarily result in high after-tax returns. For the past two decades, taxable high-yield corporate bonds have been issued with coupons near 10 percent, but the average annual return after taxes on distributions and sale of fund shares for high-yield bond funds has been a paltry 2.08 percent and 3.48 percent for ten and fifteen years (see **FIGURE 12.1**). This is even after favorable double-digit returns in 2003.

As the figure shows, municipal bonds have had vastly superior results, as compared with high-yield corporate bonds on an after-tax basis for the simple reason that you have to consider defaults as well as income or yield. One way to mitigate risk is through diversification. However, a major difference between the equity and bond markets is that diversification typically benefits stock portfolios, but it can be detrimental to high-yield bond portfolios because certain sectors are notorious for their history of persistent high default rates. High-yield managers who have been successful most likely run concentrated portfolios to avoid weak sectors. Moreover, equities trade on formal exchanges and for the most part are liquid. U.S. Treasuries are liquid, but history has shown that yield-oriented bond sectors go through periods of illiquidity that can last a quarter or more.

Many closed-end fixed income mutual bond funds employ one-third or so in leverage to boost their income generation. Leveraging can also be combined with purchasing longer-term municipal bond instruments and shorting short-term taxable bond instruments. It is not uncommon for some of these bets to be magnified eight to ten times by hedge funds using leverage to achieve tax-exempt income that may exceed a yield of 10 percent annually. This may all be fine for a short period, but the manager may not be able to sustain the strategy through a period of illiquidity, which can happen every five years or so in the fixed income markets.

When reporting yields to taxable investors, you should refrain from quoting them on a gross yield basis.

gross yield = tax-exempt bond yield to maturity / (1 – tax rate)
net yield = taxable bond yield to maturity × (1 – tax rate)

To demonstrate the calculation, let's assume we have a tax-exempt or municipal bond with a yield to maturity of 4.0 percent and the investor is subject to the maximum federal tax rate on ordinary income of 35 percent. In this case, the bond has a gross yield of 6.15 percent (4% / [1 – 35%]). If a taxable bond has a yield to maturity of 6.0 percent, it would have a net yield of 3.9 percent (6% × [1 – 35%]). Unfortunately, the practice of quoting a gross yield in mutual fund advertising gives a false impression. If you compound gross yields and then reduce the amount by an appropriate percentage of tax, you obtain a greater answer than if you compound the after-tax yields. Firms conforming to the AIMR after-tax reporting standards must report portfolio characteristics on a net rather than gross tax basis. The statement "You can't eat gross yields" is often used to highlight this issue and certainly strikes a chord with tax-aware investors.

3 *Understands the impact of premiums and discounts:* When a bond is first issued it probably offers the least value to investors, as there is great demand for bonds priced at par value. Retail investors like par bonds because their mechanics are simple to understand. Tax-aware bond managers most often go to the secondary market to hunt for value, but this means the bond most likely is at a price other than par. Most often, tax-aware municipal bond managers purchase bonds at a premium to par, because of a relatively obscure provision of the tax code known as the de minimis rule. Prior to 1993, when you purchased a bond at a discount and held it more than a year, the accretion of the principal was taxed at the rate for long-term capital gains. Since then, if you exceed the de minimis amount, the accretion is taxed at the much higher rate for ordinary income. If the amount is de minimis, which is defined as the market discount being less than 0.25 percent of the face value of the bond multiplied by the complete number of years to maturity, then the long-term capital gain rate still applies. For example, if you purchase a bond with a remaining life of ten years to maturity at 98, the discount is considered to be de minimis. However, if you purchased the bond at a price of 97.5 or below, the accretion is subject to the ordinary income rate. This feature is especially important when investors anticipate conducting a tax-loss harvesting trade when bond prices peak or yields trough, as they did in the summer of 2003. Following periods like this, you want to hold a portfolio of bonds purchased at a premium rather than at par value or at a discount, because when rates gradually increase, the market prices in an additional discount when the bonds trend toward the level at which de minimis tax provisions take hold. This causes deeper-discount bonds to accelerate downward in price. Moreover, it brings into question the viability of the tax-loss harvesting trade, because you are most likely taking a loss at the long-term capital gains rate and you do not want to purchase a replacement bond that will have accretion subject to the ordinary income tax rate. Does this mean you should totally ignore discount bonds? Not necessarily, as there have been times when deep-discount bonds became so oversold that astute tax-aware investors could extract compelling returns from them even after paying the onerous tax on the annual accretion amount.

If a tax-exempt bond is priced at a premium, no amortization is allowed. However, the reduction in basis must be accounted for when the bond is sold. This feature needs to be carefully considered when analyzing a bond on an after-tax total return basis. For taxable bonds purchased at a premium, the investor can elect to amortize the bond until maturity or not amortize and include it as part of the cost basis. This has often caused confusion for taxable investors who purchase certain Government National Mortgage Association (GNMA) mutual bond funds. If the fund elected not to amortize high-coupon bonds purchased at a premium, it paid out a high level of income over time and the price of the fund gradually fell to adjust for the treatment of the premium. In this case, there is no free lunch! This arrangement makes little sense for an investor in a high tax bracket, as he ends up paying tax on the high level of income that is not offset by the amortized amount at the ordinary income rate, and then if he holds the fund more than a year and sells it (most likely at a loss), he only gets a credit at the long-term capital gains rate. This result was quite prevalent with funds in the 1980s, when bonds could still be purchased in the marketplace with 10 percent plus coupons. The key to this element is that bond managers need to be aware of how investors evaluate bonds for tax nuances and be able to take advantage of pricing discrepancies and dislocation in the market when they can add value for their clients.

4 *Avoids phantom-income situations, if possible:* One item that perplexes individuals is the payment of tax on phantom income created by stripped Treasury zero-coupon bonds. These bonds can be ideal for funding specific cash flow requirements, as the zero-coupon structure avoids reinvestment risk. In this case, the total rate of return of the bond will equal the yield to maturity, because semiannual coupon income is not reinvested at different yield and price levels. Unfortunately, even though the zero-coupon Treasury does not distribute income, investors must pay tax on the amount of annual accretion, or phantom income. This problem also occurs with Treasury inflation-protection securities (TIPS). These are Treasury bonds that are issued a lower-than-market coupon and their principal amount is increased monthly by the percentage increase in the rate of inflation, as measured by the consumer price index. There are two ways this can be overcome. First, Christine Todd of Standish Mellon notes that the phantom-income tax does not apply to the zero-coupon municipal bonds in their portfolios. Second, Barclays has developed an innovative solution with their TIPS iShare exchange-traded fund of distributing the amount of principal each month rather than accreting it. Now individual investors desiring to invest in TIPs have a sufficient flow of funds to cover tax payments. There are now municipal inflation-protected securities, or MIPS. In these, the principal amount is fixed, but the semiannual coupon is adjusted for inflation. At this juncture, bond managers have some concerns with these issues because there is limited volume available and the semiannual coupon payment system misses some of the seasonal inflation patterns that are prevalent with TIPS.[3]

   5 *Purchases out-of-state municipal bonds when they offer superior after-tax returns.* Tax-aware municipal bond managers think of maximum after-tax versus paying no tax and are not wed to purchasing bonds solely from the client's state of residence. There is so much demand for the bonds of high-tax states like California, Massachusetts, Minnesota, and New York that local investors often pay a premium for them. When the market gets frothy, the astute investor will look to other states, where demand is lower. This will usually take the manager to low-tax states or one of the six states where local investors must still pay taxes on municipal bond income from bonds issued from their state of residence. To make matters more complex, there are states like Wisconsin where only a portion of municipal bonds are exempt from both federal and state taxes. With complexity often comes opportunity. Therefore, managers can often purchase municipal bonds at levels cheap enough that they still offer compelling value after payment of a state tax on their income. Not only does this practice serve to achieve higher after-tax returns, it also leads to a more diversified portfolio with less sensitivity to state-specific economic or political risk. While the economic output of New York or California is larger than that of many countries, they both have had their fair share of budgetary concerns over the past two decades, which have put severe pricing pressure on their bonds.

6 *Purchases taxable bonds when they offer superior after-tax returns:* Tax-aware bond managers will also consider taxable bonds for inclusion in the portfolio if the after-tax returns are more compelling than those of tax-exempt bond alternatives. The simplest example of this opportunity can be shown with money market funds. Just out of curiosity, visit the website of a favorite large mutual fund complex, check the yields on its national taxable money market fund, and multiply by 0.6 to account for the tax haircut. Then compare this number with the current yield on its California municipal money market fund. More often than not, after paying taxes, the yield on the taxable money market fund will be higher. Does that make sense? No, but it is amazing how many investors from high-tax states will purchase municipal bond products to pay no tax rather than maximize their wealth creation and invest on an after-tax basis.

To gain an understanding of the tax treatment of taxable bonds, investors should be aware that Treasury and GNMA pass-through securities are considered to be direct obligations of the United States and are exempt from state tax. Agency issues by the Federal Farm Credit Bank,

FIGURE **12.2** *After-Tax Yield Comparison*

Before-Tax Yield to Maturity

	TAX-EXEMPT MUNICIPAL	U.S. TREASURY	GOVERNMENT AGENCY	A-RATED CORPORATE
	3.20%	4.00%	4.40%	4.80%

After-Tax Yield to Maturity

FEDERAL TAX RATE	TAX-EXEMPT MUNICIPAL	U.S. TREASURY	GOVERNMENT AGENCY	A-RATED CORPORATE
10%	3.20%	3.60%	3.96%	4.32%
15%	3.20%	3.40%	3.74%	4.08%
25%	3.20%	3.00%	3.30%	3.60%
28%	3.20%	2.88%	3.17%	3.46%
33%	3.20%	2.68%	2.95%	3.22%
35%	3.20%	2.60%	2.86%	3.12%

Federal Home Loan Bank, and Sallie Mae are also exempt from state tax. Since these agency issues offer a pickup in yield over U.S. Treasuries and are very liquid, they are often emphasized by managers who incorporate the "crossover" trade (crossing over from tax-exempt to taxable bonds and back again to achieve the highest potential after-tax returns) as part of the overall strategy to enhance after-tax returns. On the surface, the trade appears to be quite simple. You just select the bond offering the highest potential after-tax return. To illustrate the opportunity for value, **FIGURE 12.2** shows before- and after-tax yields for a tax-exempt municipal, U.S. Treasury, government agency, and corporate bond at the different break points in the federal marginal tax rates.

In reality, bond prices and yields change daily, and firms that apply the crossover trade in a sophisticated manner incorporate state tax rates as well. To achieve after-tax total returns for comparative purposes, the firm may incorporate an interest rate forecast or take into account information derived from the shape of the theoretical spot rate curve to determine the impact of price movement over a defined time horizon. Tax-aware municipal bond managers incorporate this information along with other information before making buy and sell decisions. One firm that emphasizes this type of strategy to achieve its value-added proposition is M.D. Sass. Through electronic applications it can monitor the current after-tax potential of every bond in its inventory. It receives bids on its holdings from more than 200 professionals across the country having access to its inventory. This is especially advantageous for its performance; as mentioned earlier, the retail side of the business will often pay a premium for in-state bonds. You may ask, "Do tax-exempt investors ever purchase municipal bonds?" Astute tax-exempt bond managers do, especially when the yields approach 100 percent of Treasury yields. These managers realize that taxable investors will come back into the market when they realize how cheap municipal bonds are, with price movement superior to that of equal maturity Treasuries.

7 *Takes advantage of good things happening to municipal bonds:* Another element that people miss that Michael Brilley of Sit Investment Associates shares with his clients and prospects is "Good things happen to municipal bonds!" Unlike taxable bonds, with which the best thing that can happen is perhaps a credit upgrade, municipal bonds can be pre-refunded or escrowed to maturity. When rates fall, the issuer may establish an escrow account and fund the remaining cash flows from the proceeds of U.S. government bonds. When this occurs, the bonds are upgraded to AAA, causing an immediate improvement in price. Also, the bonds may become subject to a premium par call, where the bonds will be taken out at levels two to three points above par. Corporate sinking-fund bonds, which are becoming increasingly rare, are the only taxable issues that exhibit similar favorable features. An astute money manager wants to focus on bonds that are likely to have these favorable actions happen rather than purchasing those bonds where the favorable actions have already occurred.

8 *Understands that portfolios having long effective maturities offer the greatest potential:* Most bond professionals think of achieving compelling returns as the ability to produce superior risk-adjusted returns. That is fine if you limit yourself to the confines of a trading desk. What is ignored to a large extent with taxable bond portfolios is the need to match the horizon of client assets with their liabilities, which is more of a retirement-plan concept. For an individual starting a career, there is a need for a safety net and a risk-adjusted return orientation makes sense. However, if a high-net-worth family has a respectable estate plan, it can be considered to be a perpetual organization. Therefore, portfolios having a longer maturity or duration make sense, especially if you can take advantage of the tax-loss harvesting trade with more liquid securities. This does not mean you should immediately plunge into longer maturities when interest rates are near historical lows. However, over time, as opportunities present themselves, high-net-worth families especially would be financially better off extending the average life of their taxable bond portfolios. This is especially true with municipal bonds, as they are less susceptible to Federal Reserve activity. Unlike Treasuries, where shorter-maturity issues offer greater yields than longer-term bonds, municipal bonds do not experience yield-curve inversions. The municipal bond yield curve maintains its humped shape with a peak in yield typically in the fifteen- to twenty-five-year maturity range. Therefore, investors can take advantage of the higher, persistent level of tax-exempt income from this portion of the yield curve and gain some appreciation in price when their individual bonds "roll down the yield curve" with time.

9 *Can manage bond portfolios successfully for various types of taxable entities:* The property and casualty insurance industry presents a different set of challenges for the taxable-account bond manager. There are three distinguishing factors. First, municipal bond income is subject to a 15 percent haircut—meaning it is taxed at a rate of 5.25 percent (35% × 15%). Second, the property and casualty insurance industry is subject to statutory reporting requirements. Until a manager can demonstrate competence with this additional layer of complexity, companies and their advisers are usually unwilling to take them on. Third, the insurance company may, from time to time, tap the portfolio for profits when they are available. Therefore, when a manager takes a gain, he may in fact be working in the best interests of the corporation. This

thought process can be quite different than the process where a manager
may wish to take losses and delay taking gains for high-net-worth family portfolios. Also, the provisions of various tax codes that apply to the
different types of taxable account entities generally have a far greater
impact on the day-to-day management of fixed income portfolios, as
compared with equity portfolios. While everyone should know about
the tax ramifications of trading a particular client portfolio, the fixed
income professional navigating these various types of markets successfully soon finds himself almost a tax expert on each. Perhaps that is why
bond managers who started their careers originally as accountants find
this niche so rewarding.

10 *Understands how to optimize portfolios for the AMT:* The bond
manager needs to exercise caution with crossover trading when the client
is subject to the AMT.[4] The AMT is often referred to even by accountants
as "the one tax accountants do not understand." An accountant typically
thinks of minimizing the tax bite of a client, not necessarily being tax-
aware when it comes to investments. This is again a case of optimizing
the amount of dollars of net or after-tax income, as compared with paying the least amount of taxes. It is essential that the taxable-account fixed
income manager masters an understanding of the AMT, as oftentimes he
will be the one who initiates and carries the conversation as a part of or
when working with the members of the qualified triumvirate of tax-aware
service providers (see chapter 5). The AMT came about in 1986 and is a
form of the flat tax that Steve Forbes supported in his campaign for the
presidency. **FIGURE 12.3** lists the items that most often cause an individual
to be subject to the AMT.[5]

Line 42 of Form 1040 requires taxpayers to calculate their AMT according to Form 6251. AMT income, or AMTI as it is referred to, is
calculated by starting with adjusted gross income and adding back certain preference items. For married couples having more than $175,000

FIGURE 12.3 *Items Causing the Alternative Minimum Tax*

Exemptions	Interest on Second Mortgages
State and Local Taxes	Miscellaneous Itemized Deductions
Medical Expenses	Incentive Stock Options
Long-Term Capital Gains	Tax Shelters

Source: Fairmark Press

in AMTI, multiply by 28 percent and then subtract $3,500 to achieve the AMT tax. For couples having less than $175,000 in AMTI, simply multiply by 26 percent. If the AMT is greater than the regular tax dollar amount, the AMT applies. More and more individuals are finding themselves paying the AMT, especially since the maximum federal tax rate has been lowered from 39.6 percent to 35.0 percent.

The income from a subset of tax-exempt or municipal bonds known as private activity bonds is subject to the AMT. A municipal security is classified as a private activity bond if more than 10 percent of the private business activity of the issue or loans to nongovernmental borrowers exceeds 5 percent of the proceeds. As **FIGURE 12.4,** provided by Standish Mellon, shows, private activity bonds offer greater yields than similar-maturity tax-exempt bonds.

The yield differential in this chart is shown in basis points. A basis point is 1/100th of 1 percent. The trend since 2002 makes sense. Since more investors are becoming subject to the AMT, there is less demand for private activity municipal bonds. For clients not subject to the AMT, private activity bonds provide a small boost in tax-exempt income generation and should be considered. A municipal bond manager can be tax-efficient by avoiding private activity bonds for clients subject to the AMT. However, this simplistic approach typically does not provide an optimal tax-aware solution.

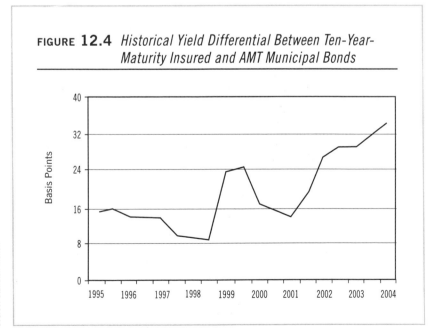

FIGURE **12.4** *Historical Yield Differential Between Ten-Year-Maturity Insured and AMT Municipal Bonds*

Source: Standish Mellon

FIGURE 12.5 *Calculating the Regular and Alternative Minimum Tax (Married Couple With AMTI Greater Than $175,000)*

REGULAR TAX		ALTERNATIVE MINIMUM TAX	
Other Income	$1,000,000		
Adusted Gross Income	$1,000,000		
Other Itemized Deductions	$400,000		
Taxable Income	$600,000		$600,000
		Preference Items	$300,000
		AMT Income (AMTI)	$900,000
Tax Rate	35%	AMT Tax Rate	28%
Tax	$210,000	AMT Tax	$248,500
		(AMTI x 28%) − $3,500	
Tax-Exempt Income	$900,000	Tax-Exempt Income	$900,000
Net Income	$1,290,000	Net Income	$1,251,500

An optimal approach for clients subject to the AMT requires modeling the allocation to tax-exempt versus taxable bonds. Adjustment of the allocation between the two types of bonds can meaningfully increase the client's net after-tax income, which is the tax-aware approach. To start the process, we select yields on representative high-grade tax-exempt and government agency bonds that have effective maturities similar to the portfolio's. For this example, the bond portfolio is $30 million and the yield on an appropriate municipal bond is 3 percent, whereas the taxable bond is offering a yield 4.5 percent. Next we construct a spreadsheet that includes the items necessary to estimate taxes and net income for the investor at both the regular tax rate of 35 percent and the AMT rate of 28 percent, as shown in **FIGURE 12.5.**

In the figure, we start with the amount of taxable security income from the bond portfolio and add to it other income to calculate the adjusted gross income. In the example, there is $0 of taxable security income, because the portfolio has a 100 percent allocation to municipal bonds. We adjust this amount for the allocation to taxable bonds (see **FIGURE 12.6**).

FIGURE **12.6** *Adjusting the Mix of Tax-Exempt vs. Taxable Bonds to Optimize Net Income*

FIXED-INCOME MIX		REGULAR TAX		AMT	
% TAX EXEMPT	% TAXABLE	TAX	NET INCOME	TAX	NET INCOME
100%	0%	$210,000	$1,290,000	$248,500	$1,251,000
90%	10%	$257,250	$1,287,750	$286,300	$1,258,700
80%	20%	$304,500	$1,285,500	$324,100	$1,265,900
70%	30%	$351,750	$1,283,250	$361,900	$1,273,100
60%	40%	$399,000	$1,281,000	$399,700	$1,280,300
50%	50%	$446,250	$1,278,750	$437,500	$1,287,500
40%	60%	$493,500	$1,276,500	$475,300	$1,294,700
30%	70%	$540,750	$1,274,250	$513,100	$1,301,900
20%	80%	$588,000	$1,272,000	$550,900	$1,309,100
10%	90%	$635,250	$1,269,750	$588,700	$1,316,300
0%	100%	$682,500	$1,267,500	$626,500	$1,323,500

Source: Thomas Lawrence, Douglas S. Rogers

Then we subtract itemized deductions to calculate the amount of taxable income. To compute the regular tax due, we simply multiply by the client's tax rate, in this case 35 percent. Last, we subtract the tax from the taxable and tax-exempt income to calculate the net or after-tax income.

For the AMT calculation, we begin with the taxable income, add back the preference items, and then multiply by the AMT rate. Since this client is married and subject to the 28 percent rate, we subtract another $3,500 to achieve the dollar amount of the potential AMT. The greater of the regular tax or AMT amount applies. In this example, the AMT amount of $248,500 is greater, so the individual would have to pay no additional tax with a 100 percent tax-exempt bond portfolio and would feel quite content. More often than not, his advisers would say, "It is unfortunate that you have to pay the AMT, but as long as you don't hold private activity bonds, you have done the right thing because you minimized your tax liability." If the investor takes this tax-efficient advice, he misses the opportunity to enhance his net taxable income by approximately $30,000 annually. This can be accomplished by holding a portfolio of slightly less than 60 percent in tax-exempt bonds and the remainder in taxable bonds. We come to this conclusion through an iterative process by adjusting the mix of bonds in 10 percent increments and recalculating the tax and net income, as shown in Figure 12.6. The shaded area in the last column highlights how gradually adding taxable bonds to the mix increases after-tax net income. While the investor's tax is higher, so is his net income.

Holding any more than approximately 40 percent in taxable bonds pushes the client out of the AMT and provides no benefit. When the client holds less than 60 percent in tax-exempt bonds, there eventually comes a point where the AMT no longer applies, he pays an increasingly higher amount of taxes, and his net taxable income continues to drop, as highlighted in the fourth column. Therefore, it is extremely naive for a manager to say, "Taxable bonds are a bargain relative to municipals, so let's move the whole portfolio in that direction." As Figure 12.6 shows, the municipal bond manager that works in a trading-room vacuum without taking the client's unique tax profile into account should be approached with a high degree of caution. This type of modeling does not require a sophisticated approach but, unfortunately, is all too rare. Each taxable client is different, and the practitioner doing this type of analysis should consider expanding the entries under adjusted gross items, itemized deductions, and preference items to gain a better understanding of the interaction between the key variables. This exercise should facilitate a healthy dialogue and may cause the client's accountant to suggest additional recommendations pertaining to income generation and preference items that can be extremely valuable in the wealth creation process.

Coupling municipal bonds with other securities can produce interesting tax-advantaged products. For years, firms like PIMCO and Metropolitan West have combined short-duration bond trading with futures to create benchmark-plus-equity returns. The same type of structure can be done with municipal bonds in lieu of taxable short-duration bonds. As unique combinations such as these become more prevalent, we are likely to uncover additional elements of taxable fixed income investing that will continue to allow competent tax-aware bond managers to outperform laddered portfolios, after fees, by a meaningful margin. Besides, the one service an investor should pay a fee for is credit analysis aimed at avoiding potential default situations.

We have shown that active fixed income portfolio management makes sense for taxable accounts when tax-aware elements are employed, but at what asset size? To answer this, we must ask two questions. First, what is the minimum number of bonds necessary to achieve a diversified portfolio? Most practitioners would answer twenty, as they do not want to have any more than a 5 percent exposure to any one credit-sensitive issuer. The number could be smaller if some of the securities are full-faith-and-credit obligations of the U.S. government. Second, what is the smallest size of bond trade that can be conducted with a reasonable amount of liquidity? The answer varies according to the sector, but $250,000 is the minimum dollar position to efficiently conduct the tax-loss harvesting trade. Therefore, investors should shy away from actively managed portfolios of less than $5 million (20 securities × $250,000 per security) in size. For amounts under this threshold, fixed income mutual funds serve a valuable purpose. Besides, with a mutual fund you can conduct the tax-loss harvesting trade with a simple phone call or two.

For taxable-bond managers, establishing the hurdle is a different process and the spread is narrower. Fees are similar for bond managers whether or not they conduct tax-loss harvesting. In any case, you should realize the tax-loss harvesting trade alone allows the investor to obtain the manager's expertise for less than cost, but this is only true for intermediate- and long-maturity portfolios. If the manager does not offer any of the tax-aware elements, he needs to have an alpha of +0.5 percent annually to be competitive. As Figure 11.3 highlights, this performance is in the top 25 percent. As with equities, fixed income managers who do not apply the tax-aware elements are at a meaningful disadvantage to those that do.

Chapter Notes

1. R. B. Davidson III, "Bond Management for Taxable Investors," *AIMR Conference Proceedings, Investment Counseling for Private Clients,* no. 2 (1999): 59–68.

2. Morningstar Principia, June 30, 2004.

3. Christine Todd of Standish Mellon, in discussion with the author, November 10, 2004.

4. The author is extremely grateful for the input received from family office executive Thomas Lawrence for his comments pertaining to the alternative minimum tax.

5. "Top Ten Things That Cause AMT Liability," Fairmark Press Tax Guide for Investors, http://www.fairmark.com/amt/topten.htm, accessed July 30, 2004.

CHAPTER **13**

The Hedge Fund Dilemma

Those that can do a good trade don't wrangle over taxes.

—Old Chinese Proverb

There is no other place in the market today where the Chinese proverb above is more applicable than in the rapidly growing hedge fund arena, where assets will soon exceed $1 trillion. Investors invest in hedge funds for two primary reasons: to lower the risk of their existing holdings or to seek superior results from other sources of return. For taxable investors, especially high-net-worth individuals, these are certainly worthwhile objectives to pursue, but if the results aren't there after taxes are paid, even so-called good trades are not worth the effort.

By their very nature, most hedge funds will be notoriously tax-inefficient. Does this mean that investors should ignore them? Absolutely not, but if taxable investors wish to pursue hedge funds, they should have an appreciation of the tax-aware opportunities that are available. There is no single solution that is suitable for all situations. Therefore, it is paramount that taxable investors and their advisers align themselves with qualified individuals who specialize in understanding and sharing how to negotiate these relatively uncharted waters. The key is to seek independent and objective advice that is not aligned with a particular product or strategy. For example, without the education the author has received over the past several years from Bob Gordon and Tom Boczar of Twenty-First Securities, this chapter would have been difficult, if not impossible, to prepare.

The first thing investors need to understand is that hedge funds utilize partnership accounting. The tax strategies of the partnership outlined in the fund's private placement memorandum should be carefully reviewed. The results of the partnership flow through to the investors and are reported on Schedule K-1. There are certain tax applications of partnership accounting that both tax-exempt and taxable investors need to be aware of.

Since hedge funds often employ leverage, they can generate unrelated business taxable income (UBTI). This is of particular concern to certain trusts, charitable organizations, and retirement plans, as UBTI can cause all income received by the entity to be taxable. Investors concerned about UBTI invest in the offshore offering, versus the onshore offering. Offshore hedge funds are structured as corporations, and generate dividend income not subject to the tax on UBTI.

Since hedge funds are partnerships, one technique that can be employed to lower the tax bite of the fund is to make an asset-in-kind distribution of assets, as was discussed with exchange-traded funds. In the case of an ETF, this typically involves a large basket of liquid securities. However, there have been instances with hedge funds where the distribution consisted of low-cost-basis securities that were extremely illiquid. It is one thing to receive an array of liquid stocks, but it is quite another to receive obscure private placements or distressed-debt issues with large bid/ask spreads where there is no orderly exchange. Therefore, it is important for investors and advisers to investigate how the hedge fund has executed past distributions, especially in challenging market environments.

Perhaps the greatest tax issue currently of concern to taxable investors is the deductibility of hedge fund expenses. Hedge funds charge a fee as a percentage of assets managed and a performance fee based on results above a predesignated hurdle rate. A typical fee arrangement is 1 percent of assets and 20 percent of the profits above the return of a benchmark like T-bills. Hedge funds of funds, which manage a basket or portfolio of individual hedge funds, typically further charge 1 percent of assets and 10 percent of profits. Therefore, if a hedge fund or fund of funds achieves a gross return in the neighborhood of 15 percent, the fees can easily be 5 percent or more. Like mutual funds, hedge funds report their returns net of all fees. However, if these fees are not tax-deductible at the hedge fund level and the investor experiences a net return of 10 percent, he may end up paying tax on a return of approximately 15 percent. This is a challenge with a fund of funds, because a hedge fund needs to claim trader status to be able to offset the fees against expenses.[1] Otherwise, in a partnership, expenses cannot be offset against income and are listed separately on the K-1 as a miscellaneous item. Most investors cannot use these miscellaneous deductions, as they do not exceed the threshold percentage of adjusted gross income need to qualify for a deduction. Recent rulings on day traders suggest that these fees are not deductible for certain hedge funds. As this book goes to press, this is the one issue to stay abreast of, as it could have a significant impact on how taxable investors allocate their hedge fund dollars in the future. Moreover, it highlights the importance of knowing the various approaches to enhancing the tax efficiency of hedge fund investing.

Factors that investors and advisers can explore to enhance the after-tax returns of hedge funds are:

1 Tax efficiency of existing hedge funds
2 Significant ownership
3 Favorable transactions
4 Allocation favoring hedge funds that offer the potential for higher after-tax returns
5 Placement of assets in individual retirement accounts
6 Investment in an offshore fund
7 Private placement life insurance (PPLI) policies
8 Shares of stock in a company whose investment portfolio consists of, or whose profits are tied to, hedge funds
9 Hedge fund derivative products
10 Derivatives on hedge fund indices

Separately or combined, these ten tax-aware facets of hedge fund investing can serve to enhance the wealth of taxable investors.

1 *Tax efficiency of existing hedge funds:* Schedule K-1 can be analyzed to determine the relatively efficiency of various hedge funds. The key to this process is you need several years of history before you can draw meaningful conclusions, which is not always possible with hedge funds. Segregating information by the tax nature of each item can prove valuable. If you serve the high-net-worth individual market, you are likely to have clients, especially those paying the alternative minimum tax, who may not be able to take advantage of certain deductions.

2 *Significant ownership:* Perhaps the best way to determine if the hedge fund is likely to be tax-efficient is to interview the senior professionals involved and determine how much of their personal wealth is invested in the fund. A manager who has a significant personal stake in a fund is likely to have a distinctly different approach toward tax consequences than another manager with a minimal commitment. Tax-aware hedge funds may apply some of the same measures as traditional managers highlighted in chapters 11 and 12, but the nature of hedge fund trading will most likely cause them to focus on the elements of item 3.

3 *Favorable transactions:* The following transactions are examples of how tax savings can be achieved in the daily management of hedge funds that Twenty-First Securities has shared with the public.[2]

a. Equity long/short funds need to be sixty-one days on the long side and forty-six days on the short side for the qualified dividend to be taxed at 15 percent and the expense to be deducted at 35 percent.

b. When cash is part of a merger, holding the target stock for at least sixty-one days will cause the amount to be taxed at the more favorable rate for qualified dividends.

c. Constructive-sale rules do not apply to fixed income transactions. Therefore, a trade that is short against the box, where you short the same appreciated security, can defer the gain. This trade alone has tremendous potential for distressed-debt specialists, who often achieve sizable profits from bonds that appreciate significantly in price after being purchased for pennies on the dollar.

d. Another trade that has wide application is the use of a broad-based listed option that qualifies for favorable tax treatment under Section 1256. If you are going to hold an index product for less than a year, it makes sense to use a qualified Section 1256 contract, because it is subject to a blended capital gains tax rate of 60 percent long-term and 40 percent short-term, or a maximum federal tax equivalent of 23 percent. When held at year-end, these contracts are marked to market and the cost basis is adjusted accordingly. Therefore, short-term trading with a Section 1256 contract in lieu of using an index fund or ETF can save one-third in tax dollars.

These are simply a sample of trades that can lead to tax savings. The tax-aware hedge fund managers work closely with tax experts who specialize in this niche so they can keep abreast of tax-minimization strategies. The hedge fund managers must analyze the tax implications of the trades that characterize their core competency and establish procedures to take advantage of certain techniques when they make economic sense.

4 *Allocation favoring hedge funds that offer the potential for higher after-tax returns:* Generally speaking, nondirectional hedge fund strategies that emphasize consistent absolute returns have lower after-tax returns than directional hedge fund strategies. Therefore, when strategies are put through a portfolio optimization process, it only makes sense that taxable accounts will rely on directional strategies more than tax-exempt charitable organizations and retirement plans will. This is why advisers serving taxable accounts typically recommend a higher allocation to equity long/short funds, as compared with the various arbitrage-related strategies.

5 *Placement of assets in individual retirement accounts:* This would be the easy solution. However, the truly affluent investors may have a very small portion of their wealth in IRAs. Also, you should keep in mind that hedge funds are limited to how much they can invest in qualified retirement plan assets.

6 *Investment in an offshore fund:* Like the IRA, this option has limited application, but it can be meaningful and should not be ignored. It applies primarily to investors in high-tax states. In most cases, U.S. individuals would not use offshore vehicles, as these entities are structured as passive foreign investment companies (PFICs). As such, their income and gains are taxed at ordinary income rates. This is not a major concern with some hedge fund strategies, because the bulk of their distributions are ordinary income. In a PFIC investment, tax is paid on your net profits, not gross,. According to tax experts in this area, PFICs have several drawbacks, one of which is a 5 percent tax on deferred income. However, one advantage is that ordinary income tax and interest charges are not included as part of federal taxable income. Since this is what most states base their tax calculation on, this feature could provide meaningful savings for individuals in high-tax states. Twenty-First Securities offers a calculator on its website to allow investors to analyze if the offshore alternative is superior to the traditional onshore or domestic option.[3]

7 *Private placement life insurance policies:* Revenue rulings in 2003 clarified the investment-related issues pertaining to the use of hedge funds as the investment vehicle for PPLI policies. To qualify for favorable tax status, insurance companies are taking measures to ensure the hedge fund options are determined by a person other than the contract holder, preferably an independent party, and offering "insurance-dedicated" products.[4] As a result, there is likely to be a proliferation of product in the years ahead, as there are three distinct tax advantages to life insurance:
- ❏ Building of principal tax-free
- ❏ Ability to make tax-free withdrawals and loans
- ❏ Avoiding the estate tax

Firms planning to enter the PPLI arena are seeking the expertise of individuals such as Leslie Giordani of Giordani, Schurig, Beckett & Tackett, who specializes in this area. This is an example of how regulatory knowledge plays a key role even in individual investor situations. Skeptics believe the insurance companies will not be able to attract top-notch hedge funds, which would not want to become captive to a single distribution channel or client where their fee structure may be brought into question in future years. If these products can be launched without outlandish fees, the benefits from tax efficiency will make them an extremely competitive tax-aware alternative that will demand serious consideration. As a result, advisers will be forced to determine which insurance companies offer the most advantageous products in response to inquiries by their tax-aware clients.

8 Shares of stock in a company whose investment portfolio consists of, or whose profits are tied to, hedge funds: One innovative way to approach this process is to start an offshore insurance company. In lieu of traditional assets, the company would utilize hedge funds for the investment portfolio. Obviously, it has to be done where the use of hedge funds would satisfy risk-based capital standards or similar provisions. While you cannot remove the company-specific risk, this is a way to achieve indirect exposure to hedge funds in a tax-aware manner. Another example of how investors can gain exposure to hedge funds is purchasing shares of a company like Man Group, an enterprise that derives profits from the management of alternative investments. These are less than perfectly correlated plays on hedge funds, but they do demonstrate insightful, tax-aware thinking.

9 Hedge fund derivative products: Playing off investors' fears following three down years in a row in the equity markets (2000 to 2002), it should be no surprise Wall Street has responded with costly principal-protected notes. From a tax viewpoint, they are less than a satisfactory solution, because they typically combine a financial derivative with a U.S. Treasury strip security. Therefore, they are subject to the phantom tax on accreted income described in chapter 12. The next step by the Street was to offer a call option on a hedge fund of funds. This product has received a lackluster response, because the premium charged for the tax-deferral mechanism is 20 to 25 percent, and many believe the structure will run afoul of the constructive sale rules. Another way to look at this offering is why would an investor pay such a high premium for an option on a hedge fund of funds with 5 to 7 percent annual volatility? In this scenario, the probability of achieving a negative return over five or seven years is near zero. Both the accounting provisions and the cost of the tax deferral or option need to be tightened up before these structures become more accepted by astute advisers. Bruce Tavel and his quantitative specialists at U.S. Trust Corporation have constructed an alternative worth considering that produces a similar outcome. They combine a QTA strategy highlighted in chapter 10 with various call and put options to truly address both the client's taxes and investment needs.

10 Derivatives on hedge fund indices: For investors that are looking for tax efficiency and liquidity, this is probably the most promising alternative today. There are now investable hedge fund indices available to investors. As a result, dealers are offering investors synthetic exposure through the use of derivatives. Structured notes are now being offered with weekly liquidity in amounts as little as $50,000. Unlike call options, tax experts believe the notes can be offered without triggering the constructive-sale rules that convert the return stream into ordinary income. Therefore, if held more than a year, they will be subject to the more favorable rate on long-term capital gains. As Tom Boczar and Mark Fichtenbaum point out in their article, "Making Hedge Fund Investing More Tax-Efficient," a hedge fund of funds would have to produce a 4.8 percent annual alpha to match the return on a seven-year note and the underlying index producing a 10 percent return.[5] Even if the fund-of-funds investor could deduct expenses, the alpha hurdle is 3.3 percent. There will be skeptics of this strategy, especially those who question the returns of a hedge fund index for various reasons. However, as in the case of Hedge Fund Research, these are investable indices with underlying managers. Will the best managers be part of their programs, and will their returns diverge significantly from the actual overall market, which nobody has yet been able to measure because of all the difficulties in obtaining meaningful hedge fund performance? Only time will tell, but what we do know is that overcoming a 3 or 4 percent alpha in any asset class is an extremely arduous task over a seven-year period, especially for hedge fund categories that have more uniform returns, such as convertible arbitrage.

This chapter explained various options available to hedge fund managers, advisers, and investors to lower the tax impact of this tax-inefficient niche of investing. With the rapid growth expected for hedge fund investing in the decade ahead, there will be new and innovative tax-aware approaches worth consideration. In the meantime, investors are applying tax-aware solutions first to those niches of hedge fund investing where the alpha, or incremental return is limited, which follows the trend of traditional assets. Therefore, we should anticipate the continual evolution of "optimal," "core and satellite," or "hub and spoke" tax-aware custom hedge fund combinations to match the client's tax profile and tolerance for risk.

Chapter Notes

1. Robert N. Gordon, "Taxing Phantom Hedge Fund Profits: Here's How to Make Sure Your Clients Pay Taxes on What They Make," *On Wall Street,* August 1, 2004, http://www.keepmedia.com (accessed November 13, 2004).

2. Robert N. Gordon, "Making Hedge Funds More Tax-Efficient," *Journal of Wealth Management* (Summer 2004): 75–80.

3. Twenty-First Securities Corporation, *Newsletter* (Summer 2004).

4. Leslie C. Giordani and Amy P. Jetel, Investing in Hedge Funds Through Private Placement Life Insurance," *Journal of Investment Consulting* (Winter 2003/2004): 77–82.

5. Thomas J. Boczar and Mark Fichtenbaum, "Making Hedge Fund Investing More Tax-Efficient," *Monitor* (July/August 2004): 31–35.

CHAPTER **14**

Amending the Search Process for Tax-Aware Manager Selection

I can't make a damn thing out of this tax problem. I listen to one side and they seem right—and then I listen to talk from the other side and they seem just as right, and here I am where I started. God, what a job!

—WARREN G. HARDING

The best tool for trying to get a grasp of the various nuances of how a firm or portfolio manager, especially one who takes his fiduciary responsibility seriously, considers the impact of taxes when making investment decisions is the formal manager questionnaire. A questionnaire—or request for proposal (RFP), as it is formally referred to—should not be issued until the sponsor, consultant, or adviser has had the opportunity to determine a short list of candidates after conducting telephone or one-on-one interviews. If questions are thought out in advance, much of the information required to make informed decisions can be obtained early on in the process and should be recorded in an organized manner for future reference. Constructing an efficient questionnaire is an art form that requires experience to master. It is an extremely important part of the search process, as by the vary nature of your questions you will be establishing the expectations for the investment manager. Therefore, you should attempt to tailor your questionnaire according to the magnitude and complexity of the relationship. Also remember that the questionnaire represents your organization and client. One of the highest compliments you can receive is when a manager calls to clarify an issue and states, "After reviewing your questionnaire I now know why your firm has such an outstanding reputation in the tax-aware investment management arena!"

The questions you list should be oriented toward the specific asset class the search is focused on. This chapter offers a detailed questionnaire for a domestic equity manager search. The questions relate only to those areas where taxes come into play, as there are numerous outstanding sample questionnaires for tax-exempt accounts that can be obtained from other books and websites. So think of each question offered as a supplement to the process for a tax-exempt account. The questionnaire was developed to cover in detail the various types of taxable accounts practitioners might serve so that it would be of value to all readers. The questions are organized according to topical areas and listed in a logical progression. Do not think that you need to use every question; the complete list of questions is most likely far more than what is required, based on the magnitude and complexity of the client situation. However, tax-aware investing is emerging as an art in investing, and professionals often interpret terms quite differently. Unless you craft questions that are consistent with your manager-evaluation process, you will receive responses that will force you to spend an inordinate amount of time following up to try to get at the actual crux of the manager's process. This is especially true with how managers address the wash sale rule and execute tax-loss harvesting trades. Quite simply, use the following as a source of questions that can be cherry-picked to focus on the needs of the specific assignment.

Supplemental Tax-Related Questions for a Domestic Equity Manager Search Questionnaire

Organization

1 How many taxable accounts and assets do you manage? Please provide breakdowns for taxable and tax-exempt assets for the firm overall and for each strategy you employ.

2 What types of taxable accounts do you manage? (Check all that apply.)

    a. Individuals and families

    b. Corporate funds

    c. Nuclear decommissioning trusts

    d. Property and casualty insurance companies

    e. Medical retirement trusts or nonprofit voluntary employee benefit associations (VEBAs)

    f. Settlement trusts

    g. Other (please describe)

3 What is the average size of your taxable accounts in each category listed above?

4 What are the products your firm recommends to taxable investors and are they listed in the _____ reporting database(s)?

5 Please list the names and the primary responsibilities of all investment professionals (portfolio managers, analysts, servicing personnel, traders, etc.) that will be involved in the management of this taxable account strategy. Please also list the number of years they have served taxable accounts, the types of taxable accounts, the time spent on taxable versus tax-exempt accounts, and their unique taxable account qualifications, if any.

6 Whom does your firm utilize for security tax expertise, as it pertains to tax-aware investing?

7 Does your compensation structure include incentives for maximizing the client's after-tax return?

8 What is your normal fee schedule, and are you willing to accept a performance-oriented fee arrangement based on after-tax returns?

Philosophy

1 Explain in detail your firm's approach to taxable account management and why it is likely to produce compelling after-tax results for this particular portfolio strategy in the future.

2 What percentage of overall assets do you typically recommend a client allocate to this strategy?

3 Do you recommend this strategy as a primary allocation for the asset class, or is it most effective when coupled with other strategies that may be different in the number of securities held, style (value, core, growth), capitalization (large, mid, small, micro), sector (technology, health care, etc.), country, overlay, or other considerations?

4 If other strategies are beneficial, do you have internal offerings you recommend to complement this strategy, or do you seek the services of other firms (please name them)?

Investment Methodology

1 Does the taxable account strategy modify an existing strategy for the impact of taxes within the firm, or has the product been developed and managed since inception solely for taxable accounts (explain in detail)?

2 Do you include the effective tax rate (consideration of federal, state, local, and other tax rates) in your management for each separate account relationship?

3 Is tax efficiency improved through analysis of the tax impact as part of buy and sell decisions, or is it best described as an overlay process?

4 Please address the following elements of tax-aware investing with a detailed description of how you attempt to add value with each:
  a. Extending the holding period
  b. Depending on the level of tax on income and long-term capital gains that are in effect, income versus long-term capital gains orientation
  c. Time horizon and step-up in cost basis at the time of death
  d. Trading activity

5 When losses are present in the portfolio, do you wait for instruction by the client or do you attempt to proactively harvest them?

6 How often is each portfolio reviewed for potential tax-loss harvesting opportunities, and how can the client audit this process?

7 If you harvest a loss at your own discretion or at the direction of the client, do you ever allow the proceeds to be in cash until it is invested at least thirty days? If so, please explain when and why.

8 Do you ever "double down" on a security position by purchasing additional shares rather then harvesting the loss when it falls substantially in price? If so, please describe when you would do this and how you might attempt to minimize the tax consequences.

9 If you harvest losses and invest in something other than cash, what type of securities do you use (e.g., stocks, bonds, mutual funds, exchange-traded funds, derivatives, etc.)? Explain the challenges with future price movement and tax consequences of each.

10 Do you use any analytical tools or software programs that calculate the tax consequences of a buy-and-sell decision before it is actually conducted? If so, were they developed internally or externally, and how do you adjust them for a particular client's tax profile and for changes in the tax code?

11 For concentrated positions, do you assist in the analysis of tax-loss harvesting strategies to gradually reduce the position, exchange funds, prepay forwards, collars, etc.? If so, what are your capabilities, and what do you charge for these services? Will you monitor and make an ongoing recommendation for the concentrated stock position(s)?

12 Do you have taxable and tax-exempt accounts using the same products/strategies you offer? If so, how do you treat them differently?

13 Can you run this strategy according to socially responsible criteria? If you have experience in this area, if asked, which criteria would you recommend a client consider and why? From your experience with socially responsible accounts for this strategy, does managing the accounts by applying the designated social criteria cause returns to differ from the standard benchmark or index?

14 How much alpha do you derive from the traditional measures (sector allocation, security selection, etc.), and how much tax alpha, if any, do you believe is reasonable? (Explain in detail and highlight with numerical examples, if possible.) How would you demonstrate the value added (net of tax and fee alpha) against an appropriate benchmark, mutual fund, or exchange-traded fund on an after-tax basis over an extended period when taxes and fees are accounted for by utilizing both the pre- and post-liquidation after-return calculation methodologies?

15 Describe your risk management process and criteria, as applied to tax management.

16 What does your firm do in this strategy that you believe truly distinguishes you in taxable account management (not what you do differently from your tax-exempt account management)?

17 If you know the mandate is to maximize after-tax performance, is there anything you would do modify to your existing strategy?

Operations

1 Do your account-opening procedures incorporate applying information pertaining to the client's tax profile and reconciling security tax lots before trading is allowed to begin?

2 Who is responsible for this process, and how does this individual maintain quality control?

3 Does your portfolio accounting system have a tax-lot accounting capability?

4 How often do you reconcile tax-lot positions with the custodian(s)?

5 What is your default accounting convention?

6 Can your portfolio accounting system maintain accounting conventions other than average cost or first in, first out (e.g., high in, first out; specific lot identification)?

7 Who do you believe are the best custodians for taxable account client relationships and why?

Trading

1 Do you use any trade-processing systems or software that offers a distinct advantage with taxable accounts? If so, was it developed internally or externally, and how do you adjust it for a particular client's tax profile and future changes in the tax code?

2 Do you attempt to harvest losses depending on whether it is advantageous for a specific account or for the composite of taxable accounts within the same strategy?

3 Do you attempt to harvest losses according to each of the various platforms you manage (separate accounts, wrap accounts, commingled funds, mutual funds, etc.) or by some other method? Please address how you prioritize the process and how you handle the challenge of potentially buying a security for some accounts, while selling the same security to harvest losses in others.

After-Tax Reporting

1 If your firm claims compliance with AIMR standards, were you able to satisfy the after-tax standards for taxable separate accounts and composites in January of 2005? If not, when do you expect to be compliant with the AIMR after-tax reporting standards?

2 What systems and providers are you utilizing to supply your clients with after-tax returns?

3 Can you supply an individual client with both pre- and post-liquidation after-tax returns?

4 If your firm maintains after-tax reporting composite information, please describe the thought process the firm goes through to determine how a particular account is assigned to a composite by addressing the following:

    a. Amount of time an account is with the firm before it is entered into a composite

    b. Minimum account size

    c. Accounts with substantial cash flows

    d. Accounts inherited with substantial unrealized capital gains or low-cost-basis concentrated positions

    e. Type of taxable entity (individual, property and casualty insurance company, nuclear decommissioning trust, medical retirement trust, settlement trust, etc.)

    f. Vintage year of inception of accounts

    g. Clients' tax domicile

    h. Clients' tax profile was what level of taxation (15 percent vs. 35 percent)

5 Please attach a sample report highlighting how you present clients with after-tax returns.

6 What is your approach toward after-tax benchmarks, and which primary and secondary benchmarks do you believe are best suited for this strategy?

7 If you cannot provide after-tax reporting consistent with the AIMR standards please complete the following table for a representative account. Please attach custodial statements that were used to complete the table.

FIGURE **14.1** *Template for Estimating Account After-Tax Return*

	YEAR 1	YEAR 2	YEAR 3	YEAR 4	YEAR 5
1 % Before-Tax Return					
2 $ Beginning Market Value					
3 $ Ending Market Value					
4 $ Contributions					
5 $ Withdrawals					
6 $ Taxable Income					
7 $ Qualified Dividends					
8 $ Short-Term Gains					
9 $ Long-Term Gains					
10 $ Estimated Total Tax					
11 % Adjustment to Return $(10 / [(2 + 3 - 4 + 5) / 2])$					
12 % After-Tax Return $(1 - 11)$					

Source: Douglas S. Rogers

Please list the anticipated tax rates that were applied in row 10 for the calculation of the estimated total tax:

Taxable income	__.__ percent
Qualified dividends	__.__ percent
Short-term capital gains	__.__ percent
Long-term capital gains	__.__ percent

Account Servicing

1 Does your firm create for each taxable account an investment policy statement or similar document that incorporates the unique tax profile of the client? Are you willing to meet with other advisers initially, and as required in the future, to gain an understanding of the client's tax profile? If so, who is responsible for the process with this potential relationship and what are his or her qualifications with taxable accounts?

2 How are adjustments made to the investment policy statement when the client's tax profile changes?

3 How does the account-servicing professional ensure that analysts, portfolio managers, and traders are incorporating the client's tax profile in the decision-making process?

4 How do the clients and their advisers receive information throughout the year pertaining to realized capital gains and losses (both short- and long-term) and unrealized positions both at the portfolio and security level?

5 Will you approach the client with recommendations with regard to tax-aware investing in a proactive manner, or will you only react to the client's direction?

6 Do you offer additional services that may be beneficial to the taxable investor beyond tax-aware investment services, such as the following:

a. Accounting services
   i. Preparation of tax filings
   ii. Form 1099-DIV and Form 1040 Schedule B and D preparation
   iii. Preparation of statutory reports, e.g., Schedule D for a property and casualty insurance company
   iv. Partnership accounting
b. Legal assistance
   i. Assistance with regulatory matters
   ii. Estate planning
   iii. Trust powers, fiduciary services, and executor services
c. Custody of assets
d. Family or back-office assistance
   i. Goal setting and generational issues
   ii. Bill-paying and payroll services
   iii. Concierge services
e. Consulting or financial-planning services

7 Will you allow the client to conduct a site visit?

8 Will you provide the client with at least two taxable account references, one of which has terminated the relationship with your firm?

Oversight

1 Who has oversight responsibility beyond the assigned portfolio manager to ensure the firm is doing what is necessary to maximize the client's after-tax return?

2 What checks and balances does the firm have in place to ensure the thirty-day wash sale rule is not violated?

3 What is your philosophy toward variability of after-tax returns for taxable accounts?

4 If applicable, what do you consider to be an acceptable level of variability of returns for your before- and after-tax composite returns for the same strategy?

5 Is there a difference in the time frame for investing a tax-exempt versus taxable account for the same strategy when you start with all cash equivalents? If so, please describe your process in detail.

6 Is there a difference in the time frame for investing a tax-exempt versus taxable account for the same strategy when you inherit a portfolio of existing securities that has an unrealized capital gains position? If so, please describe your process in detail.

7 Is there a difference in the time frame for investing a tax-exempt versus taxable account for the same strategy when you inherit a portfolio of concentrated positions of low-cost-basis securities? If so, please describe your process in detail.

When you issue a questionnaire or RFP, be respectful of the time and effort required of the investment management firm to complete the document. Depending on the size and structure of the firm, there may or may not be sufficient resources in place to return a polished product in several weeks, but this type of quick turnaround should not be expected. It is best to allow firms approximately two months to complete a tax-aware questionnaire for two primary reasons. First, tax-aware investing is still a relatively new niche, and the questionnaire provokes more thoughtful answers than the standard, cookie-cutter responses given to the traditional tax-exempt account questionnaire. Second, with boutique firms, don't be surprised if a good number of the questions will be completed by the investment professionals rather than by the marketing staff. Craft each question to elicit a specific response, and make sure you are available to answer any questions the manager might have.

Unfortunately, when tax-aware investing came into vogue during the latter half of the 1990s, there were too many instances of marketing hype, with little or no underlying tax-aware principles being applied in the daily management of the strategy. With the ethical challenges we have endured in society in general over the past decade, it is simply a good business practice to insist that the firm's compliance officer or a senior professional sign off on the response, indicating it has been reviewed by others outside the marketing department, before submitting it to you. You may even wish to tailor one or several questions in a manner that will allow you to determine if the prospect is simply telling you what you want to hear rather than how the firm philosophically goes about executing a tax-aware process. In one instance in the author's past, an investment management firm even took some of the questions and included them in future marketing materials, not realizing it was signaling it really did not understand the tax ramifications of various trading strategies on after-tax total returns. Obvious flags that you should look for in the response to a questionnaire are:

❏ Incomplete answers, indicating the firm does not take the potential assignment seriously

❏ References only to the tax-exempt account philosophy, without addressing the implications of taxes

❏ Firms that have little or no taxable assets and investment professionals who spend most of their time on tax-exempt accounts

❏ Reference to "team approach" typically means standardization, which is fine for tax-exempt accounts, whereas managing taxable accounts effectively requires a high level of personal attention devoted to each relationship

❏ Immediate transitioning of accounts to the firm's model portfolio without considering substantial embedded unrealized capital gains

❏ Inexperienced servicing personnel who provide only sales support, as compared with experienced professionals who play an integral role in developing investment policy and the like

❏ Firms that construct performance composites that do not segregate taxable and tax-exempt accounts within the same strategy

As addressed in chapter 3, achieving compelling after-tax results requires time. For seasoned accounts with high levels of unrealized capital gains, the period following the assignment of a new portfolio manager can be extremely costly to the client. Therefore, the stability of the organization and its investment professionals is paramount with taxable accounts. Since many investment management firms have been sold over the past decade and others are going through cultural change, those responsible for taxable accounts may wish to include special portfolio lock-up provisions in their contracts. This is another reason in support of passive or quantitative tax-aware strategies, which reduce or eliminate the potentially costly human factor, for taxable accounts.

The questions offered above need to be modified for searches of asset classes other than domestic equities. It would be too voluminous to include a separate questionnaire for each asset class. Therefore, the following questions have been purposely limited to fixed income and international equity taxable accounts and are intended to supplement those already presented for a domestic equity manager search.

Supplemental Tax-Related Questions for a Fixed Income Taxable Account Manager Search Questionnaire

1 Please explain in detail the firm's philosophy for managing fixed income taxable account portfolios. Be sure to address if your objective is to

a. maximize after-tax total return or pay as little tax as possible

b. manage the portfolio in the context of an isolated single account or consider the interaction of multiple classes/portfolios and their overall tax ramifications

c. manage the portfolio for the best risk-adjusted return or the maximum after-tax long-term solution

2 For the municipal bond portion of the taxable account portfolio strategy:

a. Do you purchase bonds outside the state of tax domicile? If so, do you set minimum or maximum portfolio allocations to in- or out-of-state bonds?

b. Do you favor any particular bond structures (premiums, discounts, callable, zero-coupon, etc.) as they relate to the impact on after-tax returns? If so, please explain in detail.

c. What is your approach to municipal bonds subject to original issue discount (OID) and the de minimis rule?

d. What is your approach to bonds subject to the alternative minimum tax (AMT)?

3 Does your firm believe it has sufficient internal expertise to assist clients and their advisers with issues pertaining to the AMT? If so, who is the individual most qualified to address this subject and what are his or her qualifications? If not, whom do you go to for this type of expertise?

4 What is the universe of securities for your fixed income strategy for taxable accounts?

5 If you include taxable bonds in the mix, what is the process you employ to determine when they are appropriate for taxable accounts, and who is responsible for this process?

6 Are any limits imposed on the use of taxable bonds?

7 If you purchase taxable bonds, do you rely on your municipal bond team to make individual security buy and sell decisions or on your tax-exempt account bond team?

8 Does your portfolio accounting system handle amortization and accretion of bonds purchased at a premium or discount to par value in conjunction with provisions of the tax code appropriate for the types of clients that you serve? What accounting method for amortization and accretion do you apply and why?

9 Given the way you manage fixed income portfolios for taxable accounts, do you envision that the strategy's after-tax return will be greater than the after-tax return over a ten-year period of several interest rate cycles? Explain in detail why or why not.

10 Knowing that unlike the U.S. Treasury yield curve, the municipal bond yield curve has rarely inverted, how would you manage a fixed income taxable account portfolio differently from your existing strategy if you knew the time horizon was at least thirty years and the objective was to maximize long-term after-tax performance?

With fixed income searches, be extra careful in your communication and add the terms "fixed income" or "accounts" after the words "taxable" or "tax-exempt." This will avoid possible confusion, because managers tend to think in terms of the type of bond, whereas clients tend to think of the type of the account. Obviously, using the phrase "municipal bonds" eliminates potential confusion.

Supplemental Tax-Related Questions for a International Equity Taxable Account Manager Search Questionnaire

1 Do you purchase primarily American depositary receipts (ADRs) or "ordinary" shares issued in foreign countries?

2 How does your firm handle withholding of taxes on dividends of foreign company shares?

3 Is currency management part of your process? If so, is it done any differently between tax-exempt and taxable accounts to account for the impact of tax payments, and have you analyzed the impact on after-tax returns?

Questionnaires are quite helpful, but remember they are just one of the tools required to analyze a manager's potential for achieving compelling after-tax returns. For separate account investing, there is simply no excuse for not conducting a site visit. If the initial interviews and questionnaire have been done properly, the site visit should be primarily an exercise in confirming what you believe to be true. Arrange your visit in advance, and share a copy of your checklist with your host. Make sure you have the opportunity to speak with individuals from all pertinent areas of the firm. Prior to your arrival you should carefully craft several questions that you plan to ask of every department. If there is a tax-aware process in place, expect everyone you meet to know how the subject impacts their area of expertise. It is eye-opening when you receive a questionnaire back that appears to indicate the firm considers taxes in making investment decisions, yet when you interview an analyst during your site visit you hear, "I don't know what the marketing people told you, but we don't look at the impact of taxes when recommending stocks." Another curiosity is when in its response to the questionnaire the firm highlights a particular system that assists in making tax-aware decisions, and you find during the site visit that although the firm does have the system, none of the portfolio managers are actually using it. It will become obvious after you have received several questionnaires and visited the finalists that the elite tax-aware practitioners will provide consistent answers to your questions and feel honored to roll out and share their distinctive approach to tax-aware investing.

PART FOUR

CHALLENGING TRADITIONAL ASSET ALLOCATION METHODS

Don't tax you. Don't tax me.
Tax the fellow behind the tree.

—RUSSELL B. LONG

CHAPTER 15

Challenges With Traditional Investment Policy Development

Thinking is one thing no one has ever been able to tax.

—CHARLES F. KETTERING

With the great bull market of the latter half of the 1990s, many less-than-ideal practices persisted and unfortunately have become almost accepted doctrine. The high returns during this period simply masked the lack of capability of the average adviser to serve taxable investors. These shortcomings start with the creation of the investment policy statement. Firms can make tremendous strides in overcoming the sins of the past when serving taxable-account relationships by adopting the following tax-aware procedures:

1 Listing the client's assets by the tax characteristics of the investing entity

2 Obtaining and reconciling the cost basis with custodial and manager statements of each tax lot for each security and fund held by the client

3 Addressing with the client what is required to achieve an optimal, tax-aware investment solution, versus using questionnaires focused on the client's personality traits

4 Including and revising the investment policy statement for the client's current and projected tax rates

5 Applying after-tax return and standard deviations in the asset allocation process based on reasonable assumptions, versus historical, before-tax assumptions

6 Applying an asset allocation tool that is different than the firm's standard solution to address an unique client situation

7 Avoiding the use of "cookie-cutter" asset allocation options based on historical risk profiles

8 Ensuring 401(k) presentations include the need to incorporate funds outside the employer's plan in the decision-making process for optimal tax-aware positioning

9 Reviewing the magnitude of a manager's unrealized capital gains position before terminating the manager

10 Establishing appropriate minimum and maximum allocation ranges around the strategic target allocation percentage that incorporate a balance between risk management and tax efficiency

Unfortunately, many inexperienced practitioners fall short in one or more of these procedures. All too frequently, the cost to the client is so great that it far exceeds the fee the adviser charges or the value added. With item 10, you don't want to be so tax-sensitive that you fail to maintain the overall risk profile of the mix and avoid declining markets, but at the same time you don't want to be adjusting allocations to asset classes and managers/funds so frequently that you generate excessive and unnecessary short-term gains. This chapter addresses what can be done during the construction of the investment policy statement to overcome these shortfalls and provide the client with a meaningful tax-aware solution. Elements mentioned above not directly involved with the creation of the investment policy statement listed above are addressed in other chapters.

The investment policy statement serves to drive investment decisions in accordance with the desires of the client. Because of the importance of its role, the policy statement needs to include key elements of the tax-aware process that are not part of the tax-exempt account process utilized for pension plans and charitable organizations to be effective for taxable investors. The investment management process includes the following standard steps:

1 Analyze existing holdings and needs

2 Develop the investment policy statement

3 Present tax-aware allocation and positioning solutions for consideration

4 Select managers and implement

5 Monitor and revise holdings

You can easily tell people who do not have a working knowledge of taxable accounts when they reverse steps 2 and 3, which represents the procedure used to manage tax-exempt accounts. With taxable accounts, it is impossible to develop an optimal solution, unless you get there by luck, without considering the entities available for investment and the tax characteristics that apply to each. Therefore, a large portion of the investment policy statement for a taxable account should be complete before you insert the acceptable ranges for the strategic target allocation in their appropriate location in the final document.

Before work on the investment policy statement can begin, the adviser most know the current posture of all assets, both taxable and tax deferred, listed according to their respective entity. An investment entity can be personal taxable assets, a 401(k) plan, defined-benefit retirement plan, individual retirement account, education plan, insurance, various types of trusts, and so on. The entities listed should be driven by client needs. Understanding and incorporating the characteristics of each entity is essential to achieve an optimal solution that accounts for fees and taxes.

When an adviser takes on a new relationship, it is not uncommon to find the client has financial assets with more than one provider or custodian. The inventory sheet in **FIGURE 15.1** shows a format that can be used for personal taxable assets when only traditional assets are employed. The list here is limited to major, traditional asset classes, but it should be designed in a manner to accommodate the client's current asset classes and those that may be suggested to further diversify the mix, such as TIPS and the various categories of alternative investments.

Obviously, additional inventory sheets should be created for each of the entities involved. The list should be as short or as long as needed to address the client's complete financial picture. Using a Microsoft Excel

FIGURE 15.1 *Client Asset Inventory Sheet (Personal Taxable Assets)*

ASSET CLASS	PRODUCT	$ MARKET VALUE	$ COST BASIS
Cash Equivalents	_____	_____	_____
Tax-Exempt or Municipal Fixed Income	_____	_____	_____
Domestic Large Equities	_____	_____	_____
Domestic Small-/Mid-Cap Equities	_____	_____	_____
International Equities	_____	_____	_____
Real Estate (REITs)	_____	_____	_____

Source: Douglas S. Rogers

FIGURE **15.2** *Sample Holdings Report*

SECURITY	PURCHASE DATE	SHARES	PURCHASE PRICE	TOTAL COST
Company A	3/15/2004	500	$28.50	$14,250.00
	11/2/2003	300	$31.75	$9,525.00
	10/27/2003	200	$25.50	$5,100.00
	6/1/2003	400	$26.75	$10,700.00
Company B	3/23/04	300	$34.75	$10,425.00
	8/23/02	250	$57.25	$14,312.50

Source: Douglas S. Rogers

spreadsheet rather than a preprinted form is recommended, as space can be expanded or contracted to accommodate all entries with ease. To save time, an organization should construct the form using nomenclature consistent with that used in all functional areas of the firm. For example, domestic stocks can be categorized in various acceptable ways by capitalization and/or style, but it should be done consistently to avoid confusing the client by having one nomenclature for the initial questionnaire, asset allocation, and policy statement and yet another in the reporting package. Consistency with the deliverables shows that a firm has a well-thought-out process and pays attention to quality control.

One of the biggest mistakes an adviser or client can make is to allow trading to begin with a new manager before establishing the correct cost basis of each security with the custodian. A complete reconciliation of each and every tax lot should be conducted and discrepancies resolved before trading is allowed to begin. If this is not done, someone will have to spend an inordinate of time to resolve the situation later. The custodian's statement should serve as the record of choice with the manager's report serving as a backup, but this is not always the case. There are still instances today where custodians do not have tax-lot accounting. Without accurate tax-lot accounting information it is difficult, if not impossible, for the adviser to make sage recommendations that will lower the client's tax bite.

FIGURE 15.2 represents the type of information that is required for each tax lot. Before entertaining new managers for hire, a solid understanding of the potential tax consequences of terminating an existing manager

Source: Douglas S. Rogers

FIGURE **15.3** *Risk*

LOSS	GAIN REQUIRED TO RECOUP LOSS
10%	11%
25%	33%
50%	100%
75%	300%
90%	900%

needs to be established. If the existing manager has a substantial unrealized capital gains position, it may take an excessive amount of time, if ever, to break even or get ahead with the new manager. This is the same type of analysis that is conducted by elite tax-aware equity and bond managers before they sell an existing security position (see **FIGURE 11.2**).

Determining an appropriate risk profile is the most critical element of the process, as it drives the remainder of the solution. It is also the element that requires the most education and experience to do properly. Unfortunately, until clients experience a bear market, they truly do not know what their threshold is for risk or the pain of loss of wealth. The adviser should highlight at least two concepts: First, it takes far more to recoup a loss, as **FIGURE 15.3** demonstrates, than many believe. While it is easy to play "Monday morning quarterback" and point to the Internet stock bubble, the market environment of 2000 to 2002 does provide investors with some level of sobriety toward risk. Gain and loss are not symmetrical. As Figure 15.3 shows, if you lose 90 percent of your assets, it takes a 900 percent gain to break even! Whereas the loss can occur quickly, a 900 percent return typically only comes about by compounding results over several decades or more.

Second, investors fail to realize that with greater volatility, you need more return to achieve the results of more consistent performers. In **FIGURE 15.4**, there are two return series: A and B. Both achieve an average return of 10 percent over five years. However, look at the difference in dollars between series A and B at the end of the fifth year. Series B ends up with $506 less. This is captured in the geometric return, which will always be less than or equal to the average return. The more volatile the return series, the greater the geometric return will be below the arithmetic return.

FIGURE **15.4** *The Impact of Volatility on Compound Returns*

YEAR	SERIES A	$10,000	SERIES B	$10,000
1	16.0%	$11,600	20.0%	$12,000
2	18.0%	$13,688	28.0%	$15,360
3	2.0%	$13,962	−10.0%	$13,824
4	12.0%	$15,637	14.0%	$15,759
5	2.0%	$15,950	−2.0%	$15,444
Average or Arithmetic Return	10.0%		10.0%	
Geometric Return	9.8%		9.1%	

Source: Douglas S. Rogers

After-tax returns are less volatile than before-tax returns, especially when tax-aware principles are applied. This is especially true with negative returns, because you receive a credit for the loss. If tax-loss harvesting is applied, small or negative before-tax returns will be less than the after-tax returns. Therefore, if managers embrace tax-loss harvesting, they can achieve higher returns for the same level of risk identified using before-tax assumptions.

FIGURE 15.5 lists the annual total return each profile mix achieved during the twenty five year period ending 2003. During this time, interest rates rose to double-digit levels in 1981 and then gradually declined for the next twenty-two years. As a result, equities benefited from an upward drift in their valuation, as represented by higher price-to-earnings ratios. It should be no surprise that the greater the allocation to equities for a given profile mix, the greater the annual return for this analysis. The period also had meaningful volatility, as the three-year decline in the equity markets from 2000 to 2002 is second only to the experience of the Great Depression of the 1930s. It is this recent experience that has caused investors to refocus their attention on the concept of risk.

Figure 15.5 gives historical results depending on typical industry profile mixes. It is common to use four primary client profile mixes: aggressive, moderate, conservative, and risk-averse. All equity and all fixed-income profile mixes are added here for comparative purposes, but they may or may not be used in actual practice when communicating with the client. In this example, the all-equity mix is a blend by capitalization, whereas the

FIGURE **15.5** *Profile Mix Return and Risk Information*
(for the 25 years Ending 2003)

ANNUAL PROFILE MIX	STANDARD TOTAL RETURN	DEVIATION	LOW YEAR	DRAWDOWN	DOWN YEARS	SHARPE RATIO
All Equity	13.42%	16.68%	−20.41%	−41.57%	5	0.41
Aggressive	12.90%	13.66%	−14.52%	−30.66%	5	0.46
Moderate	12.25%	11.45%	−10.33%	−22.07%	4	0.49
Conservative	11.54%	9.37%	−6.11%	−12.76%	3	0.53
Risk-Averse	10.77%	7.51%	−1.87%	−7.20%	2	0.55
All Fixed-Income	8.38%	4.54%	−0.09%	−4.72%	1	0.39

Source: Douglas S. Rogers

all-fixed-income mix combines bonds and cash equivalents. In the four primary profile mixes, the equity and fixed income components are adjusted by increments of 15 percent starting with 80 percent equities for an aggressive mix. The results in the figure are derived from the quarterly return history of the S&P 500 stock, Russell 2000 stock, MSCI EAFE stock, Lehman Brothers Aggregate bond, and Citigroup three-month Treasury-bill indices. The key here is to emphasize the measurements of risk for each profile mix with the objective of the client identifying a comfort zone with one representative profile and initial level of standard deviation to begin the more detailed analysis to follow.

For those more comfortable with statistical measures, the standard deviation statistic and Sharpe ratio work well. The Sharpe ratio measures the amount of incremental return above a risk-free rate of return (U.S. Treasury bills) compared with the amount of risk taken ([return of portfolio − risk-free rate] / standard deviation). It was originally created by William F. Sharpe, the winner of the 1990 Nobel Prize in Economics, as he believes investors should only take on risk if they are amply rewarded beyond a guaranteed rate of return. As Figure 15.5 depicts, from the perspective of reward per unit of risk, the all fixed income mix is the least attractive (0.39 Sharpe ratio). The all fixed income profile mix has a 40 percent cash equivalents component, so a low Sharpe ratio is expected. Fixed income securities and cash equivalents are not as volatile as other asset classes, but they are likely to produce just a slight premium over the general rate of inflation over the long term. Adding equities to the mix does improve the trade-off between risk and return, and it is interesting to find the risk-averse mix would have been the optimal mix (0.55 Sharpe ratio) for the truly risk-sensitive investor.

Standard deviation and Sharpe ratio information is nice for analyzing risk-adjusted returns, but it does not hit at the real pain of potentially losing money. For this requirement, the low-year return, drawdown (greatest peak to trough), and number of down years are more vivid. The drawdown statistic is very commonly used in alternative-investment analysis, and is gaining a wider following. Using several different measures just increases the chance that at least one will resonate with the client, which is the ultimate goal of the education portion of the exercise.

One must be careful with risk analysis based on historical returns, because the time frame is limited. Unfortunately, meaningful benchmark information reflective of specific asset classes is only available beginning in the late 1970s. This challenge becomes even greater when TIPS or alternative investments are included as specific asset classes. Fortunately, the experiences of 2000 to 2002 for stocks, 1994 and 1999 for bonds, 1998 for hedge funds, and vintage year 1999 for private equity/venture capital allow investors to gain insight into the potential pain of a tumultuous market environment. Education pertaining to risk profiling is important because it sets the tone for all activities to follow. Additionally, many advisers do not have sufficient experience with alternative investments, and until recently young professionals have not managed through tough market environments.

Advisers often use questionnaires to help ensure a consistent approach is used across the practice with each client and to fulfill compliance requirements. Questionnaires can be excellent tools if they serve to educate the client and establish reasonable expectations, but they can be a crutch for firms that do not have qualified practitioners capable of communicating effectively with sophisticated clients. Moreover, the ultra-affluent often find questionnaires insulting, especially those that focus on personality traits. These types of questionnaires may be able to tell if the client is perhaps conservative or aggressive by nature, but they typically offer little more than entertainment value. The obvious example is an investor who is conservative by nature. An adviser following this concept will often present a mix so conservative the potential returns will be insufficient for the investor to maintain a respectable lifestyle during retirement after taking inflation, investment expenses, and taxes into account. Likewise, entrepreneurs most often take an aggressive posture in their business dealings, but after amassing their hard-earned fortunes they are most often seeking to preserve their wealth. Regardless of what type of questionnaire is used, an experienced professional still needs to step in and be able to coach the clients and at times protect them from the characteristics of their own personality.

Organizations should provide sufficient education for their staff to ensure that inexperienced individuals do not use questionnaires as a crutch when attempting to solve taxable-account scenarios with mechanical, cookie-cutter solutions solely for operational efficiency and compliance purposes. These shortcuts are typical of financial planners offering solutions based on what the client or sponsor is willing to pay. With these types of solutions you only get what you pay for. Fortunately, there are qualified practitioners within the financial planning and consulting communities that refuse to fall into this trap and do apply a knowledgeable skill set to achieve favorable results for their clients for a reasonable fee.

The following is an outline that can be used to create an investment policy statement that will incorporate the key elements of tax-aware investing.

Elements of a Tax-Aware Investment Policy Statement

1 ***Purpose or mission:*** Outline in simple terms what is to be accomplished.
2 ***Background***
   a. Source of wealth: Describe the source with the objective of showing respect—for example, corporate source of funds, family wealth, current employment, or a concentrated stock position.
   b. *Evolution of the process:* List key events and teaching points.
   c. *Education:* Address the experience of the individuals involved in the process and how education will proceed in the future. Also, highlight licensing or certification requirements, if any, to serve in certain capacities.
3 ***Responsibilities***
   a. *Client:* Be sure to describe the role of the client, depending on whether it is a discretionary or nondiscretionary platform.
   b. *Adviser/consultant:* Outline the specific services to be rendered—for example, risk profiling, investment policy development, asset allocation/location, manager search, and monitoring. Discuss interaction with the other members of the qualified triumvirate.
   c. *Accountant:* Mention how reports will be presented and the process for interacting with other members of the qualified triumvirate.
   d. *Estate attorney/trustee:* Outline authority and how recommendations are to be presented as part of the qualified triumvirate.

    e. *Custodian:* Describe how related issues will be presented and whether and how often a representative will need to be present at meetings.

    f. *Managers:* Their specific investment criteria should be listed as a separate appendix for each strategy.

    g. *Authority for the adviser to act between meetings:* A critical item that creates flexibility and trust if sufficient procedures are outlined and adhered to.

4 **Risk profile or tolerance:** Include a quantitative measure—for example, "a standard deviation of __ percent, as represented by returns achieved by a __ / __ percent blend of stocks and bonds over the __-year period from _____ to _____.

5 **Goals and return objective(s):** Discuss these net of fees and taxes, as appropriate.

6 **Strategic target allocation**

    a. *Methodology:* Include a brief statement describing the procedure and document its approval by the investor. A copy of the exercise and a note highlighting the final decision can be included as an appendix.

    b. *Strategic target allocation:* Insert a table highlighting the allocation to each asset class by entity.

    c. *Acceptable ranges and rebalancing methodology:* Use ranges that are tight enough to maintain the general risk profile but loose enough to ensure that the frequency of rebalancing does not have an overwhelming negative impact on tax efficiency. The method for calculating the bands or ranges should be explained.

    d. *Commitment of funds and approach to tactical opportunities:* If the relationship starts with a high portion of cash equivalents, determine a timetable for the commitment of funds and add it as an appendix. For taxable accounts, items like high-yield and non-hedged international fixed income assets may be tactically employed, especially if there is a tax-deferred entity available for positioning.

    e. *Frequency:* Formally review asset class assumptions annually to account for revisions to the adviser's economic and market outlook. Revisit the exercise when the input variables will cause a meaningful modification to the strategic target allocation.

7 **Constraints**

    a. *Entities*

       i. Organization: Depending on the complexity, this may include an organizational chart, especially if multiple generations are involved. The key is to highlight relationships and flow of funds.

    ii. Parameters: Discuss the tax implications, term, possibility for valuation discounts, priority of distributions, and deductibility of fees and expenses, especially with each type of trust and retirement plan.

  b. *Time horizon:* This can be discussed under each entity or by the overall relationship.

  c. *Distribution or spending policy:* This may include a discussion regarding matters like the Uniform Principal and Income Act.

  d. *Taxes:* List current federal, state, and local rates, along with any anticipated changes.

  e. *Prohibited investments or social investing criteria:* Include a listing of restricted stock due to employment relationships and any social investing criteria the client desires.

  f. *Liquidity requirements:* This can be stated quite simply as a percentage of assets or require a more elaborate plan when private equity and venture capital are involved, which may be included as an appendix.

  g. *Currency of choice:* This item is especially important with clients living outside the United States, which may require hedging various portfolios.

8 Operational

  a. *Proxy voting:* State whether the managers, the client, or a member of the qualified triumvirate will take on this task and what parameters to follow.

  b. *Trading/commissions:* Describe in detail any variation from best-execution trading practices.

  c. *Securities lending:* For large portfolios, this may be a source of funds worth discussing with the custodian.

9 Monitoring

  a. *Frequency of reports and meetings:* Quarterly meetings are the norm for large clients, but they can be less frequent with seasoned relationships. Meetings should be scheduled after quarter-end processing when detailed reports are available, unless "flash" summary reports will suffice.

  b. *Measurement*

    i. Benchmarks and peer groups: Clearly state the benchmark and peer group universe for each asset class.

    ii. After-tax reporting: Include a discussion of any other measures besides the pre-liquidation after-tax return, if required.

10 Approval: As a minimum, the client and the adviser should sign and date the investment policy statement. It may be desirable for other members of the qualified triumvirate to sign the document as well.

There is no perfect length or amount of detail for the investment policy statement. A firm may wish to have a lengthy document that it keeps on file and an executive summary that is included in the quarterly reporting materials. It is a good practice to start each meeting by asking if there is any need to consider revising the policy statement. Thus, the document should be dynamic, rather than static. Changes can be made in the original document or by listing them in an appendix. Appendices should provide the flexibility to respond to additional requirements and detail when required. For mutual funds and partnerships, there is a formal document for each investment strategy. This is not the case for separate account managers. Rather than have each adviser in the firm craft individual investment criteria for each manager position, this process should be centralized within the research staff to achieve consistency and keep the criteria where they can be easily accessed. This will save a great deal of time and again highlight the firm's organization and attention to detail.

The type of optimization tool used depends on the amount of assets and type of situation you are modeling. For example, a mean-variance optimization may be quite suitable for an ultra-high-net-worth family. With this tool, the practitioner can share with the family the range of possible outcomes over various time horizons and the probability of not meeting a desired return objective. The value of the output can be enhanced with methods like Monte Carlo simulation, where as many as a thousand iterations are modeled to provide a feel for likely outcomes. These types of solutions are becoming more prevalent as the cost of computer memory drops.

If the return goal is not met, the family may have to adjust its style of living or philanthropic activity. Another tool that incorporates asset/ liability matching is more appropriate for critical funding issues, such as for education. In this case, if the return goal is not met, the consequences are likely to be far more severe. Therefore, rather than naively applying a given software package, the adviser should first ask what tool is most appropriate for the nature of the taxable-account scenario.

In the example of the high-net-worth family, the policy statement should attempt to identify a suitable level of risk as measured by the standard deviation of returns, whereas education funding is more oriented to achieving a desired rate of return. The current yield to maturity of a government-sponsored zero-coupon bond with a maturity date equal to the time when funds will be needed eliminates reinvestment risk and provides a guaranteed principal amount. Therefore, one or more yields from zero-coupon bonds can be entered into a program or spreadsheet to determine the level of funding required.

One area that is often overlooked is the impact of rebalancing to maintain the desired strategic target allocation on the after-tax returns of taxable accounts. A minimum and maximum percentage allocation is established for each asset class in an effort to adhere to a buy low, sell high approach and control the risk of the mix in the process. Quite often, practitioners simply pull a percentage out of the air to establish the ranges without applying any serious thought to the process. The magnitude of the ranges for taxable accounts should strike a balance between maintaining a prudent risk profile and avoiding excessive movement of assets that will lead to substantial capital gains realization, especially gains that are short-term in nature. If one asset class drops far below its cost, you may want to sell the existing position and harvest the loss. In the meantime, the proceeds from the sale should be held in a suitable alternative for thirty days to avoid violating the wash sale rule. Exchange-traded funds satisfy this need well. Then this amount, along with the additional funds required to achieve the strategic target allocation, can be invested in the long-term strategy of choice.

As Jeffrey Horvitz points out in his article, "The Implications of Rebalancing the Investment Portfolio for the Taxable Investor," there is no perfect method for establishing optimal ranges or trigger points for taking action.[1] However, he also offers a method employed by tax-aware practitioners that can reduce potentially frivolous rebalancing by taking into account the projected volatility of each asset class. To accomplish this, determine a suitable multiple of the standard deviation and then multiply it by the strategic target allocation percentage—for example, 1, 1.5, or 2 times the standard deviation of each asset class. This is one area of tax-aware investing that would benefit from additional research. Unfortunately, there is no formula available to determine the optimal factor that will take into account variables such as the investor's tax profile and the time horizon. To demonstrate how this can be done, **FIGURE 15.6** was created by taking the after-tax standard deviation assumptions from chapter 16 and applying a factor of 1.5 to achieve the +/– factor or percentage that is applied to the strategic target allocation to achieve the minimum and maximum permissible percentage allocations.

The one exception where you might not apply the methodology of Figure 15.6 is with cash equivalents, because there may be a genuine need to maintain a liquidity reserve, 10 percent in the figure. So in this example, 10 percent is entered as the minimum range for cash equivalents.

Although a great deal has been written about payout or distribution policy for charitable organizations, this subject matter is less understood with high-net-worth families. The challenge with high-net-worth families is that members of the family grow exponentially with each successive generation, while the growth in assets is linear. Therefore, sometime after the original fortune has been achieved, unless family members continue to

FIGURE **15.6** *Creating the Permissible Range for Each Asset Class (1.5 + Standard Deviation)*

ASSET CLASS	AFTER-TAX STANDARD DEVIATION	STRATEGIC TARGET ALLOCATION	+/– FACTOR	MINIMUM RANGE	MAXIMUM RANGE
Domestic Equity	15.3%	45.0%	10.0%	35.0%	55.0%
International Equity	19.1%	15.0%	5.0%	10.0%	20.0%
Tax-Exempt Fixed-Income	3.5%	20.0%	2.0%	18.0%	22.0%
Real Estate (REITs)	12.0%	10.0%	2.0%	8.0%	12.0%
Cash Equivalents	0.5%	10.0%	1.0%	10.0%	11.0%
		100.0%			

Source: Douglas S. Rogers

be economically productive, they will soon significantly dilute the amount of funds available to members of successive generations. To illustrate this concept, we will use an amount equal to the current annual estate exclusion of $2 million as the initial amount of corpus. The funds are invested in a balanced mix of 65 percent large-cap domestic stocks and 35 percent fixed income securities. The historical 10.4 percent gross return for large company stocks is applied to domestic stocks, and 80 percent of the historical 5.4 percent return for intermediate governments is used to achieve a return of 4.3 percent for tax-exempt bonds.[2] Then we apply the average fee and tax-cost ratio for the respective Morningstar category to achieve net returns of 7.8 percent for common stocks and 3.2 percent for tax-exempt bonds. This results in a blended rate (net of fees and taxes) of 6.2 percent. Applying the historical rate of inflation of 3 percent leaves a real return of only 3.2 percent. Therefore, historically, if a family invested in a typical mix of mutual funds and achieved average returns, distributions had to be 3.2 percent or less each year to maintain real growth in assets. This estimate is conservative, because fees paid to the adviser, estate attorney, and accountant are not included.

FIGURE 15.7 was created using distribution rates of 3, 2, and 1 percent annually in real terms. The available amount per family member falls precipitously with the growth in the number of individuals with each successive generation (thirty years). It is no wonder you hear stories about well-known wealthy families where current generations receive only a pittance in annual financial support as compared with earlier generations, especially if those earlier generations had lavish lifestyles. By applying historical assumptions and average fee and tax-cost ratio information from Morningstar, you find you will need to distribute somewhere less than 1 percent of assets annually if you want future generations to benefit equally. The only ways to improve on this scenario are to hope for lower inflation, have a more aggressive asset mix, achieve higher returns, pay lower fees, and/or lower the tax bite. Controlling inflation is outside the control of advisers and investors. However, by utilizing after-tax assumptions in the asset allocation process, allocating asset classes and managers/funds according to the characteristics of each entity, tax-aware equity manager positioning, and identifying tax-aware managers/funds, the taxable investor can improve performance by 1.3 to 2.5 percent annually, depending on the structure of the relationship.[3]

Tax-aware managers achieve the exposure to the underlying asset class and attempt to create alpha by combining their traditional practices and tax-aware methods that lessen the tax bite or turn the strategy into a net-loss generator. Fees and taxes can both be controlled by tax-aware practitioners and their clients. For this exercise, fees and taxes amounted to 2.2 percent annually. This percentage can be reduced to as little as 0.6 percent by using lower-cost tax-efficient mutual funds or exchange-traded funds, for an improvement in net annual performance of 1.6 percent alone! Therefore, combining these savings with the other three elements of tax-aware investing can easily produce results that are consistent with the claim of a 2.5 percent annual enhancement in performance made by many tax-aware practitioners. It has only been ten years or so since these features have begun to receive the attention they deserve. The bottom line is, if families wish to maintain their financial dynasties, they need to take seriously a tax-aware approach to investing.

Managing a trust was relatively simple in the past, when all you had to do was pay out income. Previously, trusts have had two types of beneficiaries: income and principal. Often their interests were not aligned, as when one benefits it is usually to the detriment of the other. The Uniform Principal and Income Act (UPIA) allows greater flexibility with trust distributions. Perhaps this act came about because income beneficiaries were complaining about lower distributions as a result of lower yields. Fortunately, more states are amending their rules to allow for a portion of gains to be allocated as well. This change in methodology is similar to the distribution or spending policies charitable organizations adopt. The only difference is the distributions are taxable to the beneficiary. Therefore, the UPIA heightens the importance of the trustee or members of the qualified triumvirate, as now they are investing for total return with tax implications. The trustee now needs to determine what level of distribution is just. As

FIGURE **15.7** *How the Level of Distribution Affects the Wealth of Future Generations*

GENERATION	NO. OF PEOPLE LIVING	3% DISTRIBUTION ANNUAL DISTRIBUTION	$ DISTRIBUTION PER MEMBER
		$60,000	
1	2	$60,114	$30,057
2	4	$63,516	$15,879
3	8	$67,238	$8,405
4	16	$71,178	$4,449
5	32	$75,349	$2,355
6	64	$79,764	$1,246
7	128	$84,438	$660
8	256	$89,386	$349
9	512	$94,624	$185
10	1024	$100,169	$98

a result, wealthy families are now taking the time and effort to conduct elaborate after tax asset allocation and cash flow exercises to determine a payout ratio that will be equitable to both the income beneficiaries and the remaindermen. At least for the beneficiaries involved in the process, it is to their benefit that the qualified triumvirate adheres to a tax-aware process, because if they have to pay taxes on the principal distributions it is much more favorable to account for them at the long-term capital gains rate than at the short-term rate. This process just highlights how important it is to be able to work with members of the qualified triumvirate who can comprehend and apply the various facets of tax-aware investing.

The investment industry has evolved to a point where tax-aware concepts can now be applied in a more systematic and uniform manner. However, to do so requires a plan, and there is no better place to articulate what is required than in the investment policy statement. Therefore, putting forth the effort during the creation of the investment policy statement will drive the remaining tasks to ensure a tax-aware approach can be achieved.

2% DISTRIBUTION SPENDING DISTRIBUTION	$ DISTRIBUTION PER MEMBER	1% DISTRIBUTION SPENDING DISTRIBUTION	$ DISTRIBUTION PER MEMBER
$40,000		$20,000	
$40,476	$20,238	$20,438	$10,219
$57,041	$14,260	$38,307	$9,577
$81,342	$10,168	$73,373	$9,172
$115,996	$7,250	$140,535	$8,783
$165,414	$5,169	$269,177	$8,412
$235,884	$3,686	$515,573	$8,056
$336,378	$2,628	$987,511	$7,715
$479,684	$1,874	$1,891,445	$7,388
$684,042	$1,336	$3,622,812	$7,076
$975,463	$953	$6,939,014	$6,776

Source: Douglas S. Rogers

Chapter Notes

1. Jeffrey E. Horvitz, "The Implications of Rebalancing the Investment Portfolio for the Taxable Investor," *Journal of Wealth Management* (Fall 2002): 49–53.

2. Ibbotson Associates, *Stocks, Bonds, Bills and Inflation* 2003 Yearbook (Chicago: Ibbotson Associates, 2003).

3. J. Richard Joyner, "Tax-Efficient Investing: Can It Add 250 Basis Points to Returns?" *Journal of Investment Consulting* vol. 67, no. 1 (Summer 2003): 82–89.

CHAPTER 16

Developing After-Tax Asset Class Assumptions

[American tax laws] are constantly changing as our elected representatives seek new ways to ensure that whatever tax advice we receive is incorrect.

—DAVE BARRY

A t the Association for Investment Management and Research (AIMR, now the CFA Institute) convention in 2003, economist Peter L. Bernstein shared four key points that he thought represented inflection points in the investment management industry."[1] Bernstein brought to the forefront practices that have been accepted in investment policy development almost without question for the better part of thirty years. While bear markets are painful, the experience of 2000 to 2003 brought out many of the ills that Bernstein and others had been questioning for some time. His proclamation regarding the "death of the policy portfolio" could not have been better timed, as it played to a more-than-receptive audience.

Following a thought process to similar Bernstein's, William Jahnke, in his noteworthy article, "Death to the Policy Portfolio," appropriately attacks the investment consulting community for its misrepresentation of studies pertaining to the random market hypothesis and the impact of asset allocation on future returns.[2] Jahnke highlights, "There is nothing in Markowitz mean-variance optimization or in Sharpe's capital assets pricing model to indicate that the random-walk model suggests that historical returns should be used in forecasting." Additionally, clients have been told for years that the static target allocation dictates more than 90 percent of future returns, as a result of the findings presented in "Determinants of Portfolio Performance," by Brinson, Hood & Beebower (BHB).[3] While asset allocation is important, as Jahnke points out, proper interpretation of the results suggests static target allocation explains about 50 percent of the future return over a ten-year horizon. This estimate is for tax-exempt accounts, so when taxes are included, the percentage that should be attributed to static allocation should be even less. The difference between the BHB study and Jahnke's analysis is how the R^2 measurement is applied.

Ronald Surz, Dale Stevens, and Mark Wimer have pointed out that while the BHB study has been misinterpreted, a much simpler approach provides valuable insight.[4] They believe the focus should be on the magnitude of the difference in the return of the actual portfolio mix and the investment policy weighted benchmark return. An example of an actual return of 9.01 percent versus a policy return of 10.11 percent demonstrates that the investment policy portfolio represents 112 percent (10.11 / 9.01) of the performance. Since the policy portfolio return is a combination of passive portfolios, the actual portfolio mix return is a result of the three primary effects: sponsor, manager, and cost effects. For tax-exempt and taxable accounts, the first two effects are the same. However, for taxable accounts, the tax impact is an additional cost that ranges from –0.5 to –2.5 percent. If we applied the mid-range of –1.5 percent to the example above, the policy portfolio would explain 135 percent (10.11 / [9.10 – 1.50]). What this meaningful, simplistic approach highlights is how difficult it is for taxable accounts to outperform the passive policy portfolio. However, the task is not insurmountable, and in fact, informed taxable separate account practitioners can achieve a better ratio than their tax-exempt account peers. What follows in chapters 16 through 18 are solutions to common mistakes made with taxable portfolios and solutions to narrow the gap or exceed the return of the passive policy portfolio.

Unfortunately, there is a naive audience today that still believes using historical returns to calculate a static target mix without strategic adjustments is the proper method for allocating client funds. When markets are trading at valuation levels substantially different from historical averages, using historical assumptions leads to an ill-advised solution. In the spring of 2000, advisers who utilized historical returns were subjecting their clients to the greatest equity exposure ever at precisely the wrong time, because of the robust returns of the 1980s and 1990s. Reversion back to the norm or mean is a powerful force, and when things get out of line there is a natural period of correction. While the exact timing of these points is difficult to predict, these long-term events are anything but random. This is evident by the –0.85 correlation between returns of a 60 percent equity/40 percent fixed income mix calculated by Rob Arnott when comparing the previous and following ten-year periods.[5]

The strategic ingredient or element that incorporates how the world is likely to change often gets confused with tactical allocation or quick timing mechanisms. Strategic revisions are made gradually and methodically. Like taxes, financial markets and the elements that influence them change over time. History is rife with examples of military leaders failing to adjust for change while their conquerors applied one or more strategic initiatives to defeat them. To simply accept a defeatist attitude and cling to a portfolio allocation that no longer represents reality makes little sense, but it happens all too often. Unless historical returns are representative of the future, using historical returns is simply a sign the adviser or firm simply is unwilling to devote the time and energy necessary or does not have the intellectual capital to justify its fee.

Yogi Berra of the New York Yankees, the holder of ten World Series rings, supposedly said among other things, "Predicting is very difficult, especially when it involves the future." Forecasting is difficult but it should not be neglected, and when done in a rationale, systematic manner it serves the clients' best interests. For taxable accounts, forecasting should also include the expectation for changes in the tax code. Remember, Berra also said, "It ain't over 'til it's over!" The use of Yogi Berra as an example is intentional. The answers clients receive from advisers, after being subjected to returns of portfolios created from historical return assumptions during the last bear market, have had them twisting their necks and shaking their and heads just like the AFLAC duck after a session with Berra at the barbershop!

Three primary input assumptions are required for each asset class in order to conduct a mean-variance allocation optimization exercise: the projected return, the standard deviation of returns, and the correlation coefficient between each asset class. Modifying before-tax assumptions to convert them to net-of-tax-and-fee assumptions at first appears somewhat difficult, but it can be done with relative ease if a systematic approach is taken. Specific steps required include:

1 Identify suitable asset classes.
2 Determine the before-tax asset class return assumptions to include the appreciation and income components of return.
3 Calculate the client's anticipated tax profile.
4 For the appreciation component of return, estimate the capital gains realization rate for each asset class and the percentage subject to short- versus long-term capital gains treatment.
5 For the income component of return, identify the portion of income that is taxable, is a qualified dividend, or is tax-exempt.
6 Apply an appropriate fee schedule.

7 Adjust the before-tax standard-deviation assumptions for the impact of taxes.

The purpose of this chapter is to provide the most basic approach to determining after-tax asset class assumptions, so that it will apply to the widest audience possible. Thus, if a reader's current asset allocation software package does not incorporate the impact of taxes, a simple spreadsheet can be created and modified as appropriate to create the necessary input variables.

The assumptions are not intended to be static, as this would be as faulty as applying historical assumptions. It is frequently asked, "How often should asset class assumptions be revised?" They should be formally reviewed on an annual basis, as most professional certification programs include this provision in their code of ethics or similar documents. However, key economic and political events should instigate more frequent review. The economic impact of the events of September 11, 2001, and the effects of the cuts in dividend and capital gains tax rates in 2003 are just two examples of events that should have caused practitioners to go back to the drawing board and review their assumptions. Many firms satisfy this requirement with a quarterly review of asset-class assumptions by their investment policy committee. The assumptions should also be modified when clients go through a major change in their tax profile, especially those that are creeping into the alternative minimum tax zone.

1 *Identify suitable asset classes:* First, you need to determine the permissible asset classes the client wishes to consider or the list the firm desires to maintain for general purposes. The approved list should be determined during initial communication when obtaining the information necessary to construct the policy statement. There is a fine line between offering education and taking discretion over the assets. Advisers need to be careful that they do not exceed the authority inherent in their particular type of platform. The adviser may be a strong advocate of the emerging markets, but the client may be unwilling to tolerate the volatility of the asset class. As a result, the discussion should focus on these seven primary asset classes and inflation:

1. Domestic equity
2. International equity
3. Tax-exempt fixed income
4. Real estate (REITs) and other hard assets
5. Hedge funds
6. Private equity/venture capital
7. Cash equivalents
8. Inflation

Most firms maintain a more extensive list of asset class assumptions driven by the nature of their clients. Also, refinements can be made within the broader asset classes. For example, taxable bonds may be included and domestic equity can be further delineated into large- and small/mid-cap components.

2 *Determine the before-tax asset class return assumptions to include the appreciation and income components of return:* When determining asset class assumptions, it is best to familiarize yourself with the following elements:

❑ Historical returns, standard deviations, and correlation coefficients

❑ The real return premium for each asset class in excess of the historical rate of inflation (3 percent)

❑ Economic, demographic, and political trends that are likely to have a meaningful impact on future returns

❑ Projected corporate earnings

❑ Relative valuation of each asset class

❑ Projected rate of inflation

A firm can go about establishing asset class assumptions by various accepted methods that incorporate valuation techniques in a building-block method. The key is to employ a method the firm can support and its servicing personnel can easily explain to clients. The importance of establishing assumptions is such that firms generally rally the best intellectual resources to provide meaningful input into the process. For the sake of brevity, here is a very simple method to demonstrate how this can be done even with a "back of the envelope" approach.

To start the process, calculate the difference between the yield-to-maturity of a U.S. Treasury bond and the real yield of an inflation-protection ecurity of similar maturity. As of November 2004, the differential suggests inflation of 2.6 percent over the next ten years, as compared with the 3 percent average since 1926.[6] Though it is simple, this method utilizes information from those in the market who are committing significant capital based on their outlook for inflation and future interest rate levels.

The inflation assumption can be applied to achieve a projected yield-to-maturity for a municipal bond of similar maturity, for instance, five years. First, take the inflation assumption and add to it an appropriate premium above the rate of inflation. Historically, this measure has been approximately 2.4 percent. This suggests the five-year Treasury is likely to yield 5 percent (2.6% + 2.4%) in the future. Since high-grade municipal bonds typically trade at a yield of 80 percent of Treasuries, we achieve a yield estimate of 4 percent (5% × 0.80). With the current yield-to-maturity for intermediate-maturity bonds at 3 percent, the average bond in the market is trading at a significant premium to par value at 108.45 and as of December 31, 2004, had an average coupon of 5.75 percent.[7] When the average bond in the market is trading at a meaningful differential from par (100) the bond's total return projection should include an appreciation or depreciation component of return. This is especially true for advisers who rely on their asset class assumptions for client income projections. For example, at the beginning of 2005, if the client elected to receive all income then the current payout would be equal to the current average coupon of 5.75 percent, but with bonds trading well above par there would be meaningful erosion of principal. This type of exercise is especially important for high-yield corporate bond after-tax assumptions, as the tax consequences of premiums and defaults should also be taken into consideration.

One method of addressing these concerns is to calculate the average yield-to-maturity and amount of amortization or accretion of the premium or discount of the benchmark fixed income portfolio over the time horizon of the asset class assumptions, for example, ten years. To make these calculations, we must also know the remaining life or maturity of the aver-

FIGURE 16.1 *Estimating the Average Coupon*

YEAR	YTM	FLOW	AVERAGE COUPON
1	3.06%	14.79%	4.83%
2	3.16%	14.79%	4.58%
3	3.26%	14.79%	4.39%
4	3.36%	14.79%	4.24%
5	3.46%	14.79%	4.12%
6	3.55%	14.79%	4.04%
7	3.65%	14.79%	3.98%
8	3.75%	14.79%	3.95%
9	3.85%	14.79%	3.93%
10	3.95%	14.79%	3.93%
Average Coupon			**4.20%**

Source: Douglas S. Rogers

age bond in the benchmark portfolio, which in this case is 6.76 years.

In **FIGURE 16.1**, the yield-to-maturity (YTM) for each year is the average versus the beginning or ending YTM. By taking into account the gradual adjustment in the benchmark's average coupon, we can estimate the average coupon flow (4.20 percent). Next we calculate the annual adjustment in price. In the example, bonds are priced at a premium to par value, so the average annual amortization will offset the average coupon amount just calculated to achieve an estimate of average total return (see **FIGURE 16.2**).

When we sum the average coupon (4.20 percent) and impact of amortization for bonds trading at a premium to par value (–0.81 percent), we reach an estimated annual total return of 3.39 percent.

Jeremy Siegel points out that on average, stocks have historically traded at 14.8 times earnings, and when you take the inverse of this number you come up with 6.8 percent, which is close to the real return premium for domestic stocks.[8] As of November 2004, the price-to-earnings ratio based on operating earnings is approximately 18 ($1,185 / $65.75). Therefore, the current estimate of the real return premium for domestic stocks is 5.5 percent by this approach. Since our estimate for inflation is 2.6 percent,

FIGURE **16.2** *Calculating Annual Change in Price Premium*

YEAR	AMORTIZATION	FLOW	AVERAGE PRICE	PRICE CHANGE
1	1.25	14.79%	106.13	–2.32
2	0.91	14.79%	104.45	–1.68
3	0.66	14.79%	103.23	–1.22
4	0.48	14.79%	102.35	–0.89
5	0.35	14.79%	101.70	–0.64
6	0.25	14.79%	101.24	–0.47
7	0.18	14.79%	100.90	–0.34
8	0.13	14.79%	100.65	–0.25
9	0.10	14.79%	100.47	–0.18
10	0.07	14.79%	100.34	–0.13
Average Amortization (–) or Accretion (+)				**–0.81%**

Source: Douglas S. Rogers

FIGURE **16.3** *Components of Return*

ASSET CLASS	BEFORE-TAX RETURN	APPRECIATION	INCOME
Domestic Equity	8.1%	6.1%	2.0%
International Equity	8.3%	6.8%	1.5%
Tax-Exempt Fixed-Income	3.4%	−0.8%	4.2%
Real Estate (REITs)	7.0%	3.3%	3.7%
Hedge Funds	9.0%	6.5%	2.5%
Private Equity/Venture Capital	13.0%	13.0%	0.0%
Cash Equivalents	2.4%	0.0%	2.4%
Inflation	2.6%		

Source: Douglas S. Rogers

the nominal return estimate for domestic common stocks is 8.1 percent. Returns for the remaining asset classes can be derived based on their current valuation relative to these two primary asset classes. For example, at this juncture, REITs are priced at an even higher premium than domestic equities and should be awarded an appropriate discount. **FIGURE 16.3** lists the assumptions that will be employed throughout the remainder of the chapter.

The key is to educate clients and manage the expectation of what the future is likely to bring and how best to position their overall mix of assets. Along with the total return, the appreciation and income components of return are given in Figure 16.3. This is necessary, because our tax code has different tax rates that apply to the various types of appreciation and income. As was shown with tax-exempt income, the income component should represent the average of the period rather than what is currently available in the market. There is no single time period for the analysis that is perfect. This exercise assumes a ten-year projection. The time horizon of the analysis should be established according to the needs of the client. An appropriate time horizon for a nuclear decommissioning trust may be twenty-five to forty years, whereas for a retiree it may be much shorter.

3 *Calculate the client's anticipated tax profile:* Before we begin analyzing the impact of taxes on the before-tax return assumptions, we need to develop the anticipated tax rate profile of the client. In this example, our client is subject to the maximum federal tax rates (35 percent), a 5 percent state tax, and a 1 percent local tax. Using the formula for anticipated tax rates from chapter 7, we obtain the following rates:

Ordinary income and short-term capital gains	38.9%
Qualified dividends	20.1%
Long-term capital gains	18.9%

These tax rates are applied when appropriate to achieve the after-tax returns. The example shows tax rates for 2004. However, to be consistent with the method used to determine asset class assumptions, it is also a worthwhile exercise to consider applying a forward-looking element to the client's average projected tax profile. For example, as of this writing, ordinary income, stock dividend, and capital gains tax rates are at the lowest levels ever in the post–World War II era. However, with large budget deficits, many believe tax levels will revert back to the 39.6 percent rate on ordinary income and 20 percent rate on capital gains for wealthy individuals. Therefore, you could use blended rates for the federal tax on ordinary income of 37.3 percent ([35% + 39.6%] / 2) on ordinary income, 17.5 percent on long-term capital gains ([15% + 20%] / 2) and 27.3 percent ([15% + 39.6%] / 2) on common stock dividends, if so desired. Similar analysis can be applied to state and local tax rates as well.

   4 *For the appreciation component of return, estimate the capital gains realization rate for each asset class and the percentage subject to short- versus long-term capital gains treatment:* For the appreciation component of return, there are two factors that influence the impact of taxes. First is the capital gains realization rate (CGRR). For this exercise only, the CGRR is defined as the percentage of the appreciation component of return that generates a taxable event. This should not be confused with the portfolio turnover rate, which is best suited for measuring transaction or commission costs versus tax implications. The CGRR might also be called the net taxable turnover, and some practitioners call it the effective turnover. The next step is to take into account the percentage of short- versus long-term capital gains. From this information, the tax impact for the appreciation component of return can be calculated for each asset class, as **FIGURE 16.4** shows.

   The CGRR is shown here purposely as a negative value. The negative sign is appropriate if the managers being considered have after-tax returns lower than their before-tax returns, which is typically the case. However, quantitative tax-aware equity managers discussed in chapter 10 and municipal bond managers who emphasize tax-loss harvesting do generate preliquidation after-tax returns greater than their before-tax returns. When employing these types of tax-aware managers, the CGRR percentage can be a positive entry as high as +5 percent to +15 percent, depending on the

FIGURE **16.4** *Estimating the Tax Impact of the Appreciation Component of Return*

ASSET CLASS	APPRECIATION	CGRR	SHORT-TERM	LONG-TERM	TAX
Domestic Equity	6.1%	–20%	25%	75%	–0.3%
International Equity	6.8%	–20%	25%	75%	–0.3%
Tax-Exempt Fixed-Income	-0.8%	–2%	10%	90%	0.0%
Real Estate (REITs)	3.3%	–20%	25%	75%	–0.2%
Hedge Funds	6.5%	–80%	80%	20%	–1.8%
Private Equity/ Venture Capital	13.0%	–0%	0%	100%	–0.2%
Cash Equivalents	0.0%	–100%	100%	0%	0.0%

time horizon of the exercise. As discussed in chapter 11, tax-loss harvesting is most productive during the early years of an account relationship that is funded with cash. Therefore, the longer the time horizon, the lower the percentage should be for this positive contribution to the portfolio mix. Some firms even list these managers as separate asset classes to determine an appropriate equity "core and satellite" allocation.

5 *For the income component of return, identify the portion of income that is taxable, is a qualified dividend, or is tax-exempt:* The tax calculation for the income component of return is relatively straightforward but subject to three different tax rates, as shown in **FIGURE 16.5**. If the client is also subject to the alternative minimum tax, additional adjustments may be necessary.

The area that is least specific is the percentage of REIT and international stock dividends eligible for qualified dividend tax treatment at the more favorable 15 percent rate. Coordinating with managers and calling company treasurers are sometimes necessary to acquire this information.

6 *Apply an appropriate fee schedule:* Now that the tax consequences from both components of return are calculated, fees can be included to derive the returns after taxes and fees for each asset class (see **FIGURE 16.6**).

The fee estimates shown above are for separate account managers, and for partnerships in the case of hedge funds and private equity/venture capital. In this example, a conservative approach was taken by assuming the

FIGURE **16.5** *Estimating the Tax Impact of the Income Component of Return*

ASSET CLASS	INCOME	ORDINARY INCOME	QUALIFIED DIVIDENDS	TAX-EXEMPT INCOME	TAX
Domestic Equity	2.0%	0%	100%	0%	−0.4%
International Equity	1.5%	10%	90%	0%	−0.3%
Tax-Exempt Fixed-Income	4.2%	0%	0%	100%	0.0%
Real Estate (REITs)	3.7%	90%	10%	0%	−1.4%
Hedge Funds	2.5%	80%	20%	0%	−0.9%
Private Equity/ Venture Capital	0.0%	0%	100%	0%	0.0%
Cash Equivalents	2.4%	100%	0%	0%	−0.9%

Source: Douglas S. Rogers

fees were not deductible for tax purposes. When using mutual funds and modeling for certain trust structures, fees may be offset against income and should be accounted for appropriately in the process. In the case of mutual funds, you can forgo the fee analysis and simply conduct the exercise net of fees, which is the method for reporting mutual fund before- and after-tax returns.

Each estimate should be representative of the types of separate account managers, funds, and partnerships the client is likely to hold. You may wish to apply a uniform fee for each asset class—say, for example, if you are charging an all-in fee arrangement that would be representative of a wrap provider, which on average is 1.75 percent. If a consultant is employed, you may also wish to add that fee to the manager fee for each asset class.

One area that is a bit challenging is estimating fees for hedge funds and private equity/venture capital partnerships. The typical structure of 1 percent of assets and 20 percent of profits above a hurdle rate causes a substantial difference between gross and net results even before considering the impact of taxes, and the additional 1 percent of assets and 10 percent of profits charged by a fund of funds only adds to the complexity of the calculation.

7 *Adjust the before-tax standard deviation assumptions for the impact of taxes:* Many firms start the process by taking historical standard

FIGURE **16.6** *Return Assumptions After Fees and Taxes*

ASSET CLASS	BEFORE-TAX RETURN	TOTAL TAX	AFTER-TAX RETURN	FEES	RETURN AFTER FEES AND TAXES
Domestic Equity	8.1%	−0.7%	7.4%	0.60%	7.5%
International Equity	8.3%	−0.7%	7.6%	0.70%	7.6%
Tax-Exempt Fixed-Income	3.4%	0.0%	3.4%	0.30%	3.1%
Real Estate (REITs)	7.0%	−1.5%	5.5%	0.70%	6.3%
Hedge Funds	9.0%	−2.7%	6.3%	2.10%	6.9%
Private Equity/ Venture Capital	13.0%	−0.2%	12.8%	2.90%	10.1%
Cash Equivalents	2.4%	−0.9%	1.5%	0.20%	2.2%

Source: Douglas S. Rogers

deviations and adjusting them slightly for trends in the market. For example, most recently, domestic stock returns have been less volatile than their historical average. If the adviser believes this will be a persistent trend, then an appropriate adjustment is in order. With after-tax returns, it is assumed that taxes are paid quarterly, since this type of analysis typically applies to clients filing quarterly estimated taxes. Therefore, you can review quarterly returns and focus on the variation in the appreciation component of return to come up with a reasonable adjustment factor. After-tax standard deviations are lower than their before-tax counterparts, because with appreciation, taxes are paid on realized gains and credits accumulate from realized losses. This leads to a smoother, less volatile return stream. For equities there is about a 10 percent haircut, or reduction in volatility. With taxable bonds and some hedge fund strategies, the tax haircut approaches the tax rate, since the majority of the return is taxable (see **FIGURE 16.7**).

Last, to have all the information necessary to conduct the optimization exercise, correlation coefficients between the asset classes are required (see **FIGURE 16.8**). This is the one area where there really is no need to make an adjustment, because the tax impact causes only minute differences between before- and after-tax assumptions. As a result, most firms that use after-tax assumptions simply rely on their before-tax correlation coefficient assumptions.

FIGURE **16.7** *Standard Deviation Assumptions After Fees and Taxes*

ASSET CLASS	BEFORE-TAX STANDARD DEVIATION	STANDARD DEVIATION ADJUSTMENT	AFTER-TAX STANDARD DEVIATION
Domestic Equity	17.0%	90%	15.3%
International Equity	20.5%	93%	19.1%
Tax-Exempt Fixed Income	3.6%	98%	3.5%
Real Estate (REITs)	16.0%	75%	12.0%
Hedge Funds	8.0%	70%	5.6%
Private Equity/ Venture Capital	32.0%	95%	30.4%
Cash Equivalents	0.5%	95%	0.5%

Source: Douglas S. Rogers

As with any optimization, reasonable constraints must be put in place for each asset class to prevent a "corner solution." A corner solution occurs when the optimizer selects a preponderance of one or two asset classes that simply do not represent a prudent recommendation. This can easily happen when hedge funds are included in the mix, because of their low volatility and correlations with other asset classes. Always remember that the exercise should be based on what is reasonable, as this is an art form rather than an exact science.

Once you run the optimization with after-tax asset allocation assumptions, you are likely to face three outcomes. First, since after-tax return and standard deviation assumptions are lower than their before-tax counterparts, you should expect the efficient frontier to slope down and to the left (see **FIGURE 16.9**).

Second, the after-tax portfolio will shift from tax-inefficient hedge funds to more tax-efficient private equity/venture capital, as compared with the normal before-tax mix. This is why consultants in the high-net-worth arena often recommend a higher percentage of tax-inefficient non-directional strategies in foundations and less tax-onerous long/short equity strategies for their families' taxable account hedge fund requirements.

If you adhere to the concept of speaking to clients in terms of before-tax volatility or standard deviation, the optimal after-tax solution will

FIGURE **16.8** *Correlation Coefficients*

	Asset Class	1	2	3	4	5	6	7
1	Domestic Large-Cap Equity	1.00	0.76	0.14	−0.15	0.55	0.78	−0.16
2	International Equity		1.00	0.22	0.27	0.53	0.70	−0.28
3	Tax-Exempt Fixed Income			1.00	0.12	0.29	0.12	−0.13
4	Real Estate (REITs)				1.00	0.31	0.58	−0.19
5	Hedge Funds					1.00	0.52	−0.20
6	Private Equity/Venture Capital						1.00	−0.22
7	Cash Equivalents							1.00

most likely include more equity and fewer bonds than the before-tax mix. This occurs because you attempt to target the same level of risk by applying less-volatile after-tax standard deviation assumptions, as Figure 16.7 indicates. Therefore, third and last, when you compare efficient mixes for the after-tax and before-tax solutions, the after-tax efficient mix generates a superior solution on an after-tax return basis for the equivalent level of risk. The amount of the value added typically ranges from 0 percent to perhaps as high as 0.7 percent, depending on the return assumptions and the mix of permissible asset classes.

When properly applied, use of after-tax assumptions in the asset class optimization process is one of the four key elements in the consultative process that can lead to superior after-tax results. The discussion here was purposely maintained at a basic level so that when practitioners encounter sophisticated allocation software incorporating taxes, they will be familiar enough with the approach and terminology to make informed decisions. More important, software applications have their strengths and limitations, and tax-aware practitioners need to have the experience to ensure quantitative tools are being properly employed to the benefit of clients with taxable accounts.

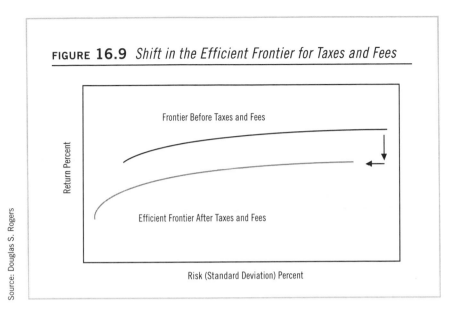

FIGURE **16.9** *Shift in the Efficient Frontier for Taxes and Fees*

Source: Douglas S. Rogers

Chapter Notes

1. Peter L. Bernstein, "Overview: A Fifth Point of Inflection," *Points of Inflection: New Directions for Portfolio Management,* CFA Institute Conference Proceedings, 2004, 1–5.

2. William Jahnke, "Death to the Policy Portfolio," in *The Investment Think Tank: Theory, Strategy and Practice for Advisers,* edited by Harold Evensky and Deena B. Katz (Princeton, NJ: Bloomberg Press, 2004), 17–37.

3. Gary L. Brinson, Randolph Hood, and Gary L. Beebower, "Determinants of Portfolio Performance," *Financial Analyst Journal* (July/August 1986).

4. Ronald J. Surz, Dale Stevens, and Mark Wimer, "The Importance of Investment Policy," *Journal of Investing* (Winter 1999): 1–6.

5. Robert D. Arnott, "Editor's Corner," *Financial Analysts Journal* (September/October 2004): 6–9.

6. Ibbotson Associates, *Stocks, Bonds, Bills and Inflation 2003 Yearbook* (Chicago: Ibbotson Associates, 2003).

7. Weighted average of Lehman Municipal Bond one-, three-, five-, seven-, and ten-year index information.

8. Jeremy J. Siegel, "The Long-Run Equity Risk Premium," *Points of Inflection: New Directions for Portfolio Management,* CFA Institute Conference Proceedings, 2004, 53–62.

CHAPTER 17

Why the Style Box Hurts Taxable Investors

Because of the income tax, a penny saved is more than a penny earned.

—Jeffery L. Yablon

The schematic that we investment professionals are introduced to during our formative years categorizes equity managers according to the average market capitalization of common stocks in the model portfolio and the style methodology employed to select them.[1] Employing multiple equity managers for taxable clients according to this process leads to nothing more than "overpriced entertainment," as suggested by David Stein of Parametric Portfolio Associates.[2] Unfortunately, trading by portfolio managers to maintain capitalization and style purity leads to premature and unnecessary realization of capital gains. Additionally, when an excessive number of managers are employed, the managers tend to come in at the high end of their individual fee schedules rather than allowing access to sliding-scale volume discounts when just a few managers are utilized. For taxable accounts, when it comes to determining the optimal number of equity managers, the rule of thumb is "Less is better than more!"

Concrete guidelines for segmenting common stocks according to market capitalization do not exist; more precisely, they differ from provider to provider. The mean and median market capitalization can be quite different. For example, the S&P 500 stock index currently has a mean market capitalization of $90 billion, as compared with a median of $10 billion.

FIGURE **17.1** *Traditional Equity Manager Style/Capitalization Grid*

	Value	Core	Growth
Large			
Middle			
Small			

Source: Douglas S. Rogers

The mean market capitalization in the Russell 1000, MidCap, and 2000 indices are $80.2 billion, $6.2 billion, and $0.9 billion, respectively for the large-, middle-, and small-capitalization segments of the domestic stock market. These values can shift dramatically, depending on the average price-to-earnings ratio of stocks and investment banking activity.[3] Corporate transactions involving initial public offerings, companies going private, mergers, and takeovers influence the composition of the various market indices.

Attempting to categorize and benchmark managers according to their purchase and sale methodology can be challenging, as managers may employ eclectic approaches. Managers selecting stocks with a growth orientation typically seek companies with superior earnings growth and correspondingly high price-to-earnings (P/E) or price-to-book (P/B) ratios. On the other hand, value managers attempt to identify stocks that are trading at a discount to others and typically have a lower P/E or P/B multiple than the overall market. A "core" or a "blend" strategy simply combines elements of both the value and growth stock-selection methodologies.

FIGURE 17.1 illustrates the traditional equity style/capitalization grid.

Over the years, the tax-exempt-account consulting industry has emphasized style/capitalization purity to create a high degree of focus and specialization, as there is an accepted belief this eliminates overlap and creates the most potential for superior returns. It is taken so seriously that managers are often terminated if they drift too far away from their perceived category. While this may benefit tax-exempt account investors, it works to the detriment of the taxable investor.

The frictional costs to taxable investors come in three ways. The first cost associated with maintaining style purity is the cost of trading. The other two costs are far more significant and involve the payment of taxes on realized capital gains. This occurs when a security must be sold, because a change in price causes the P/E or P/B ratio or the capitalization of a security to be inconsistent with the manager's style or capitalization designation.

To highlight the cost of rigid style adherence, we will investigate the capital gains realization history of several Vanguard index funds. The funds used in this exercise are intended to demonstrate teaching points and not to suggest a recommendation for or against their purchase in the future. Since we are applying information from mutual funds, the costs presented should be considered as the most conservative way to estimate what investors on average are likely to experience. With the exception of redemption activity, the only time stocks in the portfolio are sold is when the index is adjusted, or "reconstituted." There is another event that can cause a taxable transaction: the merger of two firms conducted on a cash basis, versus an exchange of shares. Therefore, the costs involved are in most cases far lower than would be the case if active managers were employed. Mutual fund capital gains generation information is taken from Morningstar Principia to highlight how easily this type of analysis can be done.[4]

First, we will examine the impact that adherence to market capitalization parameters has on generating capital gains and taxes. The challenge occurs when the sponsor reconstitutes the indices and eliminates the most successful stocks in small- and mid-cap portfolios. To maintain the integrity of the index portfolio, the manager sells stocks, which usually results in substantial gains. When small- and mid-cap stocks rise rapidly in capitalization, as with technology issues during the latter half of the 1990s, the indices have the potential to produce short-term capital gains that are taxed at the higher rates for ordinary income. This challenge is not a factor with large-cap portfolios, as there is no need to remove a long-term consistent growth stock, such as General Electric. Therefore, we should expect both small- and mid-cap index portfolios to generate meaningful capital gains in order to maintain desired market capitalization criteria. The cost of this phenomenon is shown in **FIGURE 17.2** using information taken from Morningstar Investment Detail Reports for the Vanguard 500, Mid-Cap, and Small-Cap index funds. All capital gains distributions have been adjusted to reflect a $100 investment at the beginning of the year.

FIGURE **17.2** *Impact of Capitalization on Capital Gains Realization Distribution per $100 Investment*

VANGUARD FUND/BENCHMARK	1999	2000	2001	2002	2003	AVERAGE
500 Index/S&P 500 Index	$0.88	$0.00	$0.00	$0.00	$0.00	$0.18
Mid-Cap Index/S&P MidCap 400 Index	$8.71	$8.68	$2.05	$1.10	$0.00	$4.11
Small-Cap Index/ Russell 2000 Index	$9.81	$12.80	$0.00	$0.00	$0.00	$4.52

Source: Morningstar, Douglas S. Rogers

FIGURE **17.3** *Weighted Blend Capital Gains Realization Versus Total Market Distribution per $100 Investment*

VANGUARD FUND/BENCHMARK	1999	2000	2001	2002	2003	AVERAGE
70% Large/20% Middle/ 10% Small/S&P500, S&P400 & Russell 2000	$3.34	$3.02	$0.41	$0.22	$0.00	$1.40
100% Total Market Stock Market Index/ Wilshire 5000 Index	$1.29	$0.42	$0.00	$0.00	$0.00	$0.34

Source: Morningstar, Douglas S. Rogers

Five years of information is shown, as the Vanguard Mid-Cap Index Fund began in May 1998. More important, using an average of the five years gives a more accurate portrayal of what to expect in any one year, as the bull market up to the spring of 2000 had a much greater impact on capital gains generation when compared with the bear market that followed. As expected, adherence to market capitalization parameters has a tremendous tax impact with small- and mid-cap index portfolios. From a tax standpoint alone, it is reasonable to lump small and middle capitalization together to create a small/middle-capitalization category. A typical equity allocation—or in this case, a fund allocation—of 70 percent 500 Index, 20 percent Mid-Cap Index, and 10 percent Small-Cap Index with the resulting capital gains is compared with the Vanguard Total Stock

FIGURE **17.4** *Impact of Style on Capital Gains*
Realization Distribution per $100 Investment

VANGUARD FUND/BENCHMARK	1999	2000	2001	2002	2003	AVERAGE
Value/S&P 500/ Barra Value Index	$8.71	$4.28	$4.29	$0.00	$0.00	$3.45
Growth/S&P 500/ Barra Growth Index	$3.28	$0.00	$0.00	$0.00	$0.00	$0.66
Small-Cap Value/ S&P SmallCap 600/ Barra Value Index	$5.72	$5.92	$5.70	$2.62	$0.00	$3.99
Small-Cap Growth/ S&P SmallCap 600/ Barra Growth Index	$0.00	$5.01	$0.00	$0.00	$0.00	$1.00

Source: Morningstar, Douglas S. Rogers

Market Index Fund, which attempts to replicate the overall domestic equity market (see **FIGURE 17.3**).

The capital gains distribution of the traditional blend that consultants and advisers for tax-exempt accounts use to construct client portfolios results in more than four times the amount of capital gains generation that holding the market portfolio, as represented by the Vanguard Total Stock Market Index Fund! It should be noted that the two examples represent a best-case scenario, because the primary source of capital gains realization is from trading activity conducted as a result of reconstituting the underlying index of the funds. With active management, the comparative results would most likely be far more dramatic, since managers would have additional trading activity when selling less attractive stocks for those they believe will offer superior returns in the future.

The second factor pertains to the trading activity required to maintain a particular buy-and-sell stock methodology or style that results in undesirable capital gains and taxes. In the following example, we will analyze results from Vanguard's value and growth style index funds (see **FIGURE 17.4**).

Caution should be taken in comparing the results of the style indices by capitalization, because the large-cap funds (1992) were created six years before the small-cap series (1998). Therefore, they had more time to accumulate an unrealized capital gain position. However, what the funds do show is that buy-and-hold growth is more tax-efficient when measured by the dollar amount of capital gains generated by a factor of approximately 4 to 1. For this period of analysis, Vanguard employed the index information from S&P 500/Barra, but it has recently switched to a new methodology created by Morgan Stanley Capital International.[5] Barra categorizes stocks as being value or growth according to their relative P/B ratio, as studies have demonstrated that this measure is more stable than the P/E ratio.[6] When indices are reconstituted, stocks sold from a value index portfolio are likely to have appreciated significantly, causing the realization of meaningful dollar amounts of capital gains. From a tax view, even with index funds, the value-stock selection methodology represents more of a trading strategy rather than a buy-and-hold proposition that will allow capital gains to compound tax-free until realized. On the other hand, a stock removed from a growth index is likely to have been experiencing a declining price and may have minimal appreciation, or possibly even be sold at a loss. When losses occur with taxable accounts, or in this example an index fund portfolio, they offer economic value because they will ultimately be used to offset a portion of realized capital gains.

Another factor that has contributed to lower tax efficiency for value-oriented portfolios is that dividends were taxed at the ordinary income rate before 2003.

FIGURE 17.5 shows that the value style consistently has a higher payout

FIGURE **17.5** *Income of Style of Benchmark Style Funds Distribution per $100 Investment*

VANGUARD FUND/BENCHMARK	1999	2000	2001	2002	2003	AVERAGE	FEE
Value/S&P 500/ Barra Value Index	$1.60	$1.57	$1.40	$1.69	$2.53	$1.76	$0.23
Growth/S&P 500/ Barra Growth Index	$0.73	$0.33	$0.62	$0.87	$0.90	$0.69	$0.23
Small-Cap Value/ S&P SmallCap 600/ Barra Value Index	$0.80	$0.95	$0.73	$0.87	$2.35	$1.14	$0.27
Small-Cap Growth/ S&P SmallCap 600/ Barra Growth Index	$0.42	$0.00	$0.18	$0.28	$0.00	$0.18	$0.27

Source: Morningstar, Douglas S. Rogers

in dividends, as expected. Using 2002 as an example, for every $100 invested, an investor subject to the maximum federal tax rate (38.6 percent) would have paid $0.65 ($1.69 × 38.6%) in taxes for dividends distributed from the Value Index Fund, as compared with $0.34 ($0.87 × 38.6%) for the Growth Index Fund. Many separate account investors cannot offset fees against taxable income when filing their tax return. Therefore, to gain an accurate portrayal of the tax impact of dividends from the information in Figure 17.5, they need to add back the fee to find the gross dividend yield. So in the last column, the fee or cost per $100 invested is shown for each Vanguard fund. During this five-year period, the expenses for any of the funds shown did not vary by any more than $0.01. A separate account mirroring the Vanguard Value Fund would have had a gross yield of $1.92 ($1.69 + $0.23). Therefore, for separate accounts holding the index portfolio, the difference in tax payments for the value and growth styles would be $0.74 ($1.92 × 38.6%) and $0.42 ($1.10 × 38.6%), respectively. As you can see, if the fee for separate account management was not substantially lower, the mutual fund format may offer the taxable investor an advantage from a tax standpoint, but the separate account format does have an advantage of protecting investors from the adverse impact of shareholder redemption activity.

Combining the impact of portfolio rebalancing and dividend yield dampens the value style's after-tax returns.[7] Therefore, growth-oriented index portfolios are inherently more tax-efficient than those with a value orientation. An exception to this general rule is corporate accounts, which benefit from the exclusion of 70 percent of their dividend income from taxation. In these cases, stocks that pay higher dividends, like preferreds, may offer superior after-tax returns.

The dilemma with the traditional style matrix can be solved in one of two ways. The first method, for separate accounts, is to employ a structure other than the traditional three-by-three matrix. The second method, which pertains to mutual funds, is to utilize a fund vehicle that is not victimized by capitalization gains generation from periodic reconstitution.

There are several equity allocation models that consultants and investors who manage taxable assets can employ to lessen unnecessary capital gains generation and payment of taxes. First, let's examine modifications to the traditional three-by-three matrix. A logical evolution is the "modified traditional" model. In this model, the core and mid-cap manager positions are eliminated. Additionally, small-cap managers are allowed to hold their winners longer by taking on a small/mid-cap mandate, and large-cap managers are allowed to dip down in market capitalization with perhaps as much 20 percent of assets.

The obvious intention of the modified traditional model is to reduce capitalization- and style-oriented trading and lessen the drag on after-tax performance. However, for large portfolios where separate account managers are employed, there is an additional benefit. A reduction in the number of separate account managers from perhaps nine to four will most likely lead to lower overall management fees, which is also a form of tax. This process works best with elite tax-aware managers, especially for the large-capitalization value and growth mandates. One procedure the consultant or sponsor can employ while serving as the quarterback of the process is to suggest a transfer of stock that has risen in capitalization from a small/mid-cap manager for an equal dollar amount of cash from a large-cap manager. This assumes that the large-cap manager finds the stock of the company in question to be a purchase or long-term hold candidate and has cash available. The modified traditional model is appropriate for clients who wish to have the opportunity to potentially outperform an index portfolio on an after-tax basis and are not comfortable with a quantitative tax-aware approach to equity management.

A compelling alternative to the modified traditional approach described above is the "all-capitalization/style-specific" model (see **FIGURE 17.6**). With this model, the portfolio manager is allowed to select stocks according to his particular style (value or growth) from a complete universe of securities, which may be represented, for example, by the Russell 3000 or the Wilshire 5000 stock indices. There are very few active managers that offer all-capitalization value or growth products. With the adoption of the traditional equity allocation model over the past thirty years or so, firms gradually dropped these products and focused on style/capitalization-specific strategies. However, with growing interest in tax-aware investing, all-capitalization/style-specific portfolios are experiencing a renaissance with informed investors and advisers. The advantage of the

FIGURE 17.6 *Modifications to the Traditional 3 x 3 Matrix*

	Modified Traditional			All-Capitalization/Style-Specific		
	Value	Core	Growth	Value	Core	Growth
Large						
Middle						

Source: Douglas S. Rogers

all-capitalization/style-specific model is that it allows investment analysts and portfolio managers to take a long-term approach to investing, since they are not forced to sell small- and mid-cap stocks that have had significant appreciation if they still believe it is beneficial to hold them. The worst thing that can happen with the all-capitalization/style-specific model is, for example, if the growth manager sells a company's stock at a short-term loss and the value manager purchases it within thirty days, negating the benefit of the loss sale. It is critical that the consultant or sponsor ensures that timely communication between the two managers is maintained for all trading activity that results in losses. This is often done by facsimile or, even better, by e-mail before the trade being considered is actually executed.

The next type of structure involves using a quantitative tax-aware portfolio strategy or coupling it with less tax-efficient products. These strategies, covered in detail in chapter 10, emphasize constructing a portfolio to replicate the before-tax performance of a designated stock index and then actively trading to generate net losses that can offset gains in other portfolios. It is extremely difficult to manage small portfolios profitably in a tax-aware manner, since taking taxes into account is likely to result in a more labor-intensive process. Thus, the all-capitalization/all-style, or "whole stock" model is especially beneficial for separate account assignments with a total equity allocation from $500,000 to $3 million or greater.[8] Perhaps one of the exciting developments on the horizon for taxable accounts is the creation of the all-capitalization/all-style tax-aware global equity portfolio (see **FIGURE 17.7**).

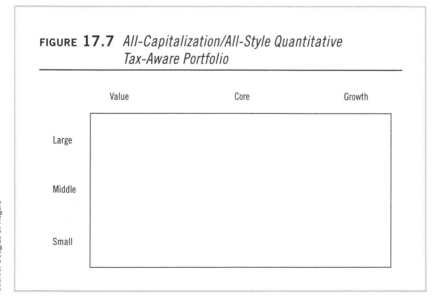

FIGURE 17.7 *All-Capitalization/All-Style Quantitative Tax-Aware Portfolio*

	Value	Core	Growth
Large			
Middle			
Small			

Source: Douglas S. Rogers

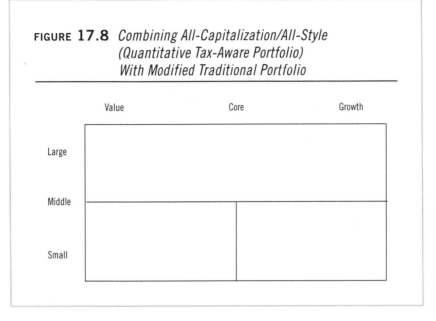

FIGURE **17.8** *Combining All-Capitalization/All-Style (Quantitative Tax-Aware Portfolio) With Modified Traditional Portfolio*

Source: Douglas S. Rogers

Astute advisers attempting to maximize after-tax returns use the quantitative tax-aware approach where the odds of outperforming an index are the least attractive and selectively place active managers where they believe they have the potential to produce an alpha of 3.0 percent or better. Therefore, the next logical extension is to combine the quantitative tax-aware approach with small- or small/mid-cap managers, as shown in **FIGURE 17.8.**

This example represents an S&P 500 quantitative tax-aware core with small/mid-cap value and growth managers, but there are many solutions that are equally attractive. For example, you could have a Russell 1000 quantitative tax-aware core with an actively managed Russell 2000 core small-cap portfolio. Additionally, instead of one or two small- or small/mid-cap managers, you could use three, depending on the amount of assets you are working with and the minimum account size managers are willing to accept. **FIGURE 17.9**, again from Barclays, shows the percentage of active managers who have underperformed their respective indices on a respective basis. Since closed funds are not included and the data suffer from survivor bias, this picture is more favorable than reality. However, it does show where it makes most sense to make your active management bets.[9]

Also, there can be a separate account for the quantitative tax-aware core and mutual or exchange-traded funds for the small-cap allocation(s). The key here is not to fall into the trap of the tax-exempt industry and drive some preconceived format or number of managers. Be creative and simply

FIGURE **17.9** *Percent of Active Managers Underperforming the Index (from 12/31/93 to 12/31/03)*

	VALUE (%)		BLEND (%)		GROWTH (%)	
	BEFORE TAX	AFTER TAX	BEFORE TAX	AFTER TAX	BEFORE TAX	AFTER TAX
Large-Cap	86	98	82	95	67	88
Mid-Cap	71	91	51	89	60	84
Small-Cap	45	81	22	43	18	34

Note: Past performance is no guarantee of future results. All total returns reflect 10-year annualized figures. Funds are categorized by Mornigstar objective.

do what makes sense with the strategies and products you have available!

Taking this process to the logical extreme results in the "optimal" tax-aware equity allocation model. It is the current rage with tax-aware consultants and advisers today, as it brings together the most compelling features of various types of managers. This model is also known as the "core-and-satellite" or "hub-and-spoke" approach to domestic equity manager positioning (see **FIGURE 17.10**).[10]

FIGURE **17.10** *Optimal Tax-Aware Domestic Equity Manager Allocation*

	Value	Core	Growth
Large	Concentrated		Concentrated
Middle		Quantitative Tax-Aware Core	
Small	Active		Active

In the optimal model, the quantitative tax-aware allocation receives the most significant level of funding and serves as the core or hub, surrounded by satellites or spokes. The satellites or spokes may be small/mid- or small-cap managers or concentrated managers that typically hold twenty or fewer securities. The reduction in nonsystematic or security-specific risk diminishes as stock portfolios hold more than twenty securities.[11] By holding this number of securities or fewer, managers have the best chance of obtaining 3.0 percent plus outsized returns through a select number of ideas they have conviction in. They may hold some of the same securities in the space the core manager occupies. If this is a concern, then core manager can be precluded from purchasing the securities held by the concentrated managers. Additionally, you should not be concerned about the lack of diversification of a concentrated manager, as the core position is already anchoring the overall mix. The concentrated approach can apply to both large- and small-cap allocations, and some firms even include equity long/short hedge funds.

The question for the practitioner is: How many managers should I deploy and what should the allocation to the various components be, especially the quantitative tax-aware core? The allocations to the large- and small/mid-capitalization equity components can be determined through the normal asset allocation optimization process using after-tax assumptions. The two percentages can then be added together for the overall domestic equity allocation. By adjusting the weights of the core and satellite

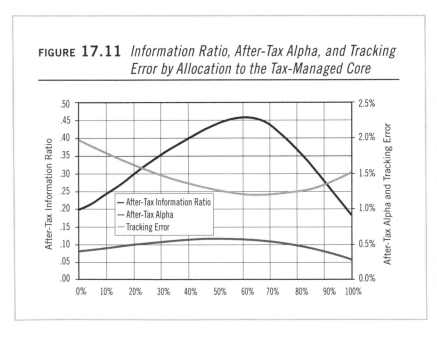

FIGURE **17.11** *Information Ratio, After-Tax Alpha, and Tracking Error by Allocation to the Tax-Managed Core*

Legend:
— After-Tax Information Ratio
— After-Tax Alpha
— Tracking Error

Source: Clifford H. Quisenberry, Jr., "Optimal Allocation of Taxable Core and Satellite Portfolio Structure," *Journal of Wealth Management* (Summer 2003): 18–26.

components for a given base-case scenario, Clifford Quisenberry of Parametric Portfolio Associates illustrates in **FIGURE 17.11** that the after-tax information ratio peaked with approximately 62 percent allocated to the quantitative tax-aware portfolio. In this case, the after-tax information is defined as "the portfolio's after-tax alpha over the tracking error."[12]

Applying the information in the figure suggests allocating approximately 60 percent to the core and 10 percent each to two satellites and two small/mid- or small-capitalization managers would produce an attractive portfolio mix to deliver compelling after-tax results that adequately represents each of the nine style boxes. Thus, the mix of managers and funds can easily be done with five or fewer managers. In some cases, there may not be a substantial fee savings, as concentrated and high-alpha managers typically charge 1 percent or more and may even apply the typical 1 percent of fees and 20 percent of profit performance typical of hedge funds. However, the net result should create the potential for much higher returns after all fees and taxes. The graph created by Parametric illustrates one approach to determining the optimal percentage for the core allocation. Consultants and advisers may wish to create their own propriety method to demonstrate their firm's distinctive competence.

The key to developing a high-performing mix of domestic equity managers on an after-tax basis is what Jean Brunel refers to as avoiding the "murky middle" (see **FIGURE 17.12**).[13]

Source: Jean L. P. Brunel, "A Tax-Efficient Portfolio Construction Model," *Journal of Wealth Management* (Fall 2001, 43-49.

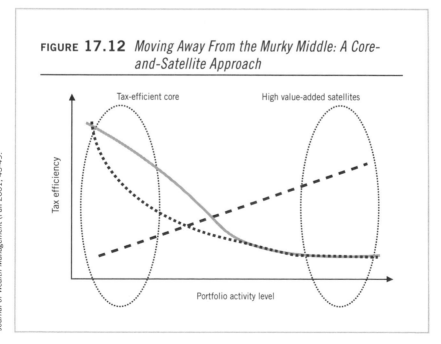

FIGURE 17.12 *Moving Away From the Murky Middle: A Core-and-Satellite Approach*

Tax-efficient core

High value-added satellites

Tax efficiency

Portfolio activity level

The murky middle consists of the vast majority of equity portfolio managers, who simply have little or no chance of outperforming the benchmark on after-tax basis. Therefore, tax-aware practitioners naturally find comfort in allocating to the extremes that consist of a core manager emphasizing the tax-loss harvesting strategy on one end of the range of choices and high-alpha-generating strategies on the other.

The second way investors can reduce the tax drag from adherence to specific domestic equity style-box allocations is to seek an investment vehicle that does not suffer from the reconstitution of the index, as do mutual funds and separate account mandates. Fortunately, exchange-traded funds serve this purpose well, especially those recently developed by Barclays in conjunction with Morningstar.[14] As described in chapter 9, the in-kind transfer allows exchange-traded funds to minimize the tax impact to investors, and in certain market environments eliminate it altogether. Since most reconstitutions are announced in advance, portfolio managers of exchange-traded funds can begin acquiring shares to ensure an orderly transition of the portfolio to the new allocation. The Morningstar methodology of style/capitalization index construction incorporates the factors listed in **FIGURE 17.13**.

The reason these are listed here is the nine iShare portfolios or exchange-traded funds are constructed in a way to minimize the problem with overlap. To address the concern with overlap, Morningstar applies a method of control called "ownership zones." This allows investors to create mixes of portfolios and funds with the confidence that they will not end up with an undesirable percentage allocation to one or more style/capitalization blocks. Moreover, they can do so with the iShares Morningstar funds and indexes in a way that is highly tax efficient. Additionally, although a

FIGURE 17.13 *iShares Morningstar Index Methodology*

VALUE FACTORS		GROWTH FACTORS	
Price/Projected Earnings	50.0%	Long-Term Projected Earnings Growth	50.0%
Price/Book	12.5%	Historical Earnings Growth	12.5%
Price/Sales	12.5%	Sales Growth	12.5%
Price/Cash Flow	12.5%	Cash Flow Growth	12.5%
Dividend Yield	12.5%	Book Value Growth	12.5%

Source: Morningstar, Barclays Global Investors

brokerage fee is charged to purchase and sell them, annual fees run from only 0.2 to 0.3 percent annually, depending on the specific product.

The Morningstar iShares index methodology is more in tune with the way the mix of portfolio holdings for taxable investors should be constructed, as compared with the Russell methodology, where approximately 30 percent of large-cap stocks are owned by both the Russell 1000 Value and the Russell 1000 Growth indices. This is fine with pension or charitable accounts portfolios where taxes are not a consideration, as you often find relative value and growth-at-a-reasonable-price (GAARP) style managers holding many of the same stocks. However, taxable accounts should avoid pairing these types of managers, as their trading often violates the thirty-day wash sale rule negating the value of selling a security at a loss, and when you combine the two you typically have little more than an expensive market portfolio. Moreover, high alpha is more often associated with managers that adhere to deep or extreme style emphasis.

The core portion of the "optimal" portfolio does not have to be an index-oriented product to be effective. There are managers who attempt to use the before-tax approach they have mastered for a decade or more and now apply a tax-loss harvesting overlay to their process. Although their before-tax return tracking error will be greater than their index-based peers, this is necessary for them to create a desirable before-tax alpha. If they can successfully achieve both a before-tax alpha driven from security allocation and security selection and an after-tax alpha from tax-loss harvesting, the investor is the ultimate beneficiary. Family offices are using this type of approach to highlight that what they offer is unique in the marketplace and really allows their managers to focus on long-term results, rather than being subject to the ridiculous pressures of the tax-exempt consulting community which wants them to pigeonhole them in one of the nine style/capitalization boxes. Moreover, this type of approach and tax-efficient exchange-traded funds can allow the manager to migrate to or overweight the portions of the matrix they feel have the opportunity for superior long-term returns based on valuation. For example, Don Phillips of Morningstar related at a Barclays iShares conference that as of the fall of 2004, small-cap value has outperformed large-cap growth over the past five years by perhaps the widest margin in the modern history of the markets.[15] This outperformance will not last forever. Therefore, if you accept a contrarian's approach, the all-capitalization-and-style tax-aware manager can gradually shift his portfolio style and capitalization to areas with the greatest return potential. Another alternative is using Morningstar iShares, since they are extremely pure in style and capitalization, allowing the adviser to use a minimal amount of dollars to achieve the desired allocation. This is the type of tactical redeployment of assets that can be executed in a tax-aware manner based on sound principles and judgment.

In summary, efficiently allocating equity managers for taxable accounts initially appears to be a more complex process than with retirement plans or eleemosynary organizations where taxes are not a factor. However, with experience, it becomes a simple and natural process of doing what is necessary to achieve the highest after-tax return possible. By taking into account the following factors, taxable investors benefit by adopting innovative equity allocation models that suit their client's needs:

❑ Establishing the total dollar amount of the equity allocation
❑ Reducing the number of equity managers employed to minimize unnecessary capital gains and taxes by adopting an allocation model other than the three-by-three matrix developed for tax-exempt accounts
❑ Positioning a quantitative or traditional manager with a focus on tax-loss harvesting in the core position
❑ Deploying traditional managers where they have the greatest probability to succeed
❑ Emphasizing concentrated or high-alpha-generating portfolios, especially in efficient market niches

Elite practitioners are embracing and will continue to refine and offer innovative tax-aware equity allocation models, because they represent an area of the investment management process that truly has the capability of enhancing the taxable client's ultimate wealth.

Chapter Notes

1. Much of the discussion on tax-aware equity manager allocation has been taken directly or summarized from Douglas S. Rogers, "Tax-Aware Equity Manager Allocation: A Practitioner's Perspective," *Journal of Wealth Management* (Winter 2001): 39–45.

2. David M. Stein, "Equity Portfolio Structure and Design in the Presence of Taxes," *Journal of Portfolio Management* vol. 4, no. 2 (Fall 2001): 37–42.

3. Barrow, Hanley, Mewhinney & Strauss, "Benchmark Review, Third Quarter 2004," listing FactSet, S&P/Barra, and Russell as references, September 30, 2004.

4. Morningstar Principia, June 30, 2004.

5. Morningstar Principia, Vanguard Growth Index Fund, June 30, 2004.

6. Barra, "Overview," http://www.barra.com (accessed September 2001).

7. Douglas S. Rogers, "After-Tax Equity Returns for Non-Qualified Nuclear Decommissioning Trusts," *Financial Analysts Journal* (July–August 1992): 70–73.

8. R. M. Ennis, "The Case for Whole Stock Portfolios," *Journal of Portfolio Management* (Spring 2001): 17–26.

9. Barclays Global Investors, The Basics of iShares, marketing document, March 2004.

10. Jean L. P. Brunel, "Asset Location: Case Study of a Critical Variable," Investment Counseling for Private Clients III, AIMR Conference Proceedings, 2001, 18-27; Jean L. P. Brunel, "A Tax-Efficient Portfolio Construction Model," *Journal of Wealth Management* vol. 4, no. 2 (Fall 2001): 43–49.

11. E. J. Elton and M. J. Gruber, *Modern Portfolio Theory and Investment Analysis,* 3rd ed. (New York: John Wiley, 1987).

12. Clifford H. Quisenberry, Jr., "Optimal Allocation of Taxable Core and Satellite Portfolio Structure," *Journal of Wealth Management* (Summer 2003): 18–26.

13. Jean L. P. Brunel, "A Tax-Efficient Portfolio Construction Model," *Journal of Wealth Management* (Fall 2001, 43-49.

14. Barclays Global Investors, iShares Morningstar Summary, marketing document, June 2004.

15. Don Phillips, "The New School of Investing Is Here," presentation at Barclays Global Investors Conference, Chicago, October 14, 2004.

CHAPTER 18

Positioning Assets by the Tax Characteristics of the Entity

Introduce a wise and efficient system of taxation, and life and energy will pervade the country. Without such a system, it will sink into general and fatal paralysis.

—ATLANTIC MAGAZINE

Positioning assets by the tax characteristics of the entity is a critical step in the logical progression of managing assets in a tax-aware manner. This step follows deriving after-tax asset class assumptions, discussed in chapter 16, and works in tandem with equity manager positioning, explained in chapter 17. Once this step is complete, managers and funds can be efficiently assigned, whether they are tax-efficient or not. This chapter explains the process at a level where it can be grasped by readers of all degrees of sophistication and experience.

Proficiency at tax-aware location requires an understanding of the various entities that investors are likely to encounter when dealing with their personal situation or when practitioners are working with taxable clients. Entities can be broken down into the following major categories for individuals:

1 Taxable assets
2 Tax-deferred retirement plans
3 Individual retirement plans
4 Education plans
5 Insurance products
6 Social security benefits
7 Trusts

FIGURE **18.1** *Schedule Y-1: Married Filing Jointly and Surviving Spouse (to Nearest Dollar)*

TAXABLE INCOME					
OVER		BUT NOT OVER	PAY +	% ON EXCESS	OF THE AMOUNT OVER
$ 0	to	$ 14,300	$ 0	10%	$ 0
$ 14,300	to	$ 58,100	$ 1,430	15%	$ 14,300
$ 58,100	to	$117,250	$ 8,000	25%	$ 58,100
$117,250	to	$178,650	$22,787	28%	$117,250
$178,650	to	$319,100	$39,979	33%	$178,650
$319,100	to		$86,328	35%	$319,100

Source: CCH Tax Law Editors, 2004 *U.S. Master Tax Guide* (Chicago: CCH, 2003).

Most taxable corporate situations typically apply a subset of the above consisting of taxable corporate assets, insurance products, and various trusts established to serve specific requirements.

A simple foundation of key elements of the tax code as it applies to individuals is also necessary to tax-aware positioning of assets. The tax code, as it applies to returns on financial instruments, is extremely complex. It takes time and substantial effort for the taxable account practitioner to obtain a level of understanding sufficient to deal comfortably with client situations. This problem manifests itself primarily for two reasons. First, tax rates evolve for individual securities and products as they are created. Second, the tax code is organized by the characteristics of the taxpaying entity—for example, an individual, corporation, or partnership. Plus, tax-related information is often presented in terms that only accountants and attorneys feel comfortable with. In this chapter, we highlight a few simple concepts and outline the history of taxes on income and capital gains and the impact of the most common rates of the post–World War II era on the net return of investments.

The appendix lists the top federal income tax rates on regular income and capital gains since 1916. The top income rate is also often referred to as the marginal tax rate, which may differ significantly from an individual's average tax rate. **FIGURE 18.1** shows the federal tax rate schedule for married couples filing a joint return for income earned in 2004.

Applying the schedule to various levels of taxable income shown in

FIGURE **18.2** *Marginal Versus Average Tax Rate*

TAXABLE INCOME	MARGINAL RATE	PROJECTED TAX	AVERAGE RATE
$ 10,000	10%	$ 0	0.0%
$ 50,000	15%	$ 6,785	13.6%
$ 100,000	25%	$ 18,475	18.5%
$ 150,000	28%	$ 31,957	21.3%
$ 200,000	33%	$ 47,025	23.5%
$ 300,000	35%	$ 80,025	26.7%
$ 500,000	35%	$149,643	29.9%
$1,000,000	35%	$324,643	32.5%

Source: IRS Schedule Y-1 (Projected 2004)

FIGURE 18.2 demonstrates that the average tax rate is typically far less than the marginal, or top, tax rate.[1]

The difference between them can be substantial, especially when the first increment on income is not taxed, as is the case for 2004 up to an income level of $14,300. This concept is quite simple but often ignored. The reason this point is made is most studies apply the maximum federal rate in effect for the year of the return to achieve a worst-case scenario. Your own tax rate or the average tax rate of your clients may differ significantly from the tax rates applied in a particular study. Therefore, it may be necessary to modify the conclusion of a particular study to accommodate the circumstances of a specific situation if another tax rate is more appropriate.

Oftentimes, the taxpayer is also subject to state and local taxes. Taxes by foreign countries may also come into play. These additional taxes are also important and should be accounted for in the analysis for a specific client. In addition to the needs of individuals, taxable account management professionals may also serve the needs of various forms of trusts established for the purpose of estate planning, property and casualty insurance companies, nuclear decommissioning trusts, settlement trusts, and nonprofit voluntary employee benefit associations (VEBAs). For corporate-related funds and property and casualty insurance companies, the maximum federal tax rate of 35 percent is phased in once a certain threshold of income is received. Short- and long-term capital gains are both subject to the 35 percent rate, but they may be eligible for a "dividends-received deduction" of 70 percent. For property and casualty insurance companies, municipal bond income is generally taxed at 15 percent of the maximum federal tax rate, or 5.25 percent. Assets in the qualified nuclear decommissioning trust are taxed at 20 percent, as compared with 35 percent in the nonqualified trust. The area of estate planning brings in an additional level of complexity, as analysis of tax implications may include the components of after-tax return from each asset class being considered in the mix, the tax characteristics of the types of trust being considered, time horizon cash flow and availability of funds, and any potential valuation discount for contributing assets to the trust. With tax-deferred accounts and insurance products, any reduction in taxable income from the contribution, withdrawal penalties imposed on early withdrawals, the level of tax on distributions, and whether distributions will be taxable to the estate are extremely important to the analysis. Any of these topics could and have been the subject in-depth articles by themselves. Therefore, it is close to impossible for any one investment professional to be completely knowledgeable about every facet of the tax code and estate planning and the impact of each on the various types of taxable accounts. However, with experience comes the ability to ask the right questions and to know to turn to qualified experts when in doubt.

For individuals, estate taxes make the planning process even more complicated. The Economic Growth and Tax Relief Reconciliation Act of 2001 affected child-related, education and tuition, retirement-plan, and estate and gift tax provisions of the tax code. The major aspects of the estate and gift tax provisions are shown in **FIGURE 18.3**.

The provisions shown above clearly highlight the importance of tax-aware practitioners' being cognizant not only of current provisions of the tax code for the clients they serve but also of changes likely to take place in the future and how these may be affected by the economic and political climate.

To establish an understanding of a client's tax profile for a particular taxable entity, the tax-aware practitioner should seek answers to the following questions from the client or his advisers.

General questions:

1 What are the types of taxable entities that need to be analyzed?
2 What are the applicable sections of the tax code that address each specific type of taxable entity?
3 Is this situation subject to any additional statutory or regulatory guidelines?
4 In the analysis of the situation, should the client's or entity's maximum or average tax rate(s) be applied?

FIGURE **18.3** *Economic Growth and Tax Relief Reconciliation Act of 2001*

CALENDAR YEAR	TOP ESTATE/ GIFT TAX RATE	ESTATE/GST TAX EXEMPTION	GIFT TAX EXEMPTION
2001	55%	$ 675,000	$ 675,000
2002	50%	$1,000,000	$1,000,000
2003	49%	$1,000,000	$1,000,000
2004	48%	$1,500,000	$1,000,000
2005	47%	$1,500,000	$1,000,000
2006	46%	$2,000,000	$1,000,000
2007	45%	$2,000,000	$1,000,000
2008	45%	$2,000,000	$1,000,000
2009	45%	$3,500,000	$1,000,000
2010	Repealed	—	$1,000,000
2011	55%	$1,000,000	$1,000,000

Source: Internal Revenue Service

5 Is the taxable entity subject to state and local rates? If so, what are the applicable rates?

6 Are there other taxes that must be considered, such as foreign with-holding taxes?

7 When all tax components are considered, what is the entity's effec-tive tax rate? (There is usually a deduction for state and local taxes on federal tax returns.)

For each taxable entity or account:

1 What are the rates for various sources of investment income?

2 Is there any type of "dividends-received reduction" (DRD)?

3 Are short- and long-term capital gains taxed at different rates?

4 Is there a defined investment horizon, for example, when the enti-ty's legal structure is terminated?

5 Do any of the holdings have substantial embedded, unrealized capital gains?

6 Does the entity allow for a valuation discount when assets are contributed?

7 When applicable, how will distributions be taxed?

8 If there is a shortfall within the entity, what impact can this have on the requirement for additional contributions or the dollar amount of distributions?

9 What is the need for funds, and how are withdrawals likely to affect potential capital gains realization?

10 Does the possibility of the alternative minimum tax need to be considered?

For tax-deferred accounts that are part of the client's overall holdings:

1 Are contributions to the account deducted from taxable income?

2 Will annual contributions be made to the account? If so, what are the dollar amounts of the anticipated contributions?

3 Are there any catch-up provisions?

4 Are there any penalties for early withdrawals? If so, prior to what time or age, and what is the penalty?

5 Can assets in one tax-deferred account be rolled over into another tax-deferred account? If so, is there a penalty associated with undertaking this exercise, or what has to be done to ensure a taxable event is not triggered?

6 At what rate(s) are withdrawals taxed?

7 If you have more than one more tax-deferred entity as an option, do any of them have a beneficial estate-planning feature? If so, what is the value of this benefit?

Tax-related information can be obtained through detailed questionnaires, conversations, or examination of previous tax return filings. There is no method that is best, as it depends on the amount of time the client is willing to devote to the process, access to members of the qualified triumvirate, and the experience of the tax-aware practitioner. Typically, junior professionals depend on detailed documentation and analysis, whereas seasoned professionals may come to the same conclusion relying more on their communication skills and past experience. The method utilized is not all that important what does count is whether the adviser captures all the relevant information, acts in the best interests of the client, and communicates effectively.

Later in the chapter, PORTAX, the most sophisticated commercially available software for taxable accounts, is mentioned. This particular tool is ideal for complex situations, especially high-net-worth families, where multiple generations and various types of estate structures are involved. However, a much simpler approach will be used to highlight the value of positioning assets by the tax characteristics of the investing entity. You do not have to be a family of extreme wealth or a large taxable corporation to benefit from this key step. Since anyone that earns income is eligible to fund an individual retirement account, almost everyone can benefit from this step of tax-aware investment management.

In the example that follows, we will start with a scenario of an individual investor with three entities: a 401(k) plan, an IRA, and taxable personal assets. Readers may even wish to follow along with their own personal situation, as they are likely to come up with a solution that adds enough value to pay for the text many times over.

The procedure for positioning assets/investment vehicles (funds, separate accounts, partnerships, and so on) in a tax-aware manner includes the following steps:

1 List existing financial assets according to their entity.
2 Conduct an optimization of all financial assets using after-tax assumptions.
3 Analyze the projected alpha and tax-cost ratio or relative wealth measure of each investment vehicle being considered:
   a. 401(k)
   b. IRA
   c. Taxable assets
4 Use an iterative process to:
   a. Utilize the most compelling and tax-inefficient choices of the 401(k).
   b. Position tax-inefficient choices not available through the 401(k) in the IRA.
   c. Use the personal taxable allocation assets to fund tax-efficient vehicles, especially equities.

Using a systematic approach simplifies the tax-aware positioning process.

1 *List existing financial assets according to their entity:* To begin the exercise, the investor or adviser simply needs to take an inventory of the existing assets, as in **FIGURE 18.4**. In this example, the three entities— 401(k), IRA, and personal taxable assets—are listed as column headings . The dollar amount of the holding within each entered is entered according to its primary asset class or major subcategory designation. This allows for the calculation of percentages by entity and for the review of the overall positioning. In the example, the total amount of assets is $100,000.

The example in Figure 18.4 is very typical of naive asset allocation and location decisions when taxes are not taken into account. The forty-year-old investor decided on a 60 percent equity/40 percent fixed income allocation after hearing an adviser make a presentation at an employee

FIGURE **18.4** *Sample Client Financial Assets Inventory*

| | TAX-DEFERRED | | | |
| | 401(K) | | IRA | |
ASSET CLASS	$ AMOUNT	%	$ AMOUNT	%
Cash Equivalents	$ 5,000	10.0%	$ 1,500	10.0%
Intermediate Fixed-Income	$15,000	30.0%	$ 4,500	30.0%
Domestic Equity	$22,500	45.0%	$ 7,000	46.7%
Large-Cap Core	$ 7,500	15.0%	$ 2,500	16.7%
Large-Cap Value	$ 5,000	10.0%	$ 0	0.0%
Large-Cap Growth	$ 5,000	10.0%	$ 2,000	13.3%
Small-Cap Value	$ 2,500	5.0%	$ 0	0.0%
Small-Cap Growth	$ 2,500	5.0%	$ 2,500	16.7%
International Equity	$ 7,500	15.0%	$ 2,000	13.3%
Real Estate (REITs)	$ 0	0.0%	$ 0	0.0%
Totals	$50,000	100.0%	$15,000	100.0%

401(k) meeting. Since the adviser recommended allocating according to the investor's remaining time horizon, the rule of thumb of 100 minus current age was applied to determine the overall equity allocation or in this case 60 percent (100 – 40 years old). Additionally, the investor thought it was prudent to place 10 percent of assets in cash equivalents as a safety net. Later, a 10 percent allocation to real estate investment trusts was recommended for the mix, using funds from personal taxable assets, resulting in an overall allocation of 35 percent to fixed income and cash equivalents, 55 percent to equities, and 10 percent to REITs. Since the investor is using mutual funds, all investments outside the 401(k) adhere to a reasonable $2,000 minimum investment.

By not being tax-aware, the investor has missed out on several opportunity costs or potential savings. Critical location errors in this example include:

1 Attempting to adhere to the same strategic target allocation across all entities.

2 Placing a liquidity reserve of cash equivalents in tax-deferred ac-

PERSONAL TAXABLE ASSETS		TOTAL ASSETS	
$ AMOUNT	%	$ AMOUNT	%
$ 3,500	10.0%	$ 10,000	10.0%
$ 5,500	15.7%	$ 25,000	25.0%
$10,500	30.0%	$ 40,000	40.0%
$ 0	0.0%	$ 10,000	10.0%
$ 5,000	14.3%	$ 10,000	10.0%
$ 3,000	8.6%	$ 10,000	10.0%
$ 2,500	7.1%	$ 5,000	5.0%
$ 0	0.0%	$ 5,000	5.0%
$ 5,500	15.7%	$ 15,000	15.0%
$10,000	28.6%	$ 10,000	10.0%
$35,000	100.0%	$100,000	100.0%

Source: Douglas S. Rogers

counts when it is not likely to be a factor for at least twenty years.

3 Holding assets that produce high taxable income in taxable personal funds rather than in tax-deferred entities.

4 Funding value-oriented equity strategies with personal taxable assets funds and placing index or buy-and-hold growth-oriented funds in tax-deferred entities.

5 Using a total of twenty-one fund positions to achieve the target allocation, which presents an administrative or logistical challenge just to keep up with the flow of information.

These types or mistakes are very typical, but costly. Over the past five years, academic research in this area has confirmed that individual households and investors have not been diligent by placing high-taxable-income-generating asset classes and products in tax-deferred accounts.[2] For example, the investor is better off financially holding an equity index fund in a taxable account and taxable bonds in a tax-deferred account in most instances. Part of the reason investors may hold a high amount of tax-exempt bonds in their personal taxable assets is due primarily to precautionary investment behavior. Since tax-deferred investments are intended to be long-term in nature, having a sufficient liquidity reserve in such "sleep-at-night" securities and funds as cash equivalents and short-term bonds is understandable.

2 Conduct an optimization of all financial assets using after-tax assumptions: In chapter 16, a procedure for estimating after-tax return assumptions was presented. Conducting the asset allocation optimization or any other financial-planning exercise on an after-tax basis is essential, otherwise the practitioner is likely to achieve inaccurate results or misleading conclusions that will be detrimental to wealth creation. Continuing with the example from step 1, calculate the before-tax standard deviation for the overall mix. Then identify an efficient mix using after-tax assumptions for the same level of risk. This serves as a focal point to ensure the client's desired level of risk is maintained. In almost all cases, the new portfolio will have a greater allocation to equities and a higher after-tax return. This exercise can be done with any asset allocation/optimization software package that allows the user to adjust the three input variables

FIGURE **18.5** *Critical Information for Entity Location*

ASSET CLASS	401(K) ALPHA	TAX-COST RATIO
Cash Equivalents	0.0%	0.8%
Intermediate Fixed-Income	0.3%	2.0%
Domestic Equity		
Index/TM/ETF	0.0%	0.4%
Large-Cap Core		
Large-Cap Value	2.0%	2.0%
Large-Cap Growth	1.0%	1.5%
Small-Cap Value	4.0%	2.0%
Small-Cap Growth	3.0%	2.0%
International Equity	2.5%	2.0%
Real Estate (REITs)		

(returns, standard deviations, and correlation coefficients for each asset class). For the remainder of the exercise, instead of a 55 percent equity/35 percent fixed/10 percent REITs allocation we will assume the new after-tax efficient mix is 60 percent equity/30 percent fixed/10 percent REITs.

3 *Analyze the projected alpha and tax-cost ratio or relative wealth measure for each investment vehicle being considered:* In this example, mutual funds are the investment vehicle of choice. By researching Morningstar Principia and analyzing the available funds in the 401(k) and those recommended for investment, we can list the estimated alpha statistic, tax-cost ratio, and the percentage of the unrealized capital gains for each option in a template similar to the one used to inventory the initial assets (see **FIGURE 18.5**).

In lieu of the tax-cost ratio or relative wealth measure, you can also use the level of taxable income to conduct the analysis. The advantage of the tax-cost ratio is it provides a more complete picture on tax implications of the fund option, since it accounts for the tax from capital gains realization as well. Additionally, this example uses mutual funds versus separate accounts. Therefore, the client is likely to be more familiar with the tax-cost

IRA		PERSONAL TAXABLE ASSETS		
ALPHA	TAX-COST RATIO	ALPHA	TAX-COST RATIO	UNREALIZED CAP. GAIN
0.0%	0.8%	0.0%	0.8%	0%
0.3%	2.0%	0.3%	2.0%	2%
0.0%	0.2%	0.0%	0.2%	–5%
1.0%	1.5%	1.0%	1.5%	1%
2.0%	1.8%	2.0%	1.8%	15%
3.0%	1.0%	3.0%	1.0%	–15%
4.0%	2.0%	4.0%	2.0%	30%
5.0%	1.5%	5.0%	1.5%	3%
3.0%	1.8%	3.0%	1.8%	12%
2.0%	3.0%	2.0%	3.0%	20%

Source: Douglas S. Rogers

ratio than with the relative wealth measure presented in chapter 8.

There are limited investment choices in most 401(k) plans, and the fund selections available may not be among the best in their respective categories. In Figure 18.5, the domestic large-cap and small/mid-cap growth equity funds are less competitive than similar options offered in the IRA and personal taxable assets entities. This is common, as we can invest in a broader universe of funds with the IRA and personal taxable assets. In this example, the only restriction is funds open to new investment and those willing to accept a minimum investment of $2,000 or below. Often, investors are limited to the products available through their fund platform, such as Schwab or TD Waterhouse, or invest all their assets with a large, single provider such as Fidelity, T. Rowe Price, or Vanguard. An additional row of information was added specifically, for index/tax-managed (TM)/exchange-traded (ETF) funds. The last column of information, the percentage of unrealized capital gains, is important to avoid investing into a potentially significant tax liability. If a tax-efficient exchange-traded, index, or tax-managed fund has a meaningful unrealized capital gains position, it usually is not a major concern. However, the same cannot be said of actively managed funds not known for focusing on tax efficiency.

4 *Use an iterative process to position the most compelling and tax-inefficient choices in the 401(k); tax-inefficient choices not available through the 401(k) in the IRA; and tax-efficient vehicles, especially equities, in the personal taxable assets:* The target allocation, dollar amount in each entity, and the desired liquidity reserve are required before starting the iterative process. In this example, the desired allocation is:

Cash equivalents	10%	
Intermediate fixed income	20%	
Domestic equities	45%	
Large-cap core		10%
Large-cap value		10%
Large-cap growth		10%
Small-cap value		7.5%
Small-cap growth		7.5%
International equities	15%	
Real estate (REITs)	10%	

The client has decided the amount of the liquidity reserve should be equal to 10 percent of assets, and the funds available in each entity is 50 percent to the 401(k), 15 percent to the IRA, and 35 percent to personal taxable assets, with a total amount again of $100,000 (see **FIGURE 18.6**). The liquidity reserve needs to be satisfied before the iterative process begins. For simplicity, we are going to assume all the personal taxable assets are being held in cash equivalents and we do not have to consider embedded unrealized capital gains. Previously, cash equivalents were assigned in equal percentages to all three entities, but they shouldn't be used in tax-deferred entities because they would be subject to a 10 percent penalty if withdrawn before age 59½. Therefore, step 1 in the table is to allocate 10 percent, or $10,000, to cash equivalents in taxable personal assets. Note the tax-cost ratio is listed at 0.8 percent, which takes into account the projected return from chapter 16 for taxable cash equivalents and the maximum federal tax rate. We could just as well have stated a municipal-bond cash-equivalent return and 0 percent for the tax-cost ratio. Which type of money-market fund does not have to be decided until the implementation phase. At this time, we can ascertain if additional taxable income might place the client in a higher tax bracket and which fund offers the maximum after-tax return. **FIGURE 18.7** (see page 258) differs from Figure 18.6, in that it highlights the steps involved in the "worst case–bottom up" and "best case–top down" iterative approach. Some people are comfortable with the table format of Figure 18.6, whereas others find the "bottom up/top down" approach of Figure 18.7 is simpler to work with. Still others start with the bottom up/top down approach and then list each step in the table. The point is there is nothing magic or sacred here. Simply do whatever works best for you and your clients.

In step 2, we look for the asset class with the highest potential tax impact. This is either taxable intermediate fixed income or REITs. In this case, REITs have a higher tax-cost ratio, so we will apply this asset class first to the IRA, where we have the benefit of tax deferral and availability. We now turn to the best case–top down selection. In this instance, the objective is to place the most tax-efficient equity option in the taxable personal assets. The analysis in Figure 18.5 shows that the index/TM/ETF option stands out with a tax-cost ratio of only 0.2. We thus assign a $10,000 allocation, and turn back to a worst case–bottom up selection. Rather than assigning a portion of the fixed income allocation to the IRA, we can assign the entire amount to the 401(k) and save the remaining $5,000 of the IRA to choices that generate higher alpha, which might not be available otherwise.

The iterative process continues until all funds are accounted for.

When using the iterative tax-aware positioning approach, international equity is quite often the last asset class to be allocated. This occurs because its relative tax efficiency is between the tax-efficient extremes of

FIGURE 18.6 *Iterative Tax-Aware Asset Positioning Process—Table Format*

ASSET CLASS	STEP #	TAX-DEFERRED 401(K)	
		$ AMOUNT	%
Cash Equivalents	1		0.0%
Fixed Income	4	$20,000	40.0%
Domestic Equity		$17,500	35.0%
Index/TM/ETF	3	$ 0	0.0%
Large-Cap Core		$ 0	0.0%
Large-Cap Value	8	$10,000	20.0%
Large-Cap Growth	5	$ 0	0.0%
Small-Cap Value	6	$ 7,500	15.0%
Small-Cap Growth	7, 9	$ 0	0.0%
International Equity	10, 11	$12,500	25.0%
Real Estate (REITs)	2	$ 0	0.0%
Totals		**$50,000**	**100.0%**

tax-managed funds and ETFs on one end and tax-inefficient taxable fixed income on the other. When the taxable personal assets are near 50 percent, you should investigate whether the international fund utilizes a currency overlay strategy, as that would increase the tax-cost ratio. International funds that hedge currency price movement are best suited for tax-deferred entities, and this may influence your selection of a particular fund or final placement.

The example presented in Figure 18.7 is quite simple and, with experience, can be done in less than fifteen minutes. As simple as it is, positioning by the tax characteristics of the entities and asset classes/investment vehicles provides the following meaningful advantages:

1 It achieves the overall desired allocation and reduces the number of holdings by one-half or more—from twenty-one to eleven in this instance.

2 It uses a liquidity reserve only where it makes sense.

TAX-DEFERRED — IRA		PERSONAL TAXABLE ASSETS		TOTAL ASSETS	
$ AMOUNT	%	$ AMOUNT	%	$ AMOUNT	%
	0.0%	$10,000	28.6%	$10,000	10.0%
$ 0	0.0%		0.0%	$20,000	20.0%
$ 2,500	16.7%	$25,000	71.4%	$45,000	45.0%
$ 0	0.0%	$10,000	28.6%	$10,000	10.0%
$ 0	0.0%		0.0%	$ 0	0.0%
$ 0	0.0%		0.0%	$10,000	10.0%
$ 0	0.0%	$10,000	28.6%	$10,000	10.0%
$ 0	0.0%		0.0%	$ 7,500	7.5%
$ 2,500	16.7%	$ 5,000	14.3%	$ 7,500	7.5%
$ 2,500	16.7%		0.0%	$15,000	15.0%
$10,000	66.7%		0.0%	$10,000	10.0%
$15,000	**100.0%**	**$35,000**	**100.0%**	**$100,000**	**100.0%**

Source: Douglas S. Rogers

3 It positions high-taxable-income-generating tax-inefficient asset classes in tax-deferred entities and funds taxable personal assets with investments that have the potential to generate meaningful long-term capital gains.

4 It ensures higher-capital-gains-generating value-oriented strategies are positioned in tax-deferred accounts, while buy-and-hold growth, index, tax-managed, and exchange-traded funds occupy personal taxable assets.

This simple example applies to any investor with a 401(k) plan, IRA, and personal taxable investments. In the sample scenario, 35 percent of the assets are taxable. By readjusting the location of the mix, the tax bite was lowered from $569 to $295 for an improvement of $274 each year. These dollar amounts were achieved by totaling the tax bite (tax-cost ratio × dollar amount of investment) for each of the equity and REIT positions in

FIGURE **18.7** *Using Best- and Worst-Case Approach*
Iterative Tax-Aware Asset-Positioning Process

STEP	PROCESS	$ AMOUNT	ALPHA	TAX-COST RATIO	GAIN EXPOSURE	ENTITY
	Liquidity Reserve					
1	Cash Equivalents	$10,000	0.0%	0.8%	0.0%	PTA
	Best Case–Top Down					
3	Index/TM/ETF	$10,000	0.0%	0.2%	-5.0%	PTA
5	Large-Cap Growth	$10,000	3.0%	1.0%	−15.0%	PTA
7	Small-Cap Growth	$ 5,000	5.0%	1.5%	3.0%	PTA
9	Small-Cap Growth	$ 2,500	5.0%	1.5%		IRA
11	International Equity	$ 2,500	4.0%	2.0%		IRA
10	International Equity	$12,500	4.0%	2.0%		401(k)
8	Large-Cap Value	$10,000	2.0%	2.0%		401(k)
6	Small-Cap Value	$ 7,500	4.0%	2.0%		401(k)
3	Fixed Income	$20,000	0.3%	2.0%		401(k)
2	Real Estate (REITs)	$10,000	2.0%	3.0%		IRA
	Worst Case–Bottom Up					

Source: Douglas S. Rogers

the personal taxable assets for the initial and recommended solution. This is a boost in overall performance of 0.27 percent ($274 / $100,000) alone. Plus, we have moved the fixed income allocation to the 401(k), where the returns of taxable bonds can compound on a tax-deferred basis.

This same thought process applies regardless of the level of complexity. You can easily add columns for additional entities, and rows for asset classes such as hedge funds and private equity. This approach provides a satisfactory approach to tax-aware positioning for 99 percent of the assignments financial planners and consultants take on for individual investors. However, for ultra-affluent clients who have numerous trusts across three or more generations, a system that has the capabilities of PORTAX is essential to achieve meaningful output for further analysis. PORTAX has the added benefit of incorporating the characteristics of each entity and cash flows into the future. Spreadsheets can be used to replicate this process in conjunction with the after-tax efficient solution from the optimization software, but it is a cumbersome process at best and subject to human error because of the volume of calculations involved. When the analysis becomes this complex, coordination with the members of the qualified triumvirate becomes more critical. The tax characteristics of each trust should be coordinated with both the accountant and the estate attorney. More important, if the estate attorney does not understand the concept of tax-aware positioning of assets, you will waste a lot of time running asset-location simulations and will have difficulty achieving consensus on an optimal solution.

When addressing this subject for the first time, it is helpful to have a financial-planning text for reference. There are about a dozen favorites used by college professors. The key is to find one that works well for your needs. A particularly good one is *Practicing Financial Planning for Professionals,* by Sid Mittra with Jeffrey Kirkman and George Seifert.[3] It is extremely well organized and thorough, which saves you time when there is a need to address a subject that you do not deal with on a daily basis. Since this area of expertise is so vast, it is difficult to keep up with changes driven by new and innovative investment products and techniques of each niche of taxable account investing, as well as the continual changes in the tax code and estate/regulatory matters.

To achieve an optimal solution, the practitioner must address elements unique to the type of taxable account investing, such as an individual, corporate fund, property and casualty insurance company, nuclear decommissioning trust, medical retirement trust, and so on. What follows is a brief discussion of key elements for investing for individuals. This area was chosen to demonstrate what is required for the majority of the reading audience. For those practitioners serving in other areas, this discussion should serve as an example of the complexity they are likely to encounter.

1 ***Taxable assets:*** Figure 18.1 shows the amount of tax married couples were subject to in 2004, based on their level of income. There are four additional items that are key for tax-aware strategy: gifting, federal estate exclusion amount, marital deduction, and step-up in basis at the time of death.

Currently, a husband and wife can each annually gift up to $11,000 free of tax to anyone they choose. Separately, during their lifetimes, they can make up to $1 million in gifts free of taxes. One important strategy with gifting is to transfer $1 million in wealth to others where the income and appreciation on the gifted amount will be subject to a lower tax rate.

With the Economic Growth and Tax Relief Reconciliation Act of 2001, the highest tax rates on the gift and the estate tax became the same, as Figure 18.3 shows. For tax year 2004, the top tax rate was 48 percent and will decline to 45 percent from 2007 to 2009. The estate tax is repealed in 2010, and then the repeal is reversed in 2011 with the tax rates reverting back to the 2001 level of 55 percent unless Congress takes action. The exclusion amount for the estate tax is $1.5 million in 2004 and 2005, increases to $3.5 million in 2009, and reverts back to $1 million in 2011 if, again, Congress does not take action. Since the estate tax is a major concern, there is likely to be meaningful change to the existing provisions sometime during the second term of the Bush administration.

The unlimited marital deduction provision of the tax code allows for the transfer of assets free of the gift and estate tax to the surviving spouse. This can be accomplished by the spouse having control of the property or through a legal structure, such as a qualified terminable interest property (QTIP) trust.

The step-up in basis currently applies to appreciated property or securities at the time of death. This feature provides the flexibility to reallocate to other asset classes without generating substantial capital gains tax. Exchange funds are structured to take advantage of the step-up in basis. A concentrated low-cost-basis stock position is transformed into a well-diversified portfolio of stocks. The beneficiaries, therefore, receive individual stocks positions where the cost basis of each security equals the market value. In 2010, the provisions of the step-up in basis are limited to $3 million for the surviving spouse and an additional $1.3 million for any beneficiaries for a total of $4.3 million. There are many nuances of the tax code, but these are the four major elements that apply to individual taxpayers and should be taken into account with any type of analysis or planning.

Key questions related to the client's personal assets are:

❑ Is the individual making annual gifts and has the exclusion been utilized? If not, is there any benefit to doing this sooner than later?
❑ What is the anticipated size of the taxable estate?
❑ Is it advantageous to take advantage of the marital deduction, or should a portion of assets remain in the decedent's estate?
❑ What are the likely estate exclusion amount and the projected rate of tax on assets exceeding this amount? Have other legal structures (trusts) been investigated to lessen the tax burden?
❑ What is the plan after the step-up in cost basis? Will this suggest a major shift in the family's strategic target allocation?

2 *Tax-deferred retirement plans:* With the exception of the ultra-affluent, these types of entities often comprise the bulk of an individual's financial assets. They can be broken down into two broad categories: defined-benefit and defined-contribution plans.

The defined-benefit plan is also referred to as an employer plan. In this case, the corporation guarantees certain benefits to qualified employees. An appropriate asset mix is developed taking into account the characteristics of the workforce and the costs of benefits offered. Returns generated by the mix attempt to match or exceed a rate-of-return objective known as the actuarial assumption. Most recently, defined-benefit plans of financially less-than-stable companies have come under pressure, because the actuarial assumption in some cases no longer reflects reality. Since interest rate levels have fallen dramatically and equities have been at high valuation ranges, assumptions of 8.5 percent to 9.0 percent have an extremely low probability of being achieved. A key element of defined-benefit plans is that funding contributions by the corporation to the plan, up to certain levels, are deductible from taxable income and their appreciation is tax-deferred until the employee elects to receive a distribution. More common today, especially for younger employees, are defined-contribution or individual retirement plans. The most familiar is the 401(k) plan, or a 403(b) plan for a nonprofit organization. **FIGURE 18.8** shows the amount that can be contributed to a 401(k) by the employee with an additional catch-up provision for individuals age fifty and older.[4]

There are also Keogh plans for the self-employed that allow for funding up to $42,000. With defined-contribution plans, the employee rather than the corporation is responsible for determining the amount of the contribution and making specific investment elections. For every dollar the employee sets aside, there is a reduction in the amount of reported income for tax purposes. Corporations typically match a portion of the employee's contribution up to a designated limit. These two favorable features almost always make funding the 401(k) plan essential and make the plan itself the most compelling alternative of any entity option. A study by Stephen Horan found the 401(k) is preferred over the tax-deductible IRA as long as the employer matches the employee contributions. Additionally, the individual is always better off when dropping from the 28 percent to

FIGURE 18.8 *Annual Employee 401(k) Contribution Limits*

YEAR	CONTRIBUTION LIMIT	AGE 50+ CATCH-UP
2005	$14,000	$4,000
2006*	$15,000	$5,000

* Indexed for inflation after 2006.

Source: Internal Revenue Service

15 percent tax bracket upon contributing to the 401(k) for any investment horizon and for employee matching as low as 5 percent.[5]

Other common types of defined-contribution plans include money purchase pension, profit-sharing, stock bonus, and employee stock ownership plans. Key questions for modeling retirement-plan entities include:

- ❑ What portion of funds contributed to the plan, if any, are deductible from income for tax purposes?
- ❑ Does the employer match any of the employee's contribution? If so, what are the limits of the employer matching?
- ❑ For defined-benefit and defined-contribution plans that are the primary responsibility of the employer, can the asset mix of the plan be determined and incorporated in the analysis?
- ❑ Will distributions be subject to tax at any other rate other than the rate for ordinary income?
- ❑ Have all the eligibility and vesting requirements been satisfied? If not, what is their impact and are there any penalties that must be considered?
- ❑ Is the viability of the plan in question?

3 *Individual retirement plans:* Individual retirement plans or accounts (IRAs) are eligible to anyone that has earned income. Individual contribution limits and catch-up provisions are shown in **FIGURE 18.9**.[6]

There are two types of IRA: traditional and Roth IRAs. Contributions can be made up to age seventy for each type of IRA. The primary advantage of the Roth over the traditional is distributions are not taxed. The taxable portion of the traditional IRA distribution is subject to tax at the ordinary tax rate, but the investor may be eligible for a full or partial deduction for the contribution. The deductions phase out in 2005 for married couples filing jointly that have taxable income of $70,000 to $80,000.

FIGURE 18.9 *Annual Employee 401(k) Contribution Limits*

YEAR	CONTRIBUTION LIMIT	AGE 50+ CATCH-UP
2005	$4,000	$500
2006–2007	$4,000	$1,000
2008*	$5,000	$1,000

* Indexed for inflation after 2008.

Source: Internal Revenue Service

There are phase-out provisions for the eligibility to participate in a Roth IRA. For married couples, the range is $150,000 to $160,000.

Investors eligible for both should take the time to analyze which type of IRA is best suited for their personal situation. Individuals can conduct the analysis themselves, using spreadsheets with present or future value computations. Fortunately, calculators are available on the Internet to allow investors to determine which IRA is most advantageous for them. Look for a site that will request the following information:

❑ Contribution amount(s)
❑ Current and projected age at retirement
❑ Expected rate of return on the investment portfolio
❑ Current and projected marginal tax rate
❑ Marital status and eligibility to participate in an employer-sponsored retirement plan

In addition to the items suggested above for comparing the two types of IRAs, you will need the dollar amount desired to be converted and the portion that was not tax-deductible.

As general rules of thumb, research conducted by Stephen Horan, Jeffrey Peterson, and Robert McLeod suggests converting from a traditional IRA to a Roth IRA is most advantageous when:[7]

❑ The conversion can be conducted optimally by paying tax consequences with non-IRA assets.
❑ There is a long time horizon.
❑ The expected return is high.
❑ The individual will be in a lower tax bracket at retirement.[8]

One of the key elements of tax-aware investing is the necessity to keep accurate records. This is especially true with determining the amount of the IRA contribution that is deductible. IRS Form 8606 should be filed for nondeductible IRAs. Another good habit to get into is to avoid mixing rollover assets with IRAs funded through annual contributions when changing employers. The accounting can consume an inordinate amount of time and effort and create a real headache in the future when you attempt to determine what portion of distributions you already paid taxes on.

4 *Education plans:* Individuals have four primary options for funding education: 529 savings plans, Coverdell education savings accounts (education IRAs), UTGM/UTMA custodial accounts, and taxable accounts. Much of the literature that has been prepared does not compare the first two alternatives with tax-efficient tax-managed funds or ETFs in the taxable account. Therefore, care must be exercised in making broad categorizations of 529 plans or education IRAs, but there is no denying that the benefit of the tax-deferral mechanism is powerful. Moreover, if earnings are to be taxed it will be at the lower rate of the student. The education IRA or Coverdell education savings account is limited to families with adjusted gross income up to $220,000 and a $2,000 annual contribution per beneficiary. The 529 college savings plans are not limited by individual's adjusted gross income and feature a maximum contribution per participant of $294,000. As a result, 529 plans are extremely popular with parents and grandparents capable of contributing a substantial amount of funds, especially when the contributions can qualify as gifts up $22,000 annually for joint filers. Additionally, couples can contribute up to $100,000 once in five years and not trigger the gift tax. There are also 529 prepaid and independent plans. Some of these plans have recently come under pressure due to concerns about the federal budget and the less than favorable returns from the financial markets since the beginning of 2000.

Earnings of the various plans are tax-deferred. If funds are used for purposes other than education, they are typically subject to a 10 percent penalty. Like so many facets of the individual tax code, 529 plans are also subject to sunset provisions in 2010. From an investment viewpoint 529 plans and education IRAs make sense if the student is age ten or less. However, some education plans include certain restrictions, like which academic institutions qualify, that should considered before investing in them.

5 *Insurance products:* Increasingly, the most controversial type of investing entity is the deferred variable-rate annuity for the simple reason that with the evolution of the tax efficient tax-managed funds and ETFs, there is less and less reason to own one when using traditional asset classes as the underlying investment. However, sales activity often exceeds $50 billion annually, because these products are sold to investors who are unaware of the better returns they could get from tax-aware choices.

There are two aspects that make deferred annuities less competitive than tax-aware products: fees and taxable distributions being subject to the ordinary income tax rate. An annuity has several layers of fees. As mentioned earlier, fees are a form of tax. Annuities have a death benefit, but interestingly enough, the cost of this benefit generally has little to do with age. When this fee is coupled with the underlying fund management fee, total fees typically equal 2 percent. Fortunately, there is a select group of discount variable-annuity providers that offer products with total fees in the range of 0.4 to 0.6 percent. This is a vast improvement over the average high-cost alternative, but this is still two times to as much as six times higher than the fee for a tax-efficient alternative mutual fund or

ETF. Funds invested in a variable annuity benefit from compounding on a tax-deferred basis, but the taxable portion of the distribution is taxed at the higher rate for ordinary income. If you have an equity mutual fund as the underlying option, you are in essence converting the long-term capital gains portion of return into ordinary income, which makes no sense. When you analyze tax-managed funds or ETFs that have little or no capital gains generation, you conclude that in many cases you are getting the tax-deferral mechanism of an annuity at a fee of 0.2 percent annually or less and the appreciation is taxed at the more favorable rate for long-term capital gains. Additionally, if the market is initially unfavorable, you can conduct tax-loss harvesting trades with funds held in personal taxable assets, which you cannot do with an annuity. This feature is not always relevant if the tax-managed fund has a steep load upon the sale of shares when the trade is likely to be consummated, which would most likely be in the first five years of ownership, if ever.

One true benefit of the annuity contract is that in about a third of the states, annuities are protected from creditors. For a physician whose personal wealth is potentially subject to patient malpractice claims, this feature has genuine value. The one exception where the structure may prove beneficial for deferred annuities is with hedge funds. Many hedge fund strategies achieve their returns though active trading that generates a high amount of short-term capital and generates income subject to the higher ordinary income tax rate. Therefore, the tax-deferral mechanism is more valuable than when the investment option is an equity index fund, for example, as the investment is already relatively tax-efficient.

Studies of variable annuities often compare the results achieved by taxable bonds held inside and outside the annuity. The projected return of the taxable bond held outside the annuity is reduced by a tax haircut reflecting a potential client's anticipated tax rate. The problem with this type of analysis is the individuals conducting these studies often do not realize is that tax-exempt or municipal bonds do not generate returns equivalent to the haircut for the maximum federal tax rate. Typically, an intermediate bond index will generate returns equal to approximately 70 percent of the index, versus 60 percent as would be suggested if the fixed income markets were perfectly efficient on a tax-arbitrage basis. So the municipal bond usually carries the day, unless a bond of lower credit rating is used inside the annuity.

6 *Social Security benefits:* This element is usually avoided. It is listed here because some financial planners consider Social Security benefits in the financial planning process. Since Social Security benefits have their own set of tax ramifications, they can be treated as a separate entity. Your eligibility for full benefits depends on the year you were born. If desired, you can begin receiving Social Security benefits as early as age sixty-two, but your benefits will be reduced. Also, there is a formula to determine the level of eligibility if you elect to receive benefits at an age between sixty-two and when you are fully eligible. Since Social Security is partially taxable income, there may be an advantage to timing the distribution depending on other personal factors if a couple's income is greater than $32,000. Additionally, depending how close the couple is to $32,000, the planner or software solution may suggest a greater allocation to tax-exempt bonds, since the income generated is not included in adjusted gross income on the federal tax return.

7 *Trusts:* Trusts can accommodate a variety of planning objectives. A trust is very simply a legal agreement under which assets are held and managed by one person for the benefit of another. The trustee is the individual responsible for managing and administering the trust assets in accordance with the provisions of the legal document. There are different types of trusts designed to satisfy specific objectives. They are often identified in terms of their relationship to the trustor's (also commmonly called the donor, grantor, or settlor) life, as living or testamentary trusts. Revocable living trusts are typically created to avoid the probate process, although they have no effect on estate taxes owed. An irrevocable living trust, which cannot be altered, may help reduce income or estate taxes by transferring assets during the trustor's lifetime. Testamentary trusts are part of the will and become effective upon the trustor's death. Their purpose is to conserve or transfer wealth. Since a will can be changed prior to death, the testamentary trust may be changed. Common types of trusts the professional serving taxable accounts is likely to encounter include:

a. Marital or QTIP trust
b. Grantor trust
c. Irrevocable life insurance trust
d. Charitable lead and remainder trust
e. Generation-skipping trust

Other types of vehicles that are similar in terms of their intended purpose are family partnerships and private foundations. In the family partnership, members of the family can essentially pool their resources and gain access to investment vehicles at a reasonable cost that may not be otherwise available. Private foundations allow families to transfer highly appreciated assets while obtaining a credit up to 30 percent of the total market value of the securities donated.

If gains and income are not distributed to the beneficiaries, then the trust must apply a tax according to the schedule in **FIGURE 18.10**.

Since reaching the highest federal tax comes quickly, trustees are gener-

Source: CCH Tax Law Editors, 2004 U.S. Master Tax Guide (Chicago: CCH, 2003), p. 30.

FIGURE **18.10** *Income Tax Rate Schedule for Use by Estates and Nongrantor Trusts—2004*

TAXABLE INCOME				
OVER	BUT NOT OVER	PAY	+ % ON EXCESS	OF THE AMOUNT OVER
$ 0	– $1,950	$ 0	15%	$ 0
$1,950	– $4,600	$ 292.50	25%	$1,950
$4,600	– $7,000	$ 955.00	28%	$4,600
$7,000	– $9,550	$1,617.00	33%	$7,000
$9,550	–	$2,468.50	35%	$9,550

ally motivated to distribute income and realized gains to the beneficiaries, where they may be taxed at a rate lower than if in they remain in the trust. Obviously, investment vehicles such as tax-managed funds and ETFs that have a history of not making random capital gains distributions can be of tremendous value, as it gives the trustee greater freedom of choice in determining on how to manage distributions in a tax-efficient manner. For example, it is much more desirable to sell a portion of an ETF knowing the proceeds will be subject to long-term capital gains treatment than to react to active managers that may randomly distribute gains subject to the higher rate on short-term capital gains.

Coordination with members of the qualified triumvirate becomes extremely important when attempting to establish payout policy, especially when certain charitable trusts are subject to priority of distribution according to ordinary income, short-term capital gains, long-term capital gains, and lastly tax-exempt income. This coordination becomes critical as it may dictate whether or not you consider hedge funds in the mix. Hedge funds can serve to reduce overall volatility and enhance the probability of achieving a target return objective, but they also generate a high level of ordinary income and short-term capital gains that may be adverse to the client's overall tax profile. Trust or estate planning can be extremely complex. When trusts are properly managed, they can truly produce fantastic results for all parties involved. However, when trusts are structured by taking liberties with estate-planning techniques, the tax code, or reasonable investment expectations, they can produce results that are less than desirable or even detrimental. The following questions are provided in the hope that investors and members of the qualified triumvirate can avoid some of the common pitfalls.

- ❑ Is the trust property or assets subject to the marital deduction?
- ❑ Are opportunities available by gifting being utilized?
- ❑ Is the best use being made of the marital deduction?
- ❑ How will the step-up in basis be accounted for?
- ❑ Will the value of trust assets be included in the decedent's estate?
- ❑ Does trust income have to be distributed annually?
- ❑ Is the value of the trust assets included in the surviving spouse's estate?
- ❑ Is the projected return on the trust's assets realistic?
- ❑ Are the philanthropic intentions of the family being satisfied, or are they so generous the trustor may have difficulty maintaining a desired lifestyle in the future?
- ❑ What impact does the structure of the trust have on the potential use of specific asset classes, styles, and manager trading strategies?
- ❑ When all fees (investment, custody, tax, legal, and so on) are accounted for, can you still justify the trust?
- ❑ Does the trustee have an understanding of tax-aware investing principles and the ability to communicate effectively with other members of the qualified triumvirate?

Questions specific to tax-aware analysis and positioning include:
- ❑ What is the term of the trust?
- ❑ Will income be distributed as ordinary income or qualified dividends, be tax-exempt, or be subject to the AMT?
- ❑ What is the project capital gains realization rate, and how it is measured for each fund/manager/partnership involved? What is the anticipated split between short- and long-term capital gains?
- ❑ What fees need to be accounted for in the process, and to what extent are they deductible?
- ❑ When assets are contributed to the trust, are they eligible for a valuation discount?

Considering the tax characteristics of each entity in the overall mix can add meaningful value on an after-tax basis. The specific amount of incremental return, when compared with naive asset location that utilizes the same percentage of each asset class across each entity, depends on the tax characteristics of the entities involved, the dollars contributed to each of them, the available universe of funds/managers/partnerships each entity can fund, and the tax profile of the investor or client. While the exercise to achieve a tax-aware solution may at first appear complex, with experience it be done efficiently. Existing optimizers can be modified to achieve efficient portfolios based on reasonable after-tax input assumptions. Using an iterative process will allow positioning of investment vehicles that are best suited for the tax characteristics of each entity. However, the most complex situations will require sophisticated software solutions. The bottom line is that tax-aware positioning by the tax characteristics of each entity involved can add consistent, positive results and should not be overlooked by practitioners when taxable accounts and entities are part of the overall asset mix.

Chapter Notes

1. CCH Tax Law Editors, *2004 U.S. Master Tax Guide* (Chicago: CCH, 2003), 28.

2. James M. Poterba and Andrew A. Samwick, "Taxation and Household Portfolio Composition: US Evidence From the 1980s and 1980s," NBER Working Paper, 1999.

3. Sid Mittra, Jeffrey J. Kirkman, and George H. Seifert, *Practicing Financial Planning for Professionals* (Rochester Hills, MI: RH Publishing, 2002).

4. http://www.ntrs.com, accessed November 27, 2004.

5. Stephen M. Horan, "A Reexamination of Tax-Deductible IRAs, Roth IRAs, and 401(k) Investments, *Financial Services Review,* 2001, 87-100.

6. http://www.ntrs.com, accessed November 27, 2004.

7. Stephen M. Horan, Jeffrey H. Peterson, and Robert McLeod, "An Analysis of Nondeductible IRA Contributions and Roth IRA Conversion," *Financial Services Review* (1997), 243–256.

8. Stephen M. Horan, "A Reexamination of Tax-Deductible IRAs, Roth IRAs, and 401(k) Investments," *Financial Services Review* (2001), 87–100.

CHAPTER 19

The Role of Systems Solutions in Tax-Aware Investing

Systems of taxation need not achieve the ideal. But the fact that the Constitution does not demand pure reason and is satisfied by practical reason does not justify unreason.

—FELIX FRANKFURTER

G radual improvement in systems technology is allowing practitio- ners to gain the information required to make more informed invested decisions when taxes are a factor. Fifteen years ago, the general consensus was the first accounts to have the sophistication to ad- dress the requirements of tax-aware investing would be the largest accounts. This was true for about a decade, but in the past five years the majority of technology spending has shifted from serving the largest accounts on a stand-alone basis to creating platforms to handle large numbers of ac- counts. The reason for this shift has to do with the economics of software development. It is far more profitable for a software firm to take on a single assignment with a deep-pocketed provider than to risk spending the time and effort to market to large taxable-account relationships that are difficult to reach, want a custom solution, and in most cases are unwilling to pay a reasonable price for the deliverable.

There have been two noteworthy cases of attempts at platform de- velopment that highlight the risks and potential for success. The case of myCFO is an example of "a bridge too far." There was a noble vision with sufficient financial backing, but the deliverable fell short of expecta- tion. On the other hand, Lockwood was able to secure the expertise and experience of industry veteran Jay N. Whipple III, the founder of Security

APL, and demonstrate how improvements in the functionality of the back office could lead to a scalable solution. Lockwood was acquired by the Bank of New York in 2002, which provided it with a technology-driven platform that offers tax-aware strategies and after-tax reporting. The success achieved by Lockwood set the rest of the industry in motion to achieve equal or greater success or else risk losing market share.

The author is extremely appreciative of James Hollis of Cutter Associates and Matt Schott of Tower Group for sharing their experience and expertise in the area of systems technology. Hollis and his associates at Cutter use the phrase "portfolio manufacturing" to describe the approach to platform development that wrap providers are embracing. Portfolio manufacturing is applying methods and procedures typical of industrial automation to the portfolio management process to achieve scale and greater efficiencies. As "just-in-time" inventory control has had a profound impact on the automotive industry, portfolio manufacturing is changing the way practitioners approach the management of accounts where taxes have an impact. The use of portfolio-manufacturing systems has three immediate benefits. First, if properly designed, portfolio-manufacturing solutions have the capability of delivering a uniform tax-aware approach across the practice. Second, it allows for quality control and compliance checks throughout the entire process. Third, a custom solution is now possible to avoid potential concerns over conflicts with Rule 3a4 covering unregistered mutual funds. If wrap account providers adhere to this rule, they do not have register under the Investment Company Act of 1940. The wrap industry has been criticized because in most instances its manner of trading is no different than a mutual fund's, and clients do not have access to a solution that truly satisfies their specific needs. As Hollis states, "portfolio manufacturing allows for customization in an automated environment."[1] This concept is not a dream or vision. Portfolio-manufacturing solutions are being now implemented that will have a profound impact on how the members of the qualified triumvirate interact with clients in the future. Unlike the trend in systems solutions for the ultra-high-net-worth market that attempt to overcome accounting challenges with partnerships and direct investments, the portfolio-manufacturing systems are providing tax-aware investment strategy and after-tax reporting. It is important to distinguish between the two deliverables. Tax solutions are favored by accounting-oriented CFOs of family offices, whereas portfolio manufacturing offers a far more comprehensive solution capable of delivering substantial investment benefits as well. An indication of the potential that can be achieved with portfolio-manufacturing solutions is Tower Group's belief that it is only a matter of time before vendors will offer systems to accommodate positioning of managers by the tax characteristics of each entity, as discussed in chapter 18.

Tower Group estimates that wrap accounts will grow by 18.5 percent a year and total assets will grow from $458 billion in 2003 to $1 trillion in 2007.[2] As a result, its analysis suggests spending on tax-aware overlay management services will grow from $6.3 million to more than $230 million over the same period.[3] The money is being spent because firms believe it is absolutely essential to have a viable technology platform to remain competitive and manage the assets of retired baby boomers. One common hurdle that almost all of the major wrap providers have had to overcome is replacing or modifying legacy systems that do not have a tax-lot accounting capability. As in the case of after-tax reporting, not having tax-lot accounting hinders the development of portfolio manufacturing.

To achieve a tax-aware solution, many wrap providers are embracing "overlay management." No knowledgeable investor can give serious consideration to traditional wrap platforms when their average fee is 1.75 percent. This is simply too high a hurdle. Once astute investors realize what they are getting for the cost, they will look elsewhere for a more cost-efficient solution. However, with overlay management the wrap platform offers the investor significant improvement in risk management and the potential to save perhaps as much as 1 percent annually in tax savings.[4] The overlay management process is administered by a qualified specialist, who often serves as both an adviser and a manager. The term "specialist" is used here purposely, so as not to confuse the function of the overlay management process with the role of money managers. The process can be accomplished by allowing the individual managers to continue to trade their portfolios and retain responsibility for their specific tax lots, or they can inform the overlay specialist of buy and sell decisions based on a model account. It is the latter format that is gaining acceptance, as it allows for greater flexibility and ease of management by the overlay specialist. Typically, this type of arrangement is done at a reduced fee, because the overlay specialist assumes operational control for activity across all the managers in the client's master account. This process may at first seem like a "black-box" solution to the investor, but it allows for enhanced risk management and tax optimization.

The overlay specialist starts the process much as an investment adviser would—by assisting the client in establishing a strategic target allocation, selecting managers, and incorporating appropriate constraints. These duties of the overlay specialist resemble the adviser function. The responsibilities of the overlay specialist may be different from firm to firm, but the objective is similar. The idea behind overlay management is to allow traditional managers to focus their attention on selecting the best securities possible and allow the overlay specialist to serve as the "quarterback" of the overall process to optimize overall tax efficiency. It should be no surprise that some of the firms offering quantitative tax-aware portfolios, such as Parametric Portfolio Associates, also offer overlay management services. Other well-known overlay management providers are Citicorp and Placemark. To assist them in their craft, the firms mentioned may employ an optimizer provided by Axioma, Barra, ITG, or Northfield. An optimizer is employed to manage the desired tracking error relative to a benchmark, the way tax losses are harvested, and the trading costs. The optimizers are often modified to provide a desired custom solution. The optimization technology must interface with the portfolio accounting and trade-order management systems, which allows for trades from numerous accounts to be batched and transacted in a cost-effective manner.

The overlay specialist plays a critical role in the allocation of assets to each manager security overlap analysis across the managers, and tax management. Challenges can arise with overlay management. For example, one manager may be selling a security at a loss, while another is contemplating purchasing it. If not checked, this type of activity has the possibility of violating the thirty-day wash sale rule. Therefore, managers need to receive information to alert them to potential wash sale violations. To overcome these types of challenges, rules-based solutions are instituted. These may address issues such as individual security constraints, changes in the target allocation, contributions and withdrawals from the account, timing of purchases and sales, different tax rates, state of residence, and the alternative minimum tax. Some money managers are unwilling to accept lower fees and turn their model portfolios and trading authority over to the overlay specialist, especially if the strategy focuses on less-liquid, thinly traded small- or micro-capitalization securities. Different challenges arise with fixed income securities, since they are traded in a secondary market rather than on an exchange with full price transparency.

When you compare the investment management industry with other fields, it is really in a primitive technological state. The real beauty of portfolio manufacturing lies in its potential to completely integrate and streamline the development of the investment policy statement, asset allocation, account-opening procedures, accounting, and performance-reporting functions. This type of start-to-finish seamless solution is being addressed in various ways by firms such as ADVISORport, Smartleaf, SoftPak, Tamarac, Vestmark, and Vista Analytics. There are also firms that specialize in trading and compliance modules, like Charles River, Latent Zero, and Linedata LongView. These firms offer complete outsourcing or an à la carte solution. The cost savings for the adviser and the solution offered the investor are far superior to anything advisers can patch together on their own. When manager recommendations and custom reporting templates are included, the adviser has the potential to brand the overall package. Getting the job done often requires hiring consulting firms like Cutter Associates or Tower Group just to gain an understanding of the landscape and who is capable of solving a specific need.

Portfolio-manufacturing platforms are not without risk. Failure to select the right provider can be extremely costly to correct, which is true of any custodial or reporting platform. While the quality and scope of these suppliers continues to improve, the primary risks to the adviser and the investor are the financial health of the supplier and the quality of the underlying managers.

Advisers need to have a high degree of confidence the software provider will be able to evolve as their business model and the industry change. Interesting technology plays are emerging daily, but only a few will be able to achieve the critical mass necessary to remain profitable. Therefore, it is important to evaluate not only the quality of the deliverable but the financial wherewithal of the company as well.

Portfolio manufacturing offers the potential to deliver a cost-effective solution, but the overall performance of the managers in the program will have the most impact on client retention. Outstanding performance still has a way of overcoming other shortfalls, but if the overall performance after fees and taxes is not on a par with a combination of less costly tax-aware mutual and exchange-traded funds, the platforms will prove to be nothing more than costly entertainment. There are four major concerns with manager selection and retention that will influence the ultimate success of individual wrap platforms and this niche of the asset management industry as a whole.

Efficiencies achieved by portfolio manufacturing are driven by volume. Therefore, the greatest inhibitor to achieving compelling investment results is employing managers in asset classes where the ability to generate alpha diminishes quickly with an increase in assets under management. Once advisers and consultants recognize this, the resulting flow of funds often drives performance more than picking the right securities does. Quite simply, if a small-capitalization manager transacting in less-liquid securities receives a higher proportion of funds than its respective asset class, continual purchasing of stocks in the model portfolio will naturally lead to superior performance. At some point, managers reach a level where the time required to sell a position becomes so great the only way they can accomplish the task without severely affecting the price of the security is through a merger or acquisition by another company. When this point is reached, or the manager experiences an outflow of funds, the performance of client accounts that remain invested with the firm suffer accordingly.

To overcome the first challenge pertaining to assets under management requires that analysts be able to identify emerging managers with short track records. Seasoned analysts with extensive industry experience who can evaluate managers on process and other intangibles versus quantitative measures are necessary to accomplish this task. Unfortunately, most firms shortchange their research function, and young inexperienced analysts base their decisions primarily on quantitative screens and measures. Therefore, the second challenge is to construct, or for the investor to identify, a platform that builds a recommended list of managers who focus on the processes that will lead to success rather than superficial performance.

The third challenge pertains to fees. Once managers are found, they need to be convinced that being captive to a wrap platform makes sense. A manager's reputation can be damaged through involvement in a wrap platform, as discriminating buyers simply will not deal with firms that yield to the asset-gatherer mentality. Moreover, other than diversifying across distribution channels, why should small-capitalization managers discount their fee when they have limited capacity? The firms that have an exclusive offering realize they don't need to bend to fee discounts and won't. Therefore, it is difficult to maintain the quality of the recommended managers list unless favorable terms can be extended to the most attractive firms. As flows to managers have slowed over the past two years, investment managers who have not received meaningful flows are now looking for ways to gracefully exit wrap and quasi-wrap separate account platforms. They are simply not being paid enough to overcome the intricacies of performance composites, higher-than-anticipated servicing requirements, and demands for fee concessions and lower account minimums. To succeed, the platform providers need to be willing to offer managers reasonable fees and demonstrate they can provide meaningful flows of funds. Additionally, they need to have the operational efficiencies necessary to respond to managers' requests for information in order to satisfy their firm's claim of compliance with AIMR reporting standards, if desired. If an investment manager is going to have exposure to wrap accounts, then it is best done with one or a few credible providers where the manager will have greater control. For the platform provider to offer a recommended list of managers of the major wrap managers just increases the probability the investor will receive no more than an expensive index solution.

The last and fourth challenge has to do with the transaction-oriented mentality of retail brokerage that can spill over to wrap platforms. While technology may provide a viable solution, someone still needs to communicate with and educate the client. Unfortunately, there is still a portion of the market that approaches wrap managers like individual stocks and terminates them far too frequently. The cost of changing managers is high enough in the tax-exempt arena but is even higher with taxable accounts that miss the benefit of compounding returns tax-free. This is one reason why the sophisticated element of the market avoids recommending managers who participate in wrap assignments, as they do not want their portfolio values influenced by the whims of the wrap market.

To varying degrees, the four challenges noted can be overcome. First, the platform needs to adopt a defined philosophy to drive the decision-making process in a manner consistent with the culture of the organization. It should be no surprise that adopting portfolio manufacturing will have a meaningful impact on the culture of the firm. Since it is process-oriented, it will naturally direct behavior in a compliance-oriented fashion. For the benefits of tax-aware investing to take hold, the overlay specialist takes on the portfolio-construction role to achieve consistency. Professionals of the firm who have had the freedom to structure client portfolios according to their own personal biases will find these platforms to be restrictive. Unless they can accept the benefit of the tax-aware approach and refocus their attention toward education, sales, and servicing activity, they will be less effective than individuals who are new to the environment and do not carry the baggage of the past with them. This is the same procedure banks go through when their internal portfolio managers must adjust to open architecture platforms, as they soon discover clients place less value on their individual security selection skills than on the overall management of the process.

A major plus of portfolio manufacturing is the ability to deliver a quality performance report. Firms are spending more and more effort on the performance report, as they realize it is the one communication tool that can distinguish the firm. To do so may require obtaining the services of other parties for pricing, security characteristics, benchmark and peer-group comparison information, et cetera. With portfolio manufacturing, these outside tools can be brought in as needed, in a cost-effective manner, to enhance the content of the report. Flash performance reports can also be created to provide more timely information. Innovative solutions are being applied to compress the time between the end of the reporting period and the delivery of the final report to the client. In particular, consultants are held hostage to waiting on peer-group information compiled from separate account managers. To overcome this challenge, mutual fund returns are being used to create custom composites, which are available within several days after the end of the reporting period. In many platforms, using separate account information makes little sense, because of account minimums. If your clients are investing in equity managers that will accept minimums of $500,000 or less, why compare these managers with a peer group universe where 75 percent of the managers have higher account minimums than the client is eligible for? Using mutual and exchange-traded fund information is actually more relevant, because it represents the results of a true investable alternative to the separate account managers available in the platform.

Adopting a portfolio-manufacturing approach makes the investor client more dependent on the platform provider. It is difficult to quantify this benefit in dollars and cents, but it is immense from a client-retention standpoint. Portfolio manufacturing facilitates creation of a variety of reporting deliverables that can be automatically sent by regular or electronic mail throughout the annual and quarterly reporting cycle. For example, the system could create a custom report in November to address year-end tax issues. During the quarter, various reports can be sent at designated intervals to keep reminding them of the brand. This capability can serve to educate clients on additional product offerings that can range from insurance products to commodities and hedge funds. These additional product offerings can increase revenue and enhance the profitability of existing investor relationships. At the same time, gradual systematic upward enhancement of the portfolio-manufacturing approach makes the investor increasingly dependent on the provider. If a complete integrated approach is achieved through portfolio manufacturing, the logistics involved simply become too onerous for the investor to even consider moving to another platform.

There are still doubters who do not believe it is possible to achieve the ideal investor experience through automation. Attorneys especially find it difficult to accept that their craft can be captured through technology, as they see estate planning as an art form that does not lend itself to a systems software solution. However, if you have the necessary input variables and the human mind can solve a problem, a systems solution is possible. Background information can now be aggregated and analyzed in a systematic fashion. Along the way, advisers assist the investor by sitting side-by-side to analyze various options. Decisions can be made quickly and documents can be printed and signed to satisfy compliance requirements. Moreover, systems solutions have the benefit of creating alternative solutions without personal bias. This allows solutions to be considered that an attorney may possibly overlook. Software developers that can capture the knowledge of qualified accountants, estate attorneys, and investment professionals have the potential to create tax-aware solutions and present information that can be easily understood by all parties involved. This enhanced capability will change the roles of the qualified triumvirate, as its members will no longer need to spend an inordinate amount of time analyzing existing holdings and preparing alternative solutions. These activities will be done for them. In the portfolio-manufacturing environment, practitioners will be able to spend their precious time on reviewing potential solutions to achieve optimal results.

With the proper security, there is nothing stopping the adviser from taking the process to the investor's home or office through the use of a portable computer. The virtual, Web-based solution is also a reality that will save time and allow for near real-time access. This type of access can unfortunately be a double-edged sword. Technology is great, but daily access often facilitates the day-trading mentality that is detrimental to wealth creation. Therefore, firms need to consider carefully how information should be represented to ensure it is consistent with a tax-aware approach to investing.

In the past, retail and ultra-high-net-worth platform providers have had difficulty establishing credibility with their client investors, because the approach to planning, investment, after-tax return reporting, and tax reporting needs is inconsistent for the assets of their typical relationship. In almost every case, one item is given priority at the expense of others, depending on the distinctive competence of the platform provider. Mastering portfolio manufacturing for the base-level investor client on the platform establishes a solid foundation for future development. The basics include items like tax-lot accounting and amortization and accretion for fixed income securities. Once the platform masters the deliverable for the simplest client on its platform it can begin to allocate development dollars to solve the needs of clients of increasing wealth. Getting this right puts the platform provider in an enviable position of being able to capture and retain a significant portion of the vast baby-boomer market that is gradually rolling over its qualified employer retirement-plan assets to IRAs. The consequences of missing this macroeconomic trend are so severe that firms feel they must commit ample resources to protect or enhance their existing market share. Therefore, the emphasis on portfolio manufacturing will ensure that tax-aware investing and after-tax reporting receive the prominence they deserve.

Chapter Notes

1. James Hollis, in discussion with the author, July 19, 2004.

2. Matt Schott, "Discretionary Overlay Management: The Route to Not so Separately Managed Accounts," Tower Group internal document, 2003, 4.

3. Matt Schott, "Developing Scale for Managed Accounts: Are Overlay Providers Sitting in the Catbird Seat?" Tower Group internal document, 2003, 4.

4. Ron Pruitt, "A Comprehensive View of After-Tax Investing and Tax Efficiency," *Senior Consultant* vol. 6, no. 5 (May 2003): 1–6.

SUMMARY

There goes another tax-aware investor laughing all the way to the bank!

—Douglas S. Rogers

Tax-aware investment management really boils down to mastering four simple steps:
1 Utilizing after-tax assumptions in the asset allocation process
2 Allocating asset classes and managers/funds according the characteristics of each entity
3 Tax-aware equity manager positioning
4 Identifying tax-aware managers/funds

At first, they may seem complicated, but through education and experience any open-minded adviser or investor who desires to capture the opportunity for wealth creation inherent in the process can master them.

While developments of the past decade have significantly enhanced our knowledge of tax-aware investment management, there are still areas that require significant research. These include topics such as determining the precise range for rebalancing target allocations, accounting for unrealized capital gains positions in the after-tax reporting process, and portfolio attribution that includes the impact of taxes on security buy and sell decisions. Solving these challenges requires solutions that might be as radical as tax-aware investment management was only a few decades earlier.

The political winds are certain to change the tax code in the future. While rates may change, deductions may be eliminated, and true simplification may even be adopted, the principles of tax-aware investment management will endure. The key for continued success of tax-aware investment management lies in education and the basic profit motive involved in the process. Education regarding tax-aware investment management will continue to gain momentum, because young degree- and certification-seeking professionals will simply demand it and seek universities and organizations capable of satisfying their thirst for knowledge. The profit incentive is already in play through portfolio manufacturing, and the spoils will go to those firms capable of delivering systems technology that will provide a clear competitive advantage in the future. Therefore, the knowledge and application of tax-aware investment management is no longer a luxury but a necessity for future success.

Top Federal Income Tax Rates on Regular Income and Capital Gains Since 1916

YEAR	TOP RATE ON REGULAR INCOME	TOP RATE APPLIES TO MARRIED TAXABLE INCOME OVER	TOP RATE ON CAPITAL GAINS	NOTES ON CAPITAL GAINS TREATMENT
1916	15.0%	$2,000,000	15.0%	Same tax rate as regular income
1917	67.0%	$2,000,000	67.0%	Same tax rate as regular income
1918	77.0%	$1,000,000	77.0%	Same tax rate as regular income
1919–21	73.0%	$1,000,000	73.0%	Same tax rate as regular income
1922	58.0%	$200,000	12.5%	Maximum rate of 12.5%
1923	43.5%	$200,000	12.5%	Maximum rate of 12.5%
1924	46.0%	$500,000	12.5%	Maximum rate of 12.5%
1925–28	25.0%	$100,000	12.5%	Maximum rate of 12.5%
1929	24.0%	$100,000	12.5%	Maximum rate of 12.5%

Source: Citizens for Tax Justice, May 2004

YEAR	TOP RATE ON REGULAR INCOME	TOP RATE APPLIES TO MARRIED TAXABLE INCOME OVER	TOP RATE ON CAPITAL GAINS	NOTES ON CAPITAL GAINS TREATMENT
1930–31	25.0%	$100,000	12.5%	Maximum rate of 12.5%
1932–33	63.0%	$1,000,000	12.5%	Maximum rate of 12.5%
1934–35	63.0%	$1,000,000	31.5%	Sliding exclusion of 70% >10 yrs; 0% <1 yr
1936–37	78.0%	$2,000,000	39.0%	Sliding exclusion of 70% >10 yrs; 0% <1 yr
1938–40	78.0%	$2,000,000	30.0%	Excl. 50% >2yrs; 67% 18-24 mos; 0% <18 mos; 30% max
1941	80.0%	$2,000,000	30.0%	Excl. 50% >2 yrs; 67% 18–24 mos; 0% <18 mos; 30% max
1942–43	88.0%	$200,000	25.0%	Exclusion 50% > 6 months; 25% maximum
1944–45	94.0%	$200,000	25.0%	Exclusion 50% > 6 months; 25% maximum
1946–47	86.5%	$200,000	25.0%	Exclusion 50% > 6 months; 25% maximum
1948–49	82.1%	$200,000	25.0%	Exclusion 50% > 6 months; 25% maximum
1950	84.4%	$200,000	25.0%	Exclusion 50% > 6 months; 25% maximum
1951–64	91.0%	$200,000	25.0%	Exclusion 50% > 6 months; 25% maximum
1965–67	70.0%	$200,000	25.0%	Exclusion 50% > 6 months; 25% maximum
1968	75.3%	$200,000	26.9%	Vietnam War 10% surtax for part of year
1969	77.0%	$200,000	27.5%	Vietnam War 10% surtax

Source: Citizens for Tax Justice, May 2004

YEAR	TOP RATE ON REGULAR INCOME	TOP RATE APPLIES TO MARRIED TAXABLE INCOME OVER	TOP RATE ON CAPITAL GAINS	NOTES ON CAPITAL GAINS TREATMENT
1970	73.5%	$200,000	32.3%	Higher rate phase-in; Vietnam War 5% surtax; minimal tax effects
1971	70%/60%	$200,000	34.3%	Higher rate phase-in; 50% top rate on earnings; minimal tax effects
1972–75	70%/50%	$200,000	36.5%	50% exclusion, minimal tax effects
1976–77	70%/50%	$203,200	39.9%	50% exclusion, minimal tax effects
1978	70%/50%	$203,200	39.0%	50% exclusion, minimal tax effects; late year reduction
1979–80	70%/50%	$215,400	28.0%	60% exclusion
1981	70%/50%	$215,400	23.7%	50% or 60% exclusion transition
1982–86	50.0%	$215,400	20.0%	60% exclusion
1987	38.5%	$192,930	28.0%	28% maximum rate
1988–90	28%/33%	see below*	28%/33%	Realized gains taxed same as as other income
1991–92**	31.0% (31.9%)	$84,300	28% (28.9%)	28% (28.9%) maximum rate
1993–96**	39.6% (40.8%)	$255,100	28% (29.2%)	28% (29.2%) minimum rate
1997–2000**	39.6% (40.8%)	$280,300	20% (21.2%)	20% (21.2%) maximum rate
2001**	39.1% (40.3%)	$297,350	20% (21.2%)	20% (21.2%) maximum rate
2002**	38.6% (39.8%)	$307,050	20% (21.2%)	20% (21.2%) maximum rate

Source: Citizens for Tax Justice, May 2004

YEAR	TOP RATE ON REGULAR INCOME	TOP RATE APPLIES TO MARRIED TAXABLE INCOME OVER	TOP RATE ON CAPITAL GAINS	NOTES ON CAPITAL GAINS TREATMENT
2003–05**	35.0% (36.1%)	$319,100	15% (16.1%)	Capital gains rate also applies to dividends
2006–07**	35.0% (35.7%)	$338,525	15% (15.7%)	Capital gains rate also applies to dividends
2008**	35.0% (35.4%)	$351,250	15% (15.4%)	Capital gains rate also applies to dividends
2009**	35.0% (35.4%)	$360,050	20% (20.4%)	Dividends return to regular tax rates
2010	35.0%	$369,050	20.0%	All Bush tax cuts expire after 2010
2011 on	39.6% (40.8%)	$378,250	20% (21.1%)	20% (21.2% maximum rate)

Notes: The definition of taxable income varied very substantially over the years. Taxable income is much less than actual income. Starting points for the top rate (indexed) are averages when multiple years are shown after 1987. Rates for 1970–81 reflect a lower top on earned income (second figure listed).

| *1988–90 detail | 28.0% 33.0% 28.0% | $31,050 $75,050 $155,780 | 28.0% 33.0% 28.0% | |

**Rates in parantheses include an additional tax on adjusted gross income (phased out starting in 2006; repealed in 2010).

Source: Citizens for Tax Justice, May 2004

Continuing Education Exam

for CFP Continuing Education Credit
and PACE Recertification Credit

Earn five hours of credit toward your CFP Board continuing-education requirement as well as PACE Recertification credit by passing the following exam online at www.bloomberg.com/ce and entering code 1576TAX8.

All the material has been previewed by the CFP Board of Standards. If you wish to find out if this book and exam can be used to fulfill the CE requirement for a different organization, please contact its governing board directly.

1. Funds in taxable accounts represent approximately what percentage of the world's liquid financial assets?
A. 10 percent
B. 25 percent
C. 33 percent
D. 50 percent

2. Which industry niche had the greatest initial impact on the evolution of knowledge pertaining to tax-aware investment management?
A. wealthy individuals
B. property and casualty insurance companies
C. nuclear decommissioning trusts
B. medical retirement trusts

3. Which investment consulting firm had a significant impact on procedures to maximize after-tax results?
A. Callan Associates
B. CTC Consulting
C. Rogers Casey
D. SEI Investments

4. The "father of tax-aware investment management" is considered by many to be:
A. Charles Ellis
B. Peter Bernstein
C. Robert "Tad" Jeffrey
D. John Bogle

5. Which of the following articles published in 1993 served as the catalyst for tax-aware investment management?
A. "Optimal Stock Trading" by George M. Constantinides
B. "Is Your Alpha Big Enough to Cover Its Taxes? The Active Management Dichotomy" by Robert H. Jeffrey and Robert D. Arnott
C. "Do After-Tax Returns Affect Mutual Fund Inflows?" by Daniel Bergstresser and James Poterba
D. "Ranking Mutual Funds on an After-Tax Basis" by Joel M. Dickson and John B. Shoven

6. A young professional aspiring to obtain a comprehensive education focused on tax-aware investment can achieve such by focusing on the following source:
A. One of the many universities teaching financial planning
B. An MBA securities analysis program
C. A professional certification program
D. None of the above

7. It has been shown that securities are efficiently priced when taxes are considered.
A. True
B. False

8. Security trading, as measured by the portfolio turnover rate, can be applied to achieve an accurate measure of a manager's tax-efficiency.
A. True
B. False

9. Which of the following events led to the creation of after-tax returns for mutual funds?
A. Mutual funds distributing capital gains of $238 billion in 1999 and $326 billion in 2000
B. The Mutual Fund Tax Awareness Act of 2000 passing by a vote of 385 to 2
C. The SEC issuing a proposal for public comment in March 2000
D. All of the above

10. What are the essential functions that must be considered for taxable accounts to maximize after-tax results?
A. Investment function only
B. Investment and tax functions
C. Tax and regulatory or estate functions
D. Investment, tax, and regulatory or estate functions

11. When a mutual fund reports after-tax performance, the after-tax return will always be less than the before-tax return for the same period of measurement.
A. True
B. False

12. At what time is the tax impact accounted for when calculating after-tax returns?
A. At the time of the transaction or distribution
B. At the end of the month
C. At the end of the year
D. April 15 of the following year

13. To calculate after-tax returns, a separate-account manager must have access to a system or custodian that has a tax-lot accounting capability.
A. True
B. False

14. After-tax returns are mandatory for separate-account clients for all firms claiming compliance with AIMR/GIPS standards.
A. True
B. False

15. With taxable accounts, what a manager has done in the past can have an impact on future after-tax performance.
A. True
B. False

16. The consultant "capture ratio" (after-tax return/before-tax return) is a measure of after-tax returns that works well in all market environments.
A. True
B. False

17. The value of the capture ratio can be greater than 100 percent.
A. True
B. False

18. The Morningstar tax-cost ratio for mutual funds is a derivation of the AIMR Subcommittee for After-Tax Return Reporting's "relative wealth measure" for separate accounts.
A. True
B. False

19. The mutual fund with the longest period since inception of not distributing a capital gain is the:
A. Vanguard Index 500 mutual fund
B. State Street SPDR exchange-traded fund
C. Vanguard Tax-Managed Growth & Income mutual fund
D. Schwab 1000 Inv mutual fund

20. "Tax-loss harvesting" is a trade conducted purposely to produce a loss that can be applied to gains in the existing portfolio or other portfolios, or deferred in most cases for future application.
A. True
B. False

21. Selling a security and investing the proceeds temporarily in cash (known as a "naked trade") makes sense from both an investment and a tax perspective.
A. True
B. False

22. From a tax-aware investment management perspective, when a security falls in value it is best to double the position and then sell the original position or tax lot when the security rebounds in price (known as the "double down" trade).
A. True
B. False

23. The preferred method for taking a loss is to sell the security at a loss and temporarily replace it with a similar security having slightly different characteristics (known as a "pair-wise" transaction).
A. True
B. False

24. A benefit of the accounting methodology for mutual funds, as compared with separate accounts, is that you cannot distribute a loss to shareholders.
A. True
B. False

25. Investors can rely on exchange-traded funds that focus on specific countries to obtain a high level of tax efficiency.
A. True
B. False

26. The tax-loss harvesting trade can add persistent tax alpha over time as the portfolio seasons.
A. True
B. False

27. Quantitative tax-aware portfolio strategies that emphasize tax-loss harvesting can be managed to generate alpha (additional return) from both security selection and tax management.
A. True
B. False

28. For an investor to justify selecting an actively managed, domestic large-capitalization portfolio strategy over a firm that applies a quantitative tax-aware methodology that emphasizes tax-loss harvesting over the first ten years of the relationship, the active manager needs to produce an alpha or return above the index of at least what percentage when the impact of taxes and fees are accounted for?
A. 0.5 percent
B. 1.0 percent
C. 2.0 percent
D. 3.0 percent

29. When an individual investor is subject to the alternative minimum tax, a ladder of non-private-activity municipal bonds will provide an optimal solution.
A. True
B. False

30. When reporting yields to taxable investors, the best practice is to "gross up" the yields for tax-exempt or municipal bonds so the investor can compare the result to yield of a similar-maturity taxable bond.
A. True
B. False

31. What can an adviser or consultant do to enhance the tax efficiency of hedge funds?
A. Look for hedge funds where the manager has significant ownership
B. If possible, locate the hedge fund in a tax-exempt account
C. Identify hedge fund derivatives
D. All of the above

32. To identify separate-account managers who practice tax-aware investment, you can:
A. purchase one of several outstanding databases available to the public
B. request that managers provide their AIMR after-tax composite with a minimum of ten years of history
C. ask managers for references rather than conduct a site visit
D. none of the above

33. When selecting a municipal bond manager, you should avoid selecting a manager who purchases bonds outside the client's state of residence and taxable bonds.
A. True
B. False

34. The primary reason why domestic large-capitalization equity managers do not show their clients after-tax returns is that their chance of outperforming the S&P 500 on an after-tax basis has proved over time to be less than 15 percent and they want to hide this from their clients.
A. True
B. False

35. When conducting an asset-allocation optimization exercise for a high-net-worth family, it is best to:
A. rely on before-tax return and standard deviation assumptions
B. conduct the optimization for taxable and tax-exempt accounts separately
C. place value-oriented managers with turnover rates of approximately 20 percent in taxable accounts
D. none of the above

36. To maximize after-tax returns, hold indexed mutual and exchange-traded funds in individual retirement accounts and bonds in personal, taxable accounts.
A. True
B. False

37. It makes sense to convert from a traditional IRA to a Roth IRA when:
A. there is a short time horizon before the investor reaches age 59½
B. the expected return is low
C. the individual will be in a lower tax bracket at retirement
D. all of the above

38. Depending on the complexity of the taxable client relationship, research has shown that applying tax-aware investment management principles is likely to add 0.5 to 2.5 percent per year in additional performance or savings.
A. True
B. False

39. Which of the following is *not* an element that can improve tax efficiency?
A. utilizing after-tax assumptions in the asset allocation process
B. allocating asset classes and managers/funds according to the tax characteristics of each entity
C. tax-aware equity manager positioning
D. when the assets are large enough, always using separate account managers rather than mutual or exchange-traded funds

40. The area that will have the greatest benefit to baby boomers for improving the net after-tax returns of their retirement assets is:
A. lower commissions by discount brokers
B. a greater number of available exchange funds
C. a significant improvement in the technological and reporting capabilities of investment platforms
D. a vast increase in the number of investment practitioners seeking professional designations

INDEX

accountant's ratio, 95–96, 136

accounting conventions, role of, 68–71

ADVISORport, 274

AIMR. *See* Association for Investment Management and Research

alternative minimum tax (AMT), 64–65, 160–164

American Academy of Financial Management, Chartered Wealth Manager program, 36–37

American Bankers Association (ABA), 39 Private Wealth Management School, 36

annuities, deferred variable-rate, 264–265

Aperio Group, 120

Arnott, Robert D., 6, 22–23, 26–27, 30, 210–211

asset allocation

appreciation and income, analysis of, 213–216

asset classes, identifying, 212–213

capital gains realization rate, 217–218

correlation coefficients, 220–222

fees, estimating, 218–219

historical returns, problems with, 209–211

income, estimating tax impact, 218

revising, 212

standard deviation, before-tax, 219–220

steps, 211–212

tax profile, calculating client's, 216–217

yield-to-maturity and inflation, analysis of, 219–216

assets, categories of, 243–244

assets, positioning

after-tax assumptions, use of, 252–253

education plans, 263–264

individual retirement accounts, 262–263

insurance products, 264–265

iterative approach, 254–259

listing assets according to entity type, 249–252

retirement plans, tax-deferred, 260–262

Social Security benefits, 265–266

steps for, 249

taxable assets, 259–260

tax-cost ratio, relative wealth measures, analysis of, 253–254

trusts, 266–268

Association for Investment Management and Research (AIMR), 7, 8, 39, 57, 60, 61, 77–78, 209

AIMR Performance Presentation Standards Handbook, 77

average cost accounting, 104

AXA Group, 137–138

Axioma, 122, 274

Bank of New York, 272

Barclays Global Fund Advisors, 106, 107, 156

Barra indices, 120, 122, 230, 274

Beebower, Gary L., 210

Beecher Investors, 145

benchmarks, 79–80, 120

Bergstresser, Daniel, 29

Berkin, Andrew L., 27

Bernstein, Peter L., 22, 209

Bernstein Tax-Managed International Fund, 113

Berra, Yogi, 211

Beyer, Charlotte B., 7, 36

ABOUT THE AUTHOR

Douglas S. Rogers, CFA, has been in the financial services industry for nearly two decades and is a leading authority on tax-aware investment management and after-tax reporting. He is a senior consultant and managing director at CTC Consulting, founded in 1981, which serves more than one hundred high-net-worth retainer relationships encompassing more than $12 billion in liquid financial assets.

Prior to joining CTC, Mr. Rogers served within the consulting industry as a chief investment officer and director of traditional manager research, where he has implemented tax-aware strategy and created open-architecture manager platforms to serve high-net-worth families. He has also worked with property and casualty insurance companies, nuclear decommissioning trusts, and medical retirement accounts.

Mr. Rogers understands the taxable-account industry from multiple perspectives, including investment policy, asset allocation, manager search activity, portfolio management, security analysis, and reporting. He is the chairman of the AIMR Subcommittee for After-Tax Performance Reporting, which was responsible for interacting with the Securities and Exchange Commission on the after-tax standards for mutual funds and made recommendations to revise the existing separate account standards to their current form.

Mr. Rogers is a graduate of the United States Military Academy and holds an MBA from Southern Methodist University. A nationally recognized speaker and author, he is also a Chartered Financial Analyst. In 2001, he received the annual Peter Dietz Award for the most significant contribution to the body of knowledge in performance measurement, for his article "The Challenges of After-Tax Performance Reporting" in the spring 2000 issue of the *Journal of Performance Measurement.*